"Elaine Ambrose and I share the need to write as a tangible expression of life's milestones. This tell-all memoir, *Frozen Dinners*, will resonate with anyone who has endured family dysfunction and will defrost the hearts of readers everywhere."

—**Joely Fisher**, actress, singer, and author of *Growing Up Fisher*

∿

"Full of luscious details, clear-eyed compassion, and enduring joy, Ambrose's memoir gives us an insider's view of one family's rocky pursuit of the American Dream. Even when she is relating personal stories of conflict, loss, and grief, Ambrose does so with a survivor's voice made strong by experience, stubbornness, humor, and love."

—**Kim Barnes**, author of the Pulitzer Prize finalist memoir: *In the Wilderness: Coming of Age in Unknown Country*

Frozen Dinners

A MEMOIR OF A FRACTURED FAMILY

BY

Elaine Ambrose

BROWN BOOKS
PUBLISHING GROUP

Books by Elaine Ambrose

Midlife Happy Hour
Midlife Cabernet
Drinking with Dead Women Writers—with AK Turner
Drinking with Dead Drunks—with AK Turner
Menopause Sucks—with Joanne Kimes
The Red Tease: A Woman's Adventures in Golf
Gators & Taters: A Week of Bedtime Stories
The Magic Potato / La Papa Mágica

∾

Elaine's Short Stories and Poems
Appear in the Following Anthologies

Faith, Hope & Healing—Dr. Bernie Siegel
A Miracle Under the Christmas Tree
The Dog with the Old Soul
Hauntings from the Snake River Plain
Tales from the Attic
Beyond Burlap
Daily Erotica: 366 Poems of Passion
Little White Dress
Feisty after 45
Angel Bumps
A Cup of Love: Stories from the Heart
Laugh Out Loud: 40 Women Humorists at Erma Bombeck
Writers' Workshop

∾

Find Elaine's books on ElaineAmbrose.com

Frozen Dinners: A Memoir of a Fractured Family

Brown Books Publishing Group
16250 Knoll Trail Drive, Suite 205
Dallas, Texas 75248
www.BrownBooks.com
(972) 381-0009

A New Era in Publishing®

Names: Ambrose, Elaine.
Title: Frozen dinners : a memoir of a fractured family / by Elaine Ambrose.
Description: Dallas, Texas : Brown Books Publishing Group, [2018]
Identifiers: ISBN 9781612542843
Subjects: LCSH: Ambrose, Elaine--Family. | Dysfunctional families. | Fathers--Death
    --Psychological aspects. | Love.
Classification: LCC PS3564.I349 Z46 2018 | DDC 818.5409--dc23

ISBN 978-1-61254-284-3
LCCN 2018946369

Printed in the United States
10 9 8 7 6 5 4 3 2 1

Cover illustration: Ward Hooper. Book cover and design by Jeanne Core, DesignWorks Creative, Inc. Author photo by Dorothy Salvatori

For more information or to contact the author, please go to www.ElaineAmbrose.com

Dedication

Dedicated to the memories of my parents,
Neal and Leona Ambrose,
and to my younger brother,
George Ambrose.

Please save me a place at the table.

Contents

CHAPTER ONE

The Quilt

Irritated clouds of old gray dust swirl behind my car and settle back onto the patches of scruffy sagebrush as I drive a back road into the village of Wendell, Idaho. I turn down 4th Avenue and stop in front of an insignificant old house where my family lived before my father became rich. Decades of decay and neglect are exposed as cheap vinyl siding sags on the outside walls and dead vines hang on crooked trellises over weathered boards thirsty for paint. I stare at the window of my former bedroom and wonder if it's still nailed shut.

I drive two blocks to the Wendell Manor and Nursing Home. Before I get out of the car to visit my mother, I follow a familiar routine: I pull the jar of mentholated cream from my purse, unscrew the cap, and dab the pungent ointment into both nostrils to mask the odors inside the nursing home. Despite the best efforts of the janitors who continually clean the facility and open the old windows on frigid winter days to exchange stale air for fresh, regular visitors anticipate the pervasive smells of bleach and urine and take necessary precautions. The analgesic rub originally was designed for temporary relief of aches and pains, but the ritual of using it in my nose enables me to enter and greet my mother with compassion. Sometimes she doesn't recognize me, and that leaves an ache that no balm or medication can soothe.

The building is a hundred years old and so are many of the residents. My father was born there in 1928 when the building was a hospital. After it became a nursing home, my grandmother died there, curled into a fetal position after several strokes. My eighty-seven-year-old mother occupies a tiny room down the hall. On good days when she can concentrate, she turns on her CD player and listens to her favorite artists: Lawrence Welk's orchestra, Tennessee Ernie Ford, several religious selections, and her collection of big band music from the 1940s. She can't remember how to use the remote control for the television, so the music is her daily companion.

Her room is simple. Furniture consists of a single medical bed, two antique nightstands from a home my parents once owned in Butte, Montana, her music table, and a wardrobe closet. Beside the unused TV sits a life-sized, wood carving of praying hands, a gift from my father after she "lost that one baby" seven years after I was born. Family pictures line the walls, and after she forgot our names I added colorful name tags to each photograph. There is a pendulum wall clock, perpetually tilted and five minutes slow. Two bookcases support scrapbooks, large-print novels, assorted knickknacks, and her Bible. A stained-glass dove hangs in the one window, and a smiling cloth doll in a frilly dress perches on the bed. A calendar on a small table notes that she is scheduled for a shower twice a week and her hair is curled on Wednesdays. My mother once lived in a mansion on a hill. Now she has one room with a private bathroom.

The room is tidy except for the scars on the corners of the wall where her wheelchair has rubbed as she maneuvers to get into the bathroom. She is completely incontinent, even after several failed surgeries to correct the problem, but she still attempts to get to the bathroom, often with disastrous results. If she falls, she pushes the call button hanging from her neck and the staff comes running to help and then lifts her back into her chair. They tried attaching an alarm to her chair so they would know when she moved out of it, but she stubbornly continues to attempt to stand. It's that feisty spirit that keeps her alive. Though her body and mind are weak, her heart and motivation remain strong.

The rules at the nursing home are strict but understandable. No hot plate, no candles, no refrigerator. Her scissors were taken after she accidentally stabbed herself and needed stitches. Her three moments of daily adventure come when she wheels herself to the dining room for meals. She usually declines the games of checkers or Bingo after lunch and returns to her solitary room after finishing a typical meal of meatloaf, warm vegetables, and soft potatoes with creamy gravy. She has been a widow for twenty-five years and is well-accustomed to living alone. I visit at least twice a month, and she has a regular group of friends from her church and from her women's association who stop by with cards and small gifts.

I enter her room with a cheery "Hello, Mom" and place a vase of flowers and a new air freshener on her table. She sits in her wheelchair, too weak to walk after breaking her back and her hip in separate falls. She looks sweet. Today's outfit is a comfortable sweatshirt covered with appliquéd flowers, black knit pants, and sturdy black shoes. And imitation pearls. Always the pearls. She has a strand of real ones but hides them in a drawer because she says they are "too nice to use." She glances up, focuses on my face, cocks her head, and then her eyes widen with a look of anticipation.

"You're finally here," she said. "I keep watching for you."

"Yes, Mom," I say as I kiss her cheek. "I'm here."

"Did you bring soup?" she asks, her face hopeful.

"No soup today. It's too hot outside. I promise to bring you some potato soup in the fall."

She loves my potato soup, made with new spuds, fresh cream, browned sausage, celery, onions, spices, and mustard seeds. One of her favorite Bible verses describes how virtuous people can move mountains if they just have faith as small as a mustard seed. Her mountains haven't budged despite a lifetime of adding countless seeds into every recipe.

I smile into the weathered face, take her eyeglasses and clean off the smudges, gently reshape the bent frames, and ease them over her ears again. She often falls asleep in bed wearing her glasses so they become contorted in various angles on her face. Today, her mood is agitated, and my filial offering of fresh flowers and clean, straightened glasses does not soothe her.

She leans forward and whispers, "They took my quilt!"

"Your grandmother's quilt?" I ask, looking quickly around the room. At almost every visit she rues the loss of one thing or another and every time the item is never really gone, just moved from its usual place.

"Yes! It was on my bed. And they took it."

I know this expertly crafted quilt, hand-stitched by my great-grandmother in the 1930s. She used one-inch scraps of my mother's baby dresses to patiently sew each section and bind and pad the cover onto white cotton material. The quilt remained in my mother's cedar chest for decades until I took it out and placed it on her bed in the nursing home. I thought it would make her feel more at home but she had been alarmed about using it.

"No, Elaine, put it back in the chest. I don't want it out because it's too good to use."

"But it was made for you," I said. "Why not enjoy it?"

"Because," she said with an unexpected tone of firmness, "someone will take it."

The quilt looked at home on the bed, a colorful and familiar splash in a drab environment. I didn't fold and store it as she requested. I wrapped her bed with the quilt, smoothed the center, and tucked in the edges. But now it was gone, just as she predicted.

Rather than acknowledge the possible theft of an old, hand-stitched heirloom, I comfort my mother and suggest that maybe the staff lost it. More than fifty residents live in the nursing home and the beleaguered workers do their best to feed and care for them as well as wash their laundry. I can only hope this was the case here, and that my great-grandmother's handiwork remains somewhere inside this old building.

Gently rubbing her stooped shoulders, I try to sound reassuring. "I'll go look. Be right back." As a precaution, I slip the jar of mentholated cream into my sweater pocket.

I find the head attendant pushing a portable shower chair on her way to the shower room. For bathing purposes, the invalid residents are undressed, lifted onto the chair, and sprayed with warm water before being dried, dressed, and returned to their rooms. The staff attempts to treat each person with kindness, but the orderly system doesn't provide attention to the resident's dignity or personal needs. My mother hates shower day.

"Excuse me," I interrupt the attendant. "Can I talk to you about my mother's missing quilt?"

"Gotta go, hon," she replies. "You should talk to the director."

The attendant disappears into a room and I hear her cajoling a woman named Mildred to get ready. Mildred doesn't want to go. The attendant closes the door and I assume the shower will soon take place. I turn to find the director's office. We've never met because she's new at the job, and my first impression is that she's in her late twenties. My mother was the town's matriarch before this woman was born.

"Hello, I'm Elaine, Leona's daughter," I say, stretching out my hand.

5

Miss Evans looks up from behind the piles of paperwork on her desk and sighs as if to acknowledge another family member with yet another complaint. She nods but doesn't shake my hand or ask me to sit.

"My mom's quilt is missing, and I need to find it. Do you know where I can look?"

The director is young and has no idea why this quilt is so important. She also has no clue that my mother, the feeble old woman in Room 17, was once the matriarch of the town, or that a gentle pioneer woman patiently weaved tiny stitches through bits of cloth by light of a kerosene lantern.

"A quilt? Well, is her name on it?"

"No," I reply. I'd thought about that when I placed it on her bed but hated the idea of marking the delicate fabric. "I didn't want to write on the quilt."

Miss Evans shakes her head and sighs again. "I can take you down to the laundry room," she says. "You can go through all the nameless stuff."

Nameless stuff. I wince.

Heels clicking on worn linoleum, I follow her through several hallways, down two steep staircases, and then down a ramp into the basement. Carved into the ground a century ago, the dark and dank room would never pass any official inspection today. Electrical wires hang exposed overhead, an old boiler sits useless in the corner, too big to extract, and several industrial washing and drying machines hum and rattle in another corner amid waiting lines of burdened baskets. Several bare bulbs hang overhead, casting low shadows in the corners of the windowless room.

"There," she says, pointing to six long tables burdened with mounds of limp clothing and blankets. "This is where the nameless things go. It might be in there. Let me know if you have any trouble."

And with that she leaves me alone in the basement surrounded by rejected artifacts. I don't know if these items belong to someone still living or not. Most of the residents are incontinent, and despite regular changing and showers, many sit around in soaked adult diapers. The smell remains in the rooms, the hallways, and in the walls. I pat the cream into my nostrils and go to work. As I sort the garments, I practice Kegel exercises to strengthen my pelvic floor muscles and vow to visit the gym after I return. One pair of sweatpants equals five Kegels, a camp t-shirt requires ten. I regret not asking for gloves as I rummage through the dark pants with elastic waistbands and well-worn sweatshirts. I know these outfits; my mother wears this uniform, too. A few brightly colored, lacy blouses interrupt the mundane garments, and I imagine they were worn by spirited women who refused to wear more sensible clothes.

As I move from table to table, I consider the sights and sounds as well as the smells that had permeated the building through its various incarnations. From the hospital, I hear cries from newborn babies, and from the nursing home, sighs from the dying as they take their last breaths. The industrial kitchen somewhere overhead echoes through the vents with the clattering of pans, dishes, and non-threatening silverware. Every Christmas local church groups visit and choirs sing to residents huddled in wheelchairs and leaning on walkers. People bring little sacks of donated socks and hand lotion, the most requested gifts. Many of the decorations remain up all year.

I grew up in Wendell and attended the same schools as my parents before me. We even had some of the same teachers, and several of them ended their days at the Manor. At age eleven, I had a newspaper route and rode my bicycle every day to deliver papers to seventy customers. The Manor was on my route. I remember dashing in with the paper and seeing the elderly people sleeping in their chairs. The ones who were awake begged me to stay and talk.

"Hey, Missy," said a man everyone called Shorty. "Why don't you stop and chat. Did I tell you about the farm I had?"

"I can't stop today, Shorty. I need to finish my route. Some day you can tell me about it."

"Are you coming tomorrow?" asked a toothless woman with wispy patches of hair on her head. "Can you bring me some milk?"

I stopped and placed the newspaper in her lap. "Sorry, June, I can't carry milk on my bike."

I always hurried out the door and continued my route. Now I've returned, forty years later, and my mother lives here, and the sights, sounds, and smells remain the same.

By the fourth table, I have the uneasy feeling that someone is watching me. I turn to study the room. Perhaps it's just the century of spirits that return to see the place of their birth and death. Mysterious shadows caused by the hanging lights move over the walls in the far corner, cold and damp beneath a canopy of cobwebs. A faded, illegible chart is nailed onto a dusty bulletin board, and a stiff mop tilts from an empty bucket. One of the dryers stops and the loud buzzer makes me gasp. No one comes to empty it, and I don't need another task. I move to the fifth table, laden with blankets and towels.

This one? No. This one? No. I find a few quilts, but not the right one. As I search, I consider taking one of the quilts just to convince her I had found it. But she would know. She can't remember what day it is, but she knows that quilt. No, it's not on this table either. One more table, it has to be here. With the determination of an explorer seeking lost treasure, I plunge my hands into the stack and begin to sort.

Why am I so driven to find the quilt? This fragile, patchwork fabric is a symbol of my family's tattered, traditional history.

After so much time and neglect, I can't afford to allow any more reminders to be lost.

I find it.

Beneath the last lump of discarded remnants of strangers, I see the rumpled edge surrounding the cherished quilt made from dresses my mother wore as a toddler. I see patches of green and blue, red and yellow, black and red, and orange and white secured by a checked binding. The colors of the past are faded but familiar. I pull out the quilt and wrap it around my shoulders like a religious shroud. Cocooned in that dark, dank basement, I am a good daughter. My mother will be happy. I say goodbye to the room and to whatever spirits surround me and find my way back up to the light.

"Mom." She is asleep in her wheelchair. I lean in closer. "I found it, Mom. I found the quilt."

I pile it into her lap and guide her hands to the fabric. She arouses, smiles, and presses her face into the old quilt and mumbles something about my great-grandmother.

Then she notices me. "Oh, it's you. Could you go get Elaine?" she says. "It's time for school to be out."

I leave the Manor and emerge into the sunshine. During the two-hour drive home, my mind is a patchwork of memories: lost wealth, calamity, a family fractured, with no chance of redemption. Once at home, I go to my storage closet and pull out several old photograph albums and my mother's hand-written journals. I want to piece together all the unorganized scraps from my past and create something meaningful. I pour a glass of red wine, sit at the large table in my fresh-smelling kitchen, and open the oldest book, dated 1950, the year before I was born.

~

CHAPTER TWO

The Trucking Company

During the harvest of 1950, disaster came to potato farmers in southern Idaho. Bad weather, bad luck, and bad timing resulted in a poor yield, and after the meager harvest the farmers were paid less than what it cost them to grow the crops. The local bank managers demanded that loans be paid or else farms that had been bartered for collateral would be seized.

My father clenched his teeth as he watched the local banker, who was now his former friend, pound No Trespassing signs on the farm he was renting. For nine months, he had worked to plant, weed, and harvest a worthless field of potatoes. Now the bank owned the farm, and he owned nothing but debt.

These circumstances prompted my dad to distrust banks and vow to make it on his own. By the spring of 1951, his biggest regret, after losing the farm, was that my mother was pregnant. They already had a one-year-old boy, and Dad, only age twenty-three, didn't know how he could support his growing family. My mother did her best to conceal her pregnancy to minimize his distress, but the charade became more difficult because she carried twins. I was one of them.

Dad's older brother lived in Hawthorne, Nevada, near the US Army Depot. The brother wrote that there was a job for a mechanic at a local truck stop, so my father packed his family and their few possessions into a battered Ford station wagon and left Wendell for Hawthorne. Mom was sick during the ordeal, but concentrated on supporting her husband and caring for her baby boy. She left behind her parents, her sister, her friends, and her church.

Dad quickly learned how to service the eighteen-wheel diesel trucks that rolled day and night between Montana and California. Through the grease, the clamor, and the meager pay, he focused on ideas that could improve his life. Something in his gut told him there was opportunity beyond the noise of the pneumatic torque wrenches he used to change hundreds of dirty tires. He just had to find it.

My mother sweltered in the Nevada heat. They had rented a cramped, one-bedroom, half of a duplex without air conditioning in the village of Babbitt. The town was a World War II housing project, later abandoned in the 1980s. On the morning of September 8, my father drove her to the hospital and then paced the floor in the waiting room, wondering how his life had turned so stressful. Three babies in twenty months. Losing his farm. Working manual labor in a sweat-filled shop with grease under his fingernails, in his nostrils, and matted through his black hair. Living in a government housing project. This wasn't the life he wanted.

When the doctor emerged, Dad sensed something was wrong. "We lost one," the doctor said slowly. "But one survived and she is one healthy baby! She came out hollering!"

Dad suppressed a smile. He didn't know if his relief was because there was one less mouth to feed or because his daughter seemed to be boisterous. "Let me see her," he said as he passed the doctor and marched through the door.

My mother was still in recovery, but Dad noticed two bassinets in my room. One was empty. "That was for the other baby," he said to the nurse. He looked at the healthy, eight-pound baby in the next bassinet. "Should have been a boy," he said. Then he went back to work.

Christmas of 1951 was bleak. My parents missed their own parents and siblings back in southern Idaho, but no one had any money to travel. It didn't feel like the holidays anyway because the weather was warm. They entered the New Year with a determination to return to Idaho. Dad worked overtime at the shop, and Mom took in a little boy to babysit. She cared for three children in cloth diapers, washed clothes in the sink, and hung them to dry on a line in the backyard. Back in that hot, temporary home in Nevada, Mom took life one day at a time to do the best she could for her children. One day she found that someone had left a new high chair on the front step. She never knew who gave such a wonderful gift, but she promised to return the favor someday to another woman in need.

Dad watched and learned as the big trucks continued to pull into and out of the shop. He worked on the refrigerated units on the trailers going south, added propane to the cooling units and diesel to the trucks. These same rigs came back through with empty trailers, and he realized that if the trucking company could still make a profit with empty trailers, it could make a much larger profit if the trailers were loaded. He tabulated how much diesel it would take at 14.9 cents a gallon to drive 1,100 miles. He talked with drivers as he serviced their trucks and asked them about their wages and expenses. He learned how payments were made for deliveries and which loads were more profitable.

He was a visionary and studied the opportunities of the time. The 1950s brought economic advantages and posterity for many people living in post–World War II America. The automobile industry successfully produced cars and trucks, and new industries capitalized on consumer demand for more electronics and household conveniences. Most homes had one black-and-white television set, and families often ate dinner while watching TV.

For the next two years, he read newspapers and business magazines during his work breaks. He was interested in the latest innovation in the food industry: frozen food that was inexpensive and easy to cook. The public craved these products, but couldn't always get them because of distribution problems. My father had the answer. He would haul them in refrigerated trucks.

One day one of the drivers who came through on a regular basis told him that a small trucking company in Montana was looking for drivers. Dad decided he would become a truck driver. He quit his job as a mechanic, left Mom with three small children, and hitched a ride in a truck going to Montana. On the way, he learned how to drive an eighteen-wheeler.

When my father walked into the office of Hansen Packing Company in Butte, Montana, Alvin Williamson, the owner, eyed him with suspicion. Dad wore wrinkled clothes, he was unshaven, and he had grease around his fingernails. But he was impressive, a big man; he stood six foot two, ruggedly handsome, with black hair and intense green eyes.

"I'm here for a job," he said.

"Can you drive?" Alvin asked.

"Yes, sir," he replied, not admitting that he had just learned how to maneuver a truck by hitchhiking with a Montana Express driver. "And I have an idea that will make you more money."

Alvin leaned forward in his chair. He wanted to hear what this skinny twenty-four-year-old stranger had to say. Within two hours, Neal Ambrose and his dream of making money had convinced Alvin to give him a job. Ambrose saw his future fortune packed tightly and conveniently into a refrigerated trailer on the back of a diesel truck.

"You'll need a co-driver this time out," Alvin said. "Driving in Los Angeles ain't easy." Dad nodded and stuck out a grease-stained hand. They shook. "There are showers and a cot upstairs," said Alvin. "Be ready to go by six in the morning."

My father hardly slept that night. Three other drivers shared the dormitory, and they all seemed to compete for who could snore the loudest. He wished he could talk with my mother to tell her about the job. He made another promise to himself: someday they would have a telephone.

Three days later, Mom was hanging diapers on the line when she heard a diesel truck pull up in front of the house. She laughed as Dad jumped out of the cab and ran toward her. "I got the job!" he yelled as she ran to him.

"Are you driving that?" Mom was amazed.

"Yes, I am," he answered as he kissed her. "And I'm on my way to California. See you in a few days."

"Do you want to see the kids?"

"Don't have time," he hollered and climbed back into the cab. "But I'll have a paycheck in two weeks."

As the truck rumbled out of sight, my mother wondered what she should do. She had five dollars to her name, the rent was due, and the babies needed food. That night, someone left a bag of groceries and an envelope with one hundred dollars on her front step, and she had never been so grateful in her entire life. Before going to bed, she prayed for her husband somewhere on the road, she prayed for her children, and she prayed for her mysterious angel. Then she dried her tears and, mentally and physically exhausted, fell asleep.

"This here is L.A.," said Marvin Titus, Dad's co-driver. Dad's eyes widened as he sat in the passenger seat. He had never seen so many cars and buildings. Three lanes of traffic moved in each direction, and there wasn't any lane separating the oncoming traffic. "These roads can't handle big rigs," Marvin said as he maneuvered the truck.

"I've read that a new interstate system will be built soon," said Dad. "It will connect the country from coast to coast, and there will be north-south freeways that connect to the interstate. We'll be able to drive from Butte to Los Angeles in two days."

"That's impossible," Marvin muttered. "They can't do that."

"Interstate I-5 will be built soon, and I'll drive on it."

Dad and Marvin had shared the cab for five days and 1,100 miles. One of them slept on a crude bed behind the seats while the other drove. They cleaned up at truck stops along the route and shared the ten dollars a day that Alvin gave them for food. Through the trip, my father learned a lot from Marvin and he admired the driver's knowledge of trucking, but the confined quarters went against his need for space. He knew that he had to have his own truck.

Marvin turned into the warehouse district and found the Safeway store's loading dock. "I'll take it in this time," he said. "You can pull 'er out." He backed the forty-foot trailer down the ramp and shut off the engine. The two drivers got out to watch as the dock workers unloaded the trailer. They logged every pallet of frozen groceries and then exchanged paperwork with the workers. There were no shortages, no broken cartons, and no thawed food. Any one of those possibilities could have resulted in the load being declined. A declined load meant no paycheck.

"Okay, your turn," said Marvin as he climbed into the passenger seat.

Dad adjusted the mirrors and put the truck into gear. He slowly eased the rig up the ramp and into the truck yard. Then he noticed that no other trucks were waiting to unload. He stopped the truck, shoved the gear in reverse, and moved the trailer backward.

"What the hell you doing?" shouted Marvin.

"I need to know how to do this," Dad said as he watched the mirrors and backed down the ramp. It took ten tries until he got the trailer lined up and the dock workers stopped to watch. When he finally got the trailer safely down to the loading dock, they all clapped and cheered. Dad saluted and drove back into the yard.

"Show-off," muttered Marvin.

The two drivers cleaned up in the driver's lounge of the main trucking center. Then my father scanned the message board until he found the notice he needed. A broker had a load of frozen Morton chicken pot pies that needed to go north. Consumers were demanding the new innovation of frozen food, and Neal Ambrose was ready and willing to bring them their dinners.

"Bingo," he said and wrote down the number.

It took several calls and all of his spare change, but Dad finally contacted the broker and secured a deal between the broker and Hansen Packing. Five hours later, Marvin and my father were hauling 40,000 pounds of Morton frozen chicken pies to Montana. Night fell as Dad drove the truck away from the city, and he was relieved to see the lights of Los Angeles in his rearview mirrors. Marvin climbed into the sleeper and was snoring before the rig turned north.

Dad drove through the desert and noticed that the stars were extraordinarily brilliant. He felt more alive than ever, and his heart beat in rhythm with the rumbling engine of the truck. He was a trucker, and people needed the pies, soup, detergent, and toilet paper that he would deliver. He was intoxicated with the open road. When he crossed the state line into Nevada, he began to think about his family. For the first time in two weeks, he wondered how his kids were doing.

It was daylight when my father pulled into Hawthorne and stopped at the shop where he used to work. He jumped out of the cab and called for the attendant to fill the tanks. The boy looked at Dad with surprise and envy. Marvin crawled out of the truck, sleepy and disheveled.

"We have to make one quick stop," Dad said. "Then you'll drive."

After the rig was serviced and the men had grabbed some food, my father drove the truck to his rented home. Mom hustled the children out to the lawn and they waited until he stopped.

"Can't stay long," he said as he hugged his wife and patted his children and the other little boy. "But I'll be back in a week with my paycheck."

He gave my mother a bag of groceries from the truck stop and all of his extra food allowance. "It's going to be okay. I promise." Then he climbed into the sleeper and Marvin drove away. Mom counted twenty dollars and waved goodbye. With the money she made from babysitting, she had just enough for groceries until he returned.

A week later, she heard the familiar rumble in front of the house. She ran out and met her husband with another driver. He lifted her in the air and twirled her around. "Hey, sweetheart," he said. "Look here!" He handed her an envelope with his paycheck for $300 plus a bonus of $50 for instigating the frozen dinner loads. They had never seen so much money at one time.

"Can you get to the bank?" he asked. "Keep some for yourself! Maybe get a new dress!" He searched for the kids, gave them a quick hug, and hurried to the truck. "Be back in two days. Hustle. Hustle. Time is money," he called, fired up the diesel engine, and drove away.

Mom couldn't think. A new dress? The kids needed shoes. And how was she supposed to get to the bank with three small children? She waited until her sister-in-law stopped for a visit later that afternoon and begged her to watch the kids for an hour. The woman agreed and Mom hurried to the bank to make the deposit. She reserved enough money to pay for rent, groceries, and essentials. Then she stopped at the dime store with the intention of buying new shoes for her son. That's when she saw the rocking chair.

Forgoing the dress, my mother eagerly bought the shoes and the chair and drove home, the chair tied with ropes into the open trunk of the old car. That night, after the working mother picked up her son, and my brother was in bed with his storybooks, Mom rocked her daughter and smiled. "It's going to be better," she said.

By the spring of 1952, my parents had saved enough money to move back to their hometown of Wendell, Idaho. They rented a two-bedroom house across the street from the Presbyterian Church, and Mom found a young widowed woman who needed babysitting for her two kids while she worked. Mom took care of four children during the day and then typed for the church in the evening. When money was lean, she added a third job and typed for Bradshaw's Honey Plant late at night. I often fell asleep listening to the clacking of the typewriter keys.

Dad was gone on the truck most of the time, and Mom found companionship in the church women's group. When she could get a babysitter, she would wear her best dress and attend the church luncheons. She carried her porcelain platter piled with homemade cookies, sure to write LA on the bottom in fingernail polish to make sure the platter was returned.

Dad leased a truck in 1953 and became an independent owner/operator. His nonstop truck driving and Mom's three part-time jobs paid the bills with enough money left to buy a few Christmas gifts that December. The New Year promised prosperity, even if Mom still didn't own a car.

Dad was an avid reader, and during the fall of 1954 he noticed news articles about a new invention: frozen TV dinners. A national food company named Swanson misjudged how much turkey would be sold for Thanksgiving that year and after the holiday the company had 260 tons of leftover turkey. A clever salesman noticed how meals were served in compartmentalized aluminum trays on Pan American Airways planes. The salesman convinced Swanson to develop a convenient meal, served in trays, that could be frozen and delivered across the country. Swanson gambled on the concept and packaged turkey, corn bread stuffing, peas, and sweet potatoes and initiated a nationwide advertising campaign. The company sold more than 25 million TV dinners to Americans who demanded the convenience and low cost of frozen dinners. The meals cost 98 cents per package, and people enjoyed eating them in front of their television sets.

Dad continued to develop relationships with key contacts in the Los Angeles area. Soon, he had brokered regular shipments of Swanson TV dinners. He continued to haul meat from Montana to southern California and return with pallets of frozen food to distribute to warehouses and stores in Idaho and Montana. He knew the route by heart and drove from daybreak to late at night.

Every time my father drove through town, he left a box of frozen TV dinners. Mom didn't have enough freezer space, so we ate the dinners for every meal. Salisbury steak, little trays of corn, cherry cobbler, meat loaf and potatoes. We sat around the table scraping the bland food from the tin trays. Sometimes, to be fancy, Mom would spoon the food onto real plates. She said we were lucky that Daddy could bring home food for the family.

I remember my father bringing random surprises from his travels, and we eagerly waited at the door when we heard his truck rumble to a stop in front of the house. One time he maneuvered a large wooden crate into the living room, and my mother seemed excited as she tore open the box. Her expression changed from hopeful to confused as she uncovered four life-sized busts of Aborigine Indians. The two men and two women were carved from dark wood and each had a hole at the side of the mouth to hold a wooden pipe. The women were bare-chested.

"Aren't these great?" my father asked, enthusiastic as a schoolboy. "I got them at an Indian trade market on the California border. They'll look perfect in the living room. Gotta go. See you next week."

Those four busts remained in Mom's living room for the next forty years. At Christmas, I would add red bras on the women, much to the chagrin of my mother and the laughter of my brothers. Other "rare" gifts included a large metal shield with five swords, an adult-sized metal breastplate, an Indian shield made from painted buckskin supported by two iron arrows, a wooden Indian throwing an arrow, and a wooden Indian sitting on the ground smoking a peace pipe. He complemented the theme with several framed prints from western artist Charles Marion Russel. Mom tried to balance the cowboy and Indian theme with watercolors of flowers and pastoral landscapes. She added candles and crosses arranged on hand-crocheted doilies. As a result, our home resembled a pawn shop in a truck stop.

Life changed dramatically again in the spring of 1955. Dad borrowed money to lease seven diesel trucks and named his company Montana Express. Mom was pregnant with their third child.

~

CHAPTER THREE

Lullabies and Work Songs

The song "You'll Never Walk Alone" was a popular 1955 show tune from the Rodgers and Hammerstein musical *Carousel*. We didn't yet own a piano, but my mother used to keep sheet music so she could sing her favorite songs in her soft, off-key voice as she went about her daily activities. I vaguely remember as an active three-year-old that I didn't understand the song because my mom was usually alone except for her two children and the two kids she babysat.

One of my first memories is of her being sick. She was throwing up in the kitchen sink and could barely stand. Finally, she gathered up the four children—all under the age of six—and told us to hold hands and walk with her. We were nervous because of her desperate voice and her hunched posture, but we grabbed hands and marched several blocks across town to the local doctor's office. As we walked in silence, I heard my mother whispering the words from the song about never walking alone. I walked on with her, with hope in my heart.

My mother, eight months' pregnant, was having an appendicitis attack. She was rushed to the hospital and we waited in the doctor's office for Grandma to drive from Jerome to get us. Grandma took all four of us home and told us to take a nap. I remember burying my head under my pillow so no one could hear me cry. My fourth birthday that week passed without notice. I have a black-and-white photograph of me during that time with my arm in a sling. Years later when I asked my mother what happened to my arm, she couldn't remember.

My mother stayed in the hospital for several days after her appendix was removed. My dad was hauling loads to and from California and stopped briefly at the house once a week. My brother was born in October and wasn't named for four days until Dad came home.

"We'll call him George," he said. "George Patrick is a solid name."

To celebrate my brother's birth, my dad said my older brother and I could ride in the eighteen-wheeler parked in front of the house. I remember climbing up into the cab and sharing the passenger seat with my brother. The truck rumbled to a start and Dad drove around town pulling on the air horn. My most vivid memory of that ride was to see my thighs jiggling as the diesel engine rattled the cab.

Then he was gone again. He was making payments on seven trucks for Montana Express, and he had to keep them running all the time. He didn't want to move his growing family to Montana because he needed us to stay in Wendell so my mom's parents could help when he was gone. He hired his friends and former army buddies to be drivers and learned on the road how to manage a business. The fleet grew and he continued to buy more trucks. On his trips home, he would bring damaged goods that his customers refused to accept: broken cases of frozen TV dinners, dented cans of soup, and unlabeled jugs of bleach. For years, my mother kept gallon jars of capers that we eventually threw away.

Frozen TV dinners continued to be popular as Americans gathered around their television sets to watch the pioneer shows and programs. Our black-and-white set only could reach one station: CBS. We didn't watch when Dad was home but when he was gone driving, I sat with my dinner and watched *I Love Lucy* and *The Jackie Gleason Show*. Dad resembled Gleason in appearance, and the show made me laugh.

Money was tight, and my mother kept detailed records of every penny spent. Her ledgers were neatly written in pen and included expenses such as 25 cents for four root beer drinks, $25 for rent, and $8.61 for groceries. Donations for church ranged from 20 cents to a dollar. She also included refunds on pop bottles in the income column. She paid $15 a month to Sears for a wringer washer and hung the clothes to dry outside on a line. She also paid $10 a month on a set of Childcraft books to read to her children.

Our family of five had outgrown the tiny two-bedroom rented house. In 1956 my dad purchased the house on 4th Avenue with two bedrooms, one bathroom, a screened back porch, and a huge backyard. I remember walking into my own room and falling in love with the knotty-pine walls, hardwood floor, and built-in bookshelves. It would be my private sanctuary for the next eight years.

Wendell Public Schools didn't offer kindergarten in 1956 so I started first grade at age five. My brother was a year ahead in school even though he was twenty months older. My mother ordered a fifteen-book set of Childcraft books for children, and we eagerly ran home after school each day to look through the pages. I kept the books and read them to my children and grandchildren, even though now they can quickly look up animated stories on the Internet.

By the start of 1959, my mother's songs had improved in spirit and voice. Her favorite artists were Doris Day, Bing Crosby, and the McGuire Sisters. By then, the success of the trucking company meant that she no longer babysat other children and she reduced the amount of nightly typing jobs. After my brothers and I were in bed and my father was still gone, she would play Tennessee Ernie Ford records. Many times, I fell asleep to the slow and comforting crooning of Ford's spirituals. My favorite song was "His Eye Is on the Sparrow."

This brief time of happiness ended during that summer. One morning when Dad was out of town, my brothers and I woke to find my mother unconscious on the floor. We dialed my aunt's telephone number and she came quickly to offer assistance. I remember looking at my mother's white face and being too afraid to touch it.

My mother was seven months' pregnant and we learned later the baby had turned several times so that the umbilical cord was twisted around her neck. Mom was confined to bed rest for two months and an older woman came to stay with us. In August, Grandma drove Mom to the hospital to give birth. The baby was kicking and emerged feet first, but the cord was wrapped too tightly around the neck. They didn't do emergency caesarian sections then, so the doctor was helpless to save the baby and she strangled to death. I never again heard my mother sing.

I remember seeing the dead baby wrapped in a pink blanket and lying in a tiny white casket at the funeral home. On August 15, 1959, I attended the quiet, small service at the cemetery and then she was buried. I sat next to my father and brothers and stared at the tiny white casket, fighting the urge to run away. My mother remained in the hospital, lamenting the fact that she had never seen the baby and couldn't attend the service. The following month my mother gave me a big doll for my eighth birthday and added all the unused baby clothes for the doll to wear. No one ever spoke again about the baby. Her name was Carol.

In December of 1959, my parents incorporated a company called Wendell Gas and Oil. Their partner, Nolan Cooper, operated the existing gas station located on the north end of Wendell. The company secured a contract to distribute Union Oil products for the county and supplied home heating oil. They hired mechanics to work on trucking and farming equipment and offered loans to ranchers and farmers.

The building was expanded to include truck bays and a parking lot for trucks. One of the lots was across the street from the Mormon Church. Refrigerated trailers, called reefers, needed the diesel engines to be running constantly to maintain the cooling system, and church members complained about the noise interrupting their Sunday services. My dad responded by adding more running reefers to the lot.

Dad's office was on the second floor of what we called "The Shop." The walls were covered in walnut paneling and adorned with prints from noted western artist Charles M. Russell. Uncle Muncie built him a massive desk of solid walnut with a large letter "A" fixed to the front. A low leather couch sat across from the desk, and guests, salespeople, and drivers sitting on the couch had to look up to see Dad. He kept a cardboard box on his desk to collect bills and receipts. He studied every invoice and often would quarrel over a dollar before the bill was paid or adjusted.

As the fleet of trucks increased, salesmen from Kenworth and Peterbilt came from Boise to convince Dad to buy their trucks. Kenworth featured him in an advertisement with its Model 923 that was used to haul grain and groceries. Montana Express expanded its territory from Montana throughout the Northwest and Southwest.

The 1960s brought a new prosperity for my family. My father remodeled the terminals in Wendell and in Butte, Montana. His fleet grew to thirty eighteen-wheel trucks and trailers. From the playground at the elementary school, I stood with the other children and watched as the trucks rolled through town to delivery locations throughout the northwest. We pulled our arms in the air and the truckers blasted their horns. I felt a strange proudness to be connected with the big rigs.

During 1961, Montana Express trucks covered almost two million miles throughout eleven western states and Canada. The driver's payroll exceeded $210,000—a sizeable amount for the time. Dad's company, Wendell Gas and Oil, continued to supply fuel for his trucks and for agriculture customers in the area. The business provided home heating oil and offered discounts for farmers and ranchers during harvest season. The mechanics at the shop kept the trucks running and worked on local vehicles. To show appreciation for the community support, my parents sponsored a free open house with dancing at the American Legion Hall. After the Christmas of 1961, my mother wrote in her journal that Dad gave her an electric skillet. She added several exclamation points for joyful emphasis.

As my dad's business grew, so did his temper. He was under a lot of stress with so many trucks on the road. We were not allowed to use the one telephone at home because a driver might call with a problem. Or it could be the dispatcher or an upset customer or bad weather on the mountain passes. Any small quarrel between siblings could result in my dad's rage coming down on us. He used the wooden board to spank all of us, regardless of guilt or innocence. His key employees remained loyal, and they understood and respected his moods. However, employees who didn't perform suffered the consequences. Once he found a male and female worker kissing in the parts room and he fired them on the spot.

I envied Dad's relationship with his longtime employees who helped him grow and maintain his businesses. He rewarded them with large cash bonuses at Christmas, a butchered hog, and a case of apples. Every summer, he organized a company picnic and prizes included camping gear and a car. Employees received one raffle ticket for every year of service and the winner claimed a trip to Hawaii or the monetary equivalent. Most of them had no desire to travel across the ocean, so they took the cash. Dad also offered and contributed annually to employee individual retirement accounts, but most of them cashed the accounts and paid the penalty.

When he conducted business in Montana, Dad stayed at the Butte Hotel. Then he bought a big furnished home that we visited during the summers. I never questioned why he lived there so much, and it always amazed me when I visited my friends' homes and both parents were there. In my home, the children lived with the familiar adage, "Just wait until your father gets home!"

I know my mother was frustrated with all the responsibilities of raising children and keeping the household while my father was gone. But the only way she could get his undivided attention was to exaggerate our misdeeds. He would come through the door, and she would grab his arm and relate the transgressions of the nearest child—usually me—and he would listen to her for a brief moment before the spankings would commence.

The family routine changed in 1963, when my father stopped living in Montana and came home every night. Mom's food selections moved beyond TV dinners, and after our silent meals, she washed the dishes as my brothers disappeared to do whatever boys did back then. We owned one black-and-white television but were only allowed to watch a few programs, including *Gunsmoke* and *Friday Night Fights*. If we had the television on when my father came home from work, he would turn it off and instruct everyone to do chores.

Dad completed the purchase of Montana Express and continued to add trucks, trailers, drivers, and prestige. By 1966, the fleet grew to 21 trucks and trailers. Many of the fathers of my classmates were employed by my father. Sometimes they would make comments about me being rich, and I didn't know how to respond. I wore the same type of clothes they did and owned one pair of black shoes and one pair of boots. To me, the rich families existed only in the movies.

I became friends with many of the drivers and admired their dedication to their jobs. I often listened to their conversations as they relaxed at the shop between assignments.

"I can't believe all the new government regulations on trucking," muttered a driver known as Hohnhorst. "Now I need to show my log books at every port of entry."

"Just keep that sweet smile," replied Preston Hughes, the main truck mechanic. "You can charm your way across the country."

"We're hauling more Campbell's soup and Clorox now," Hohnhorst replied. "Who knew there were so many clean soup-eaters?"

"We've hauled some exciting cargo," Hughes replied. "I remember we once rigged a trailer to haul a helicopter down the freeway. No one ever caught us."

They laughed and continued their stories. I maintained my respect for the long-haul road warriors who transported products to warehouses and pantries from the southern border to Canada. They were gone from their homes most of the week, but Dad rewarded them with good salaries and benefits. His drivers were non-union so Dad paid them the same rate as union drivers.

Montana Express trucks and trailers were painted in Dad's favorite colors of red and black. He took pride in his rigs and traded cabs and trailers every few years. By 1969, Montana Express had rotated through seventy-two trucks.

With the trucking company running smoothly, my father decided to return to his farming roots and hired some friends and relatives to help him establish Ambrose Farms. He started buying sagebrush for $25 an acre, which made him the laughing stock of the county. But he had an idea to dig wells, add pumps, and bring in sprinkler pipe irrigation to turn the worthless land into fertile acres of crops. Within a decade, the land was worth more than $2,000 an acre.

September of 1963 was dry. The wind blew constantly, turning green fields into ragged clumps of struggling potato vines. A growing concern among the farmers soon became a collective fear shared by all the residents of Wendell. When the farmers lost crops, the entire town suffered. Farmers bought supplies and groceries from local stores. Farmers put money in the banks, provided jobs, and shared their extra crops. This fall harvest would be critical, and there was no rain in sight.

I could tell that my father was agitated with worry. I went with him one day as he drove his pickup truck around his farms, plowing through the mounds of dirt and topsoil that blanketed the country roads.

"Six months of work is about to blow away," he muttered to himself. "These potatoes are just too small. I need water!"

I knew it was best to keep quiet. I pressed my nose against the window and studied the fields as we drove.

"I'll have to sell them for less money than I've already spent on seed and labor." Dad pounded the dashboard. "Somehow, I have to find a better way!"

October blew into southern Idaho with a fury. Local farmers huddled over coffee every morning at The Little Pig Cafe, lamenting their woes. Each one owed money to the bank, and they were deciding whether to let the crops rot in the field or try to salvage what was left so they could make a payment on their loans. Together, they decided to go for the harvest, and each man promised to help the other.

By the second week of October, the mammoth potato harvesters were lined up in the fields. Empty trucks would travel alongside the harvesters to collect the small potatoes that rolled off the harvesters. The potatoes would then be taken to the dirt cellars located around the valley. Buyers from major grocery and

31

food processing plants would assess the quality and, if acceptable, would offer a price that the farmers had to accept.

The monthlong harvest was half over when the rain came. It started as a drizzle and increased to a downpour that lasted for two weeks. The thirsty fields became seas of mud. To save the crops, farmers began to work through the night. The soggy harvesters churned angrily through the muddy fields, guided only by the weak lights on the trucks. The rusty wipers slapped at the windows as the drivers struggled to see through the solid sheet of water. The mornings brought only more rain, and the potatoes started to rot in the mud. School was canceled so all the farm children could help salvage the crops. Even the teachers came out in the storms to help. Women brought baskets of food, jugs of hot coffee, and dry clothes to the fields. When the weary workers took a short break, no one spoke as they huddled in the rain, gobbled a sandwich, and then returned to the machines.

I stood in the mud on the platform at the end of the lurching harvester, barely able to see through the rain as I fought to pull wet weeds off the potatoes. My back ached and I was hungry. The harvester had been groaning through the mud for nine hours, halting only for fuel that was brought to the fields in tanker trucks. Suddenly the huge machine stopped dead, mired in mud. It could go no further.

My brothers and I trudged, dirty and exhausted, to our father's pickup truck waiting at the end of the field. We avoided his eyes, climbed in the back, and rode quietly to the house. We hosed off the mud from their clothes, and I turned the hose on my head for several minutes, trying to wash away the grime. I left my muddy clothes in a heap and washed up at the kitchen sink. Rejecting my mother's offer of some warm potato soup, I escaped to my room, pulled on a clean nightshirt, and fell into bed.

CHAPTER FOUR

Rebel Daughter

My roots are in Wendell, Idaho. My father was born there in 1928 and met my mother in Wendell High School before they married in 1948. My brothers and I also graduated from the same high school. A hanging sign straddled Main Street and proclaimed that Wendell was "The Hub City of Magic Valley." In the tiny farming community, population around 1,000, hard work and men were valued above all else. Next in priority came the hired help, the crops and livestock, and the paying customers. And, in terms of real value, a bumper yield of hogs would leap ahead of the hired help. The women were necessary to keep the household, tend the children, and pleasure the men, and the boys were appreciated as potential workers. Girls were insignificant. They were an expense item on a profit and loss statement that included assets of pigs, potatoes, and property.

During the first twelve years of my childhood, I rarely saw my father. He worked all the time, and when he came home, my mother and brothers became apprehensive. The stresses of his business caused him to become more detached from the family, and his health began to deteriorate. He developed an appetite for Crown Royal whiskey and a spontaneous reaction to punish his children. He used a wooden board and I remember the blows. I refused to cry, which greatly irritated him, and if I asked what I had done wrong, the blows only increased in intensity. My only escape was to crumple onto the floor and pretend to be dead. Even he wouldn't hit a dead girl. Then he would stomp from my room and slam the door. I laid there, my cheek against the cool wooden floor, and pretended to fly away. My mother? She never interfered as her children were beaten.

At the beginning of seventh grade, I was a gangly, goofy girl with eyeglasses and weird clothes. My mother sewed many of my dresses, and I never was too concerned about fashion. That's why I was amazed when Debbie and Sylvia, the most popular girls in my class, asked me to join them for cheerleader tryouts. At the time, girls didn't play sports, so being a cheerleader was the prize for the ultimate popularity contest. Debbie and Sylvia knew I had a lot of friends and we needed their votes.

We practiced during our lunch breaks and learned energetic routines. I wanted to be a cheerleader and knew I could do it. At our school, the cheerleaders chosen in seventh grade usually were the cheerleaders throughout junior high and high school. It was my only chance.

Two nights before tryouts, my father announced at the dinner table that I wasn't allowed to try out.

"Why?" I asked. "We already have our routines."

"Cheerleaders only jump around to show off their legs," he answered. "You're not doing it."

I fumbled for the right words. "But I have good legs!" I pleaded. "And I love to cheer."

"The answer is no. No more discussion."

The next day I told Debbie and Sylvia I couldn't join them. They asked Leah, and the three of them were cheerleaders until our senior year.

Family life at home consisted of moments of tension interrupted by bursts of confusion. My father would arrive for dinner at any time and my mother would scurry around fixing him something to eat. Her great creative culinary abilities included cooking some frozen dinners, removing the food from the packages, and hiding the empty boxes. Or she would mix two cans of different soup and serve it with potato chips. We would sit stoically like monks at the table, silently hoping to make it through the meal without drama.

One evening my father sat down and happened to look at me. He noticed that my bangs were almost long enough to touch my eyebrows. That was the style of the time, made popular by the new and sensational singing group, The Beatles. My father had warned me about growing my bangs too long because he didn't like the "long-haired hippies" in the band from England, and my bangs were an insult to clean-cut Americans. I grew my bangs, anyway, and attempted to clip them to the side when I was home. But that one evening I forgot.

He glared and dropped his fork, and I could see his mouth trembling as he scrambled for words. The air was electric with tension as if I had committed the ultimate sin against my family and all of our ancestors. My heart raced as I moved mashed potatoes around my plate. My breath came in shallow puffs, and I closed my eyes in preparation.

I tried to distract myself from my fear by concentrating on some of my favorite Beatles' songs. I focused on "I Want to Hold Your Hand" because I could visualize the singers tossing their shaggy heads in exaggerated desire for the thrill of touching a lover's hand. I really needed someone to sing about feeling happy, inside, with a feeling I couldn't hide. But no, there was no secret lover coming to save me, and I couldn't escape the pending consequence.

My father jumped from his chair, stomped to the kitchen, grabbed the kitchen scissors, turned my chair around, and told me to sit still. Then with swift and deliberate cuts from the blades he slashed off my bangs until there was only a half-inch jagged fringe of hair sticking straight out around my forehead.

Nobody spoke. I remember my mother disappeared into the kitchen and returned with dessert with extra whipped cream topping. My brothers refused to look at me, secure with their cropped crew-cuts. I caught a glimpse of my reflection in the window and felt the death of my inner fire. I knew the other students would laugh at me at school the next day, but going to school would be better than staying home. As instructed, I swept up the hair from the floor and dumped it into the garbage.

After the humiliation with the haircut, there came a worse incident a few months later. I dressed for school in a cute plaid dress with a white collar. I had grown several inches and was one of the tallest girls in my class, but I liked the dress and was eager to wear it again. My father sat at the table reading the morning newspaper and glanced at me as I walked toward the door. He threw down the paper, and I froze.

"Get back to your room and change your clothes," he ordered. "That dress is too short!"

Instead of obeying, I grabbed my books and ran out the door. I was running down the alley when I heard him start his pickup truck and squeal out of the driveway. I felt like a desperate fugitive as I ran down a side road and ran four more blocks. I glanced back and saw him coming so I ran faster.

A carload of high school kids drove past me and I stared at them with a look of desperation. I knew them because they lived in my neighborhood, so I waved to see if they would stop and give me a ride. They drove on, laughing at the silly seventh grader running to school.

His red and black pickup was getting closer. I ran into the playground of the elementary school near the junior high and stood in the middle of the field, my breath coming in gasps of fear. My dad continued to drive around the block, and I turned to watch him circling past my two escape routes. The bell rang from the junior high, and I knew I was late. I looked for someone to help me, but the streets were quiet. School had started, and I was alone in the playground wearing my cute, but short, plaid dress.

Finally, I gave up and dutifully walked to his truck. He took me home, spanked me fiercely with a wooden board, and then left for work. I changed my clothes and walked to school, where I refused to undress for gym class. I stood alone with my hideous bangs and long skirt while the other girls exercised and ignored me. Mrs. Trounson, the PE teacher, asked if I was okay, and I nodded yes. The bruised but defiant girl didn't want any pity. When I returned home after school, the dress was gone.

I felt completely worthless and irrelevant. No one valued me for my uniqueness. I had developed a passion for music, reading, and writing but those attributes became more difficult while living in a home that prohibited emotions and rewarded constant work without play. I wanted to sing and dance and laugh and tell stories, but such frivolity wasn't allowed in our strict household. No one cried in my family, and I don't remember any times of boisterous laughter. Alone in my room, I wrote short stories and poetry, reread *Little Women*, listened to my music, and longed to be free.

My angst consumed me, and I believed there was something wrong with me. A few days after the dress incident, I was home alone when I took a bottle of aspirin and a glass of water into my bedroom and shut the door. I used a red plastic cup because I didn't want to accidentally break one of the good ones. I poured the white tablets onto the top of my brown dresser and counted eighty-three pills. Wanting even numbers, I lined up eight rows of ten aspirin and then dropped three tablets back into the bottle and replaced the lid. I started swallowing two at a time with a sip of water until they were gone.

I took a last glance at the sad reflection in the mirror. My ragged bangs stuck out straight and taunting. Then I lay on my bed and closed my eyes.

I felt the warmth of Idaho sunshine spilling through my window onto the yellow chenille bedspread. I heard the ticking of a clock from the hallway and the muffled, lonely coo of a mourning dove outside my window. Then I imagined my bedroom detaching from the rest of the house and floating away. I was happy because I still had my books, my record player, and my collection of records. Gerry and the Pacemakers were singing "Don't Let the Sun Catch You Crying" as everything faded to black.

I don't remember much of what happened next. I woke vomiting all over the floor, and my mother demanded that I put on a dress so I would look nice to go to the doctor. It was a blue dress with white polka dots and a ribbon for a belt. It was the outfit I wore to church and to family gatherings, and apparently now it was appropriate to wear when seeking medical attention after attempting suicide.

After much confusion, stomach pumping, and low mutterings from the doctor, my mother silently drove us home in the Ford station wagon. I was lying on the green fabric couch in the living room when my father burst into the house, his face red, his eyes wide.

"What have you done now?" He stood above me, his arms flailing in the air. He paced across the floor, then stopped. "Don't you ever tell anyone about this!" he demanded, and then added for extra impact, "You're grounded for a month, young lady!" With that, he stomped out of the house, slammed the door, and returned to his office at the truck stop. My mother looked at me with pity and disgust until I closed my eyes.

"Your father works so hard, and he gives us so much," she said. I knew she was shaking her head. "There are plenty of poor children in the world who would gladly trade places with you." She retreated to the kitchen to make dinner.

I was too weak to dig out my well-worn copies of *National Geographic* so I could see photographs of all the children who wanted to swap homes with me. I was rather partial to that smiling girl in Ireland. I thought I would enjoy living in a thatched-roof cottage and walking beside the sea. Or the places in Austria and Italy looked inviting. I had read about those locations and looked at the pictures until the pages were all loose in the magazines. I promised myself that if I lived through this horrible day, that someday I would travel the world and do whatever I wanted. I would follow the winding Snake River and find joy. Someday.

When I finally had the strength to stand up, I went to my room and noticed the aspirin bottle and glass were gone and a Holy Bible was strategically placed on my dresser. My mother had removed the evidence of my shameful act and substituted what would surely cure me, once and for all. I slipped out of the dress, hung it in the closet, and never wore it again. I took a marking pen and drew a picture of my favorite dodo bird caricature on the inside wall of my closet. The caption said, "Why?" as the silly cartoon questioned everything about my life.

I didn't mind being grounded. It wasn't much different from being ungrounded. I sat in my room, listened to my records, and wrote short stories about girls who could fly. On this particular afternoon, with my stomach churning and my head pounding, I stopped writing and stared out the window at the huge willow tree in the yard. For years, I had escaped out the window to climb up into the tree house, but my father had nailed shut my window so I couldn't open it. I remembered the pounding: bang, bang, bang, as he drove the nails into the wood.

"Silly man," I thought at the time. "If I wanted to get out I would just break the glass."

Sitting in my room, grounded for swallowing eighty aspirin, I wondered why my life was so strange. My two brothers never seemed to have any problems. They were spanked and hit occasionally, but they never talked back or got into as much trouble as I did. They were good boys. I was the bad girl, and I carried the heavy burden of being the family's failure. My father often threatened to send me away to boarding school, but I didn't know what that meant. Every time I asked, he would turn red and grumble, "Don't get smart with me." I concluded that I should remain stupid in his presence.

On the evening of my bad deed that could never be discussed, my father was late for dinner. My mother stood in the kitchen, adding milk to the gravy and arranging tin foil over the roast because she wanted the meal to be more than just another TV dinner. The siblings waited in their rooms. When he finally arrived, we gathered around the table and ate in silence. My brothers stirred lumps of butter into the mashed potatoes, took extra helpings of the bland meat to please my mother, and focused on their plates. Finally, near the end of the meal, my father spoke.

"It's time for you kids to do more work," he declared. "Besides your regular duties, you are to find jobs to earn money. The boys can work in the shop, and Elaine can get a newspaper route." He stood, poured himself a tall glass of Crown Royal, and walked outside to sit on the patio. The intermittent glow of his cigarette penetrated the darkness, and the ice clinked in the glass with every long draw. We all knew he'd rather be just about anywhere else instead of dealing with the burden of a family.

"Know how to work?" I said. "I finish my chores every day. Doesn't that count?"

"Elaine, please," whispered my mother. "Don't irritate your father any more today."

To teach me how to work, and obviously how to earn my keep, my parents had found a daily newspaper route for me. I was twelve years old. Most of my friends were trading in their jump ropes for lipstick and hugging boys instead of their fathers. Not me. I was Faithful Paper Girl, ever ready to deliver the *Twin Falls Times-News* on my shiny red, one-speed Schwinn to hungry customers. Not the heat of summer nor the chill of winter nor the teeth of vicious dogs kept me from my appointed routes.

My route was three miles long, mostly uphill, through the twilight zones of Wendell. The speed of my route ranged from two hours on easy days to four hours in the winter. If an emergency occurred, sometimes the papers didn't get delivered at all. I made thirty dollars a month, if every customer paid.

Weather was the chief obstacle of my paper route. Summer afternoons provided opportunities for leisurely sidetracks—a stop at the candy store or a meander through the city park. Some of my school friends lived along my route, and I would often stop to visit. Once I stopped at Cindy Brown's house and we created a fun trick to play on her older brother. We took some cat poop from the litter box, covered it with frosting, and gave it to him. The resulting commotion resulted in Mrs. Brown calling my parents and forbidding me to ever come inside her home again. I was to leave the newspaper at the door and go away. Another time I stopped at my friend Leah Geisler's home, and we practiced our drill team maneuvers until we broke a lamp. I was banned from another home.

I hated winter. Pedaling a bike up an ice-covered hill with seventy soggy newspapers was no thrill. Sometimes, if I shivered a lot, the nicer ladies would offer me hot chocolate. My pants would freeze stiff, my nostrils filled with ice, and I often had to take the route on foot and push my bike through the deep snow. In the spring, I could anticipate a sudden cloudburst that would drench my newspapers, despite the heavy canvas bags.

Besides the weather, the worst part of my route was dealing with dogs. To this day, my legs sport an assortment of various scars inflicted by the savage beasts. I quickly learned that the cutest poodle could tear into a leg as efficiently as any bulldog.

An experienced paper girl can anticipate a ferocious dog. The big ones that lie and growl are considered dangerous. Dogs that run around yelping are annoying but harmless if ignored. Any house with a high barbed-wire fence covered with shredded bits of clothing was to be avoided. Far too many times, I would cram the newspaper in the can and ride away as if my life were in danger, because it was. Angry, barking dogs would chase me down the street, biting my legs. A casual yell by their owners rarely stopped the attack. I started to carry a bottle of ammonia, and when a snarling beast came after me, I gave it a squirt right in the eyes. The attacks ended and I felt powerful, even though some friends and dog owners referred to me as a barbarian. I threatened to squirt them in the eyes.

Collecting money at the end of each month provided my first experience into the cruel world of entrepreneurship. I heard excuses from the older lady who hadn't received her Social Security check, or the couple with ten children who couldn't find the necessary $1.50, or the grinning old man who wanted me to come inside and have some tea. I learned that people try to take advantage of others, especially a twelve-year-old girl on a bicycle.

After a year of the paper route, I had mastered the art of delivery. I could ride by a newspaper can, reach into the bag for a paper, slap it on my knee to fold it twice, shove it in the can, and never slow down. Or I could throw a newspaper fifty feet with 80 percent accuracy. My biggest stunt was to pedal my bike, steer without using my hands, and read one of the newspapers. It was classic, and I owned that route.

I was thirteen when my mother noticed that I was a girl. My parents called a family meeting and decided I should give my route to my cousin, a good boy who would never cover cat poop with frosting. I was sad. After all, I knew seventy families and all their strange kids. I had heard their fights, eaten their cookies, and been invited inside to get warm. We shared stories as I traded the news for their quarters. I could outride the meanest dogs, and I had the best legs in class. I reluctantly handed over the collection book and canvas bags to my cousin. On the first snowy day, his mother drove him on the route, and I wanted to chase them and bite his leg.

The biggest lesson of having a daily newspaper route is I learned how to meet and talk with people. I came to their house every day, so I decided I might as well get to know them. I remembered the lonely ones who wanted to chat, the busy ones who only read one or two of the newspapers each week, and the struggling ones who begged me to give them another week to get the money. Some of them still owe me.

My paper route days were ones of independence and youthful energy. Decades later, I couldn't ride a bicycle laden with heavy newspapers three miles through gravel and over hills, but I continued to enjoy meeting people. And I continued to read the daily newspaper long after everyone else read the news online. Some habits were hard to break.

After I quit the newspaper route, my father decided to move into the country. In addition to the trucking company, he was starting a farming operation. He bought land on top of a hill overlooking rolling acres of pasture and decided to build a castle.

In May of 1965, the family moved to a new home two miles outside of Wendell. The unique design of the house attracted attention from curious people who drove for hours just to see it. For many years after that, strangers would think nothing of driving up to the house and asking if they could look inside. My father got a mean watchdog and often left his shotgun near the door as a warning to unwanted guests.

The house was built by Muncie Mink, my mother's brother-in-law. He was a talented local carpenter, but this became his largest project. Because the kitchen was round, the plans called for curved doors on the kitchen cabinets. Uncle Muncie learned how to construct and create the elaborate doors and install a huge skylight on the roof over the kitchen. He hired a crew to lay the massive stones for the walls and spread the concrete for the floors. At my request, he added a secret compartment in my closet for me to store gossip magazines and a pack of cigarettes that were never smoked.

According to my father, the house was designed by a student of the famous architect Frank Lloyd Wright. I don't remember the name of the original architect. From a distance, it looked like a massive ship marooned on a rock. Surrounded by 180 acres of farm land, the structure was designed of rock and cement and became both palace and prison. The house was built in a semi-circle with two main towers in the center. The floors were polished cement, and the ceilings were sprayed with glitter. The round kitchen had a huge bubble skylight and curved cabinet doors. The kitchen countertops were white marble, the two bathrooms had purple toilets, and my father's bathtub had red and black tiles. Padded doors covered with orange leather lined the hallway.

The outside walls were constructed of white stone with a slash of green glass on the wall of the living room. A screened porch circled around the back. The four bedrooms opened onto the porch and overlooked the countryside. We could walk up a jagged stone wall to get on top of the flat roof.

An upper clerestory of windows circled the entrance, and on the inside rock tower, my father hung the huge silver shield with four steel swords that he brought from one of his long-haul road trips. Over the fireplace, he hung his favored metal breastplate. The rest of his trucking treasures were stationed around the living room. An attractive but unused pool table took center stage in the living room as a repository for magazines, books, coats, and various knickknacks. I guessed that the original architect would have been dismayed at the altered house plans.

The house was the first in the county to have music and speakers wired into every room. In the evening, Dad would play his favorite records, which included an eclectic variety from Strauss waltzes to *The Six Fat Dutchmen*. Every morning at 6:00 a.m. my father would blare John Philip Sousa marches into our rooms, bang on the doors, and holler, "Hustle, hustle. Time is money!" Then my brothers and I would hurry out of bed, pull on work clothes, and get outside to do our assigned farm chores. As I moved sprinkler pipe or hoed beets or pulled weeds in the potato fields, I often reflected on my friends who were gathered at their breakfast tables, smiling over plates of pancakes and bacon. I knew at a young age that my home life was not normal.

I remember the first time I entered my friend's home and gasped out loud at the sight of matching furniture, floral wallpaper, delicate vases full of fresh flowers, and walls plastered with family photographs, pastoral scenes, and framed Norman Rockwell prints. On the rare occasions that I was allowed to sleep over at a friend's house, I couldn't believe that the family woke up calmly and gathered together to have a leisurely, pleasant breakfast. Obviously, they didn't know time was money.

The variety of crops around the house rotated through the years and included potatoes, corn, wheat, or sugar beets. Black Angus cattle grazed in the pasture, and my horse, Star, had a stall in the barn at the west end of the property. The pastoral scene was quite ideal until my father discovered that agricultural entrepreneur J.R. Simplot was selling his hogs. My father knew that sows would have up to thirteen babies at a time, a considerable economic advantage over cows that only produced one calf a year. So he went into the hog business and within a few years there were over 4,000 hogs grunting, squealing, and pooping just a half mile from the front door. My mother would sit at the table in our custom house and swat flies during dinner. The odor was horrific, but my father said it was the smell of money.

I have no idea why my father paid to build that house. Even though he was becoming the major employer and the most successful businessman in the county, he always kept a low profile. He wore polyester work shirts, faded workpants, and old boots. He was so frugal that he would wait in airports that had pay toilets until someone came out and he'd grab the door so he didn't have to pay a quarter to use the bathroom. Yet here it was— this dazzling stone estate on a country hill. And in that house, I wrote poems and stories, my brothers loaded shotgun shells to shoot rockchucks from the porch, and my father suffered from various illnesses until he died. After Dad's death, my mother lived alone in the house for sixteen years. At age seventy-nine, she was manipulated by an unscrupulous Realtor from Twin Falls to sell the house and surrounding acreage for one-fourth of the value and to carry the mortgage contract. The shameful real estate transaction caused the inglorious demise of the Ambrose castle on the hill.

~

CHAPTER FIVE

Bringing Water to the Desert

By the spring of 1965, I noticed that my father was captured and motivated by his vision of bringing water to his crops. Some farmers bought sprinkler pipe on a trial basis, but Dad gambled on thousands of dollars of pipe and then introduced lines suspended on huge wheels that ran on motors to move the pipes in a circular pivot. It consumed him, and he talked of nothing else. It provided him with an answer to the challenge of competing with nature for his crops. He had analyzed the situation, spent hours working with a pencil and paper, and consulted agriculture experts and magazines. Now he was ready to fulfill his dream to bring sprinkler pipe irrigation on moving pivots to southern Idaho.

Farmers usually watered their fields by subscribing to a series of canals and ditches running through their land. Landowners bought water rights to a certain amount of water and could take no more than their share. In a drought year, water allotments were limited to the meager portion released from upstream reservoirs.

Dad gathered his best employees for meetings around the Ambrose kitchen table. I remember them well: Keith Wert,

Preston Hughes, and Dad's brother-in-law, my uncle Henry Winterholler. I quietly supplied plates of fresh pie and mugs of hot coffee as I listened to their plans.

"If we can guarantee water, we'll always have crops to sell," Dad said, frustrated that his vision took months to implement. "The only way to guarantee water is to pump it from underground, use sprinklers to cover the crops. Someday we'll have sprinklers that rotate on giant pivots."

"It's a gamble, and it's risky," cautioned Keith. He took his role seriously of managing the farm's books and providing the necessary skepticism. "Sprinkler pipe and pumps cost thousands of dollars. And we'll need more employees to move the pipe and maintain the pumps."

"Listen to the facts," Dad persisted. "We'll install pumps throughout the fields and then we'll lay permanent main line pipe. The moveable sprinkler pipes will hook into the mainline and be rotated every twelve hours." He pointed to a series of charts and graphs he had drawn. The men leaned forward to study the graphs.

"This system is designed to provide the most efficient balance between the cost of the pipe and the cost of the power to run the pumps. We can even adjust the nozzles on the sprinkler heads to reduce the pressure on windy days. We also can adjust the pump to avoid soil erosion." He looked each man in the eye and then continued.

"Yes, we'll have to hire labor to move the pipe, but the increased yield will cover that cost. And what's wrong with providing more jobs?"

The men nodded their approval.

"How much water will be used?" Keith asked.

"Sprinklers result in better water conservation," Dad declared, resembling a preacher in a revival tent. "The lines will be fifty feet apart and each sprinkler will spray five gallons per minute.

That's one-fourth inch of water an hour. The consistent coverage eliminates the stress and low yield caused by drought and reduces the soil erosion and wasted water caused by irrigating the rows from the canal."

The mood in the room lifted as the men caught Dad's vision.

"I can't ignore this opportunity," he said intently. "I promise you it will work and in two years, we'll own five thousand acres of land! But we must hurry. Time is money."

The men were speechless at the thought of such an incredible goal. They returned to their figures and notes and waited for the final word.

"Let's do it," Dad whispered. They nodded in agreement and attacked their pie.

The group met again the following evening and, again, I remained within hearing distance as they studied financial figures and discussed their strategy.

"I can get a fair price for the cattle," said Keith. "With that money we can purchase the pipe and pumps. I still think we should borrow from the bank to get more land."

"No!" Dad stood up, knocking some papers to the floor. "We will never borrow from the bank. We can do this. Besides, I already bought five hundred more acres."

The men gasped. "Where? How?" they said in unison.

Dad sat down, enjoying their surprise. He relished the risk he had just taken.

"I bought five hundred acres of sagebrush along the canyon rim south of town. It's the old Scott farm."

"You what?" cried Keith. "That's nothing but sagebrush and sand! It's worthless. Three different farmers have gone broke on that barren wasteland."

Dad smiled. "I paid twenty-five dollars an acre for it," he bragged. "In a couple years, it will be worth five hundred an acre."

Keith shook his head and scribbled frantically on his paper. "I sure hope you know what you're doing."

News of the land purchase spread quickly at school.

"Hey, Elaine!" shouted Warren Block, a stocky farmer's son who was the leader of a pack of gregarious seventh-grade boys. "I hear your dad bought a bunch of sand and sagebrush. My dad said that's the dumbest thing he's ever heard of!"

A chorus of boys joined in. They had heard their parents joking about the land purchase. What was Neal Ambrose going to do with five hundred acres of sand? Did he have that much money to waste?

I burned at the criticism of my father. For the first time in my life, I defended him.

"You just wait and see," I said. "Someday he'll own all your farms!"

At the end of March, several loads of sprinkler pipe were delivered to Dad's new property south of town. Each pipe was forty feet long, three inches in diameter, with a sprinkler stand in the middle and metal hooks on each end that could be hooked into the main line or onto another pipe.

Dad hired men to dig wells and install pumps. Machines worked from dawn until dusk to clear the sagebrush and level the ground to prepare for miles of twelve-inch main line pipe that stretched from the pumps across the new fields. Each half mile of main line had thirty-two joints, or valves, that connected to the pipe. The valves were spaced fifty feet apart along the line. It would take two weeks, with crews of men moving several lines of pipe twice a day, to reach the end of the field, and then start over and move back.

My brothers, some cousins, and I joined the workers as they practiced carrying the pipe. The trick was to grab the sprinkler stand with one hand and support the pipe with the other and then carry the bobbing pipe to the next hookup along the main line. When the pipes were full of water, they were too heavy to carry, so each one had to be tilted to empty it. My older brother, Tom, could carry a pipe by himself but it took both George and me to balance another one. The pipes were to be changed at 6:00 a.m. and again at 6:00 p.m.

At first, there were problems with the pumps. To save money, the first pumps installed were diesel-powered. The noise could be heard for miles around and the equipment couldn't handle the constant use. Dad decided to bring in electric generators to power the pumps. Often, the generators would quit or a part would break. Preston Hughes, the main worker on the pumps, lived in the fields that spring, his hands and overalls black with grease and his heavy work boots caked with mud. Despite the hard work, Preston always had a contagious grin and his eyes sparkled beneath the dust and the sooty bill of his cap that touted a crusty fertilizer logo. He knew he was part of some great experiment and it was the highlight of his life. He often went out in the middle of the night, flashlight in hand, to repair the pumps and anticipate any trouble.

Other problems were created when one pipe came loose from the next one and the water washed a gully in the land. Several times, the sprinkler heads blew off; creating a geyser that could be seen for miles around. The high school Future Farmers of America took a field trip to the site and the teacher explained what a folly it was to install sprinkler pipe on land that was only sand and sagebrush.

Dad drove around the fields making regular inspections as the pipes were installed and flushed. My brothers and I rode in the back of the pickup truck, and at each stop we listened as the men discussed the day's gains and failures. I knew that each new problem only made my father more determined. It was time to plant the crops, and the sprinkler pipes had to be ready. Finally, the system worked for three days without a problem, and my father was elated.

"It's time to plant!" he said. And they did.

Farmers usually started planting potatoes on Good Friday, and huge tractors crisscrossed the fields turning and cultivating the land. Several trucks loaded with seed potatoes arrived from Montana and eastern Idaho, and the budding chunks of russet potatoes were dropped in the rows and covered with loose topsoil. The crew finished the planting two weeks later and laid the sprinkler pipe in long rows stretching from the main line.

My brothers and I stood beside our father as the valves were twisted to turn on the sprinklers. A gushing sound came from the main line, the sprinkler heads sputtered and turned aimlessly on their stands, and then water burst from the nozzles onto the waiting ground. The spring sunlight danced in the drops of man-made rain, creating thousands of temporary rainbows across the field. A rhythmic pattern of squirts rotated the sprinkler heads as the water sprayed forty feet in overlapping circles. It was music to our ears, and the surrounding workers hollered their approval. Only six months to wait for the harvest.

Two months later the potato plants were only a few inches high but still bigger than any other crops in the area. My brothers and I left early each morning, responsible for the forty acres around our house. Tom turned off the main line, unhooked the valve on the first pipe and carried it forty feet to the next valve on the main line. Then he walked back to the line, lifted the next pipe, emptied the water, and carried it to the new line, hooking it into the first pipe. It was a trick to balance the end of the pipe and make the connection to the other pipe from twenty feet away.

The wet, muddy ground made walking over the rows difficult, but Tom moved quickly, carrying the awkward pipes. George and I tried to maneuver a pipe, but I kept slipping in the mud and finally fell, much to the delight of my brothers.

Tom lifted a pipe at the end of the line and then threw it down in disgust. A drowned muskrat was stuck in the pipe, waterlogged and eyes bulging. It must have crawled into the pipe before it was hooked, and then it was trapped inside.

"Hey, George," Tom called. "Come and get this out."

Dropping the ends of pipe, George ran over to stare at the dead animal. He kicked it with his rubber boot and jumped back as the muskrat oozed from the pipe.

"What should we do with it?" asked George. Just then our father stopped his pickup truck at the end of the field, walked over, picked up the soggy muskrat, and threw it into the canal. Then he told us to get back to work. The job moved a bit slower as we cautiously checked the ends of the pipes for drowned varmints.

Several vehicles drove slowly past the fields south of Wendell, the drivers checking to see how the crops were doing on the sandy soil. No one was laughing at Neal Ambrose anymore. Especially those who wanted a job. Dad had hired several men to help with the pipe during the week and word was out that more jobs were available.

One day we finished moving the pipe and were returning to the pickup truck when an old Chevy truck stopped by the field. It was Warren Block, the boy who had teased me at school, and his father.

"Good morning, Mr. Ambrose," said Chester Block as he stepped out of his truck and stuck out his hand.

"Morning," said Dad, quickly shaking the hand. "What can I do for you?"

"That's a fine crop of potatoes you have there. I guess they will grow in sand," Chester said, shaking his head and grinning too much.

Dad was busy and had no time for small talk. He started to leave, so Chester Block quickly said what was on his mind.

"My boy, Warren, is a strong worker. He'd like a job moving those pipes. He can do it before and after school."

Dad looked at Warren. "Is that right, Warren?"

"A fine worker," said Chester.

"I'm asking Warren."

"Yeah, I can move the pipe," the boy said, avoiding my smug look.

"Be here Monday at 6:00 a.m.," my father said. "You'll get done in time for school, and then come back at 6:00 in the evening. We pay one dollar an hour."

"Thank you, Mr. Ambrose," Warren and his father said in unison. Then they hurried back into their truck and drove off.

"Do I have to work with that bully?" I asked.

"No," my father replied as he surveyed the field. "From now on, you will have other chores. The weather's getting warmer and we'll have to move the pipe faster. It's too hard for you, and we've got plenty of hired help now."

Dad got in the pickup and Tom quickly jumped in the front seat with him, eager to demonstrate that he was now with the working men. George and I climbed in the back and sat quietly during the ride home. I was sad because my father didn't want me moving any more sprinkler pipe, and I felt as if I had just flunked a test.

By late May, it was time to begin the preparations for Memorial Day. Mom and I cleaned the house, polished the good silverware, washed the good dishes, and ironed the table linens. The day before the holiday, Mom was up at 5:00 to start on the pies. The fruit on the trees wasn't ripe yet, so she had purchased apples and cherries at Simerly's Grocery Store. She worked the pie dough and then started on the bread dough. A twenty-pound ham was soaking in the sink and would be cooked overnight. I retrieved jars of home-canned beans, red beets, jam, and relishes from the cellar.

The Ambrose family celebrated Memorial Day for two reasons: to honor the deceased relatives and to clean out the pantry to make room for the garden produce and the fall harvest. Even in drought years, the pantry was emptied. It was bad luck to anticipate a meager harvest.

On Monday morning, my mother and I cut purple and white irises from the garden and arranged the flowers in jars covered with tin foil. The family piled into the car and drove to cemeteries in Twin Falls, Jerome, and Wendell, where at each stop, flowers were placed beside the grave of some relative who had gone on to his or her final reward. At the Wendell Cemetery, I found a clump of dandelions to put on the unmarked spot that held the coffin of my baby sister.

At 11:00, the American Legion Army volunteers conducted a program at the cemetery that concluded with rifles being fired into the air. The shots echoed in the breeze and the small American flags waved against the headstones. After paying our respects, we hurried home to prepare for company.

The relatives started arriving at the Ambrose house at 1:00 p.m., bringing salads and desserts. Aunt Billie brought her famous chocolate pie and Dad tried to hide it in the cupboard. Aunt Buff presented her sweet potato salad, bringing raves from everyone in the kitchen. At last count, there were twenty children and fifteen adults. The house soon resounded with the sounds and smells of family and food.

It was time to eat when Dad carried the heavy platter of ham into the dining room and placed it in the center of the massive wood table. When the other dishes were arranged around the ham, the adults gathered around the table to admire the feast. After a brief blessing by Uncle Jesse, the adults lined up to select their portions and sit at card tables scattered throughout the house. The children were last, scooping up mammoth servings before sitting down at big tables in the kitchen and on the porch.

I hadn't sat at the children's table for several years because I took care of Grandma Ambrose. I filled a plate for my grandmother and then sat beside her. The room buzzed with animated discussions and I knew the conversation would soon turn to the crops. As the only child in the room, I sat quietly and listened.

Uncle Mac was the first to ask. "How are those sprinklers doing, Neal? You sure know how to get the gossip going for miles around."

All eyes were on my father. They waited for his answer.

"Soon, every farm in the county will have sprinkler pipes on pivots," he predicted.

"Impossible!" gasped Uncle Mac. "Who can afford that?"

"Those who want to stay farming," came the reply.

"I heard that if everyone gets sprinklers, the underground water will dry up forever," Aunt Ruth said. Ruth ran a beauty shop in Jerome and had accumulated the wisdom and opinions of her faithful customers.

"The Snake River aquifer is the largest natural underground reservoir in the world," Dad said. The others looked at him with admiration and amazement. "It stretches 250 miles from Eastern Idaho to Hagerman. I've read studies that say the aquifer is between three thousand and six thousand feet deep and can hold about two billion acre-feet of water."

Two of the uncles let out a low whistle. Aunt Ruth grabbed her purse and dug for a pen so she could write down this fact to tell her customers.

"Is there any danger that the water would decrease if, say, we had several more years of drought?" asked Uncle Cleo.

"Actually, sprinklers use less water than canal irrigation and we can irrigate more land with the same amount of water," Dad responded. "And it's more flexible and less wasteful. On cool or cloudy days, we can cut back and not pump so much water."

"What's the biggest concern now?" asked Ruth, pretending to be a journalist.

Dad looked out the window at the surrounding fields in the distance. "Our biggest goal is to keep our water rights," he said. "Make sure no one ever takes your water rights."

"Is that possible?" Uncle Henry was concerned.

"It's possible because water rights are more valuable than gold," replied Dad. "Most of us bought our water rights years ago and staked a legal claim to the water we take for our crops. Now more farmers are coming into the area, and they will want water rights. Don't allow them to get yours."

The adults nodded in agreement, and I was proud that my father knew so much. He was tired of the conversation, however, and stood to go find Aunt Billie's chocolate pie. That signaled the beginning of the last course, and the crowd headed for the dessert table.

Aunt Billie stopped to hug me. "Are you still writing?" she asked.

"Yes, Aunt Billie," I replied, pleased that my aunt appreciated my short stories and poems. "I'll bring you some more poems this summer."

"Oh, that would be wonderful," Aunt Billie said. "I do enjoy reading your whimsical poems."

After dinner, the children ran outside to play and the women and older girls went quickly into the kitchen to hand-wash the dishes. The men gathered in the living room for a smoke and a cup of coffee, duplicating a familiar routine practiced by their own fathers.

I dried the dishes with my cousin Macie, a tiny and delicate girl I thought looked like an angel because her short blonde hair framed her face like a halo. Macie's skin was milky white and her blue eyes seemed on the verge of tears as she moved quietly, almost invisible in the room.

"After we're done with the dishes, do you want to go see my horse?" I asked.

"No," Macie replied softly. "I would like to go swing in the big willow tree in the back yard."

I thought that would be pretty boring but I knew Macie could spend hours in a swing, riding down and pushing up, singing an unknown song. After we finished our chores and ran to the yard, I pushed Macie, watching the back of the beautiful, mysterious child swing away from me. Macie seemed too perfect for such a confusing world. Later that year she was diagnosed with leukemia and died within two months. The family had another grave to visit the following Memorial Day.

When the last group of relatives left at 6:00 that evening, my father and brothers left to drive around the farms, and Mom and I sat on the front porch.

"I'm still stuffed," I moaned, rubbing my stomach.

"It was a great meal, wasn't it," said Mom. "It's such an honor to feed so many fine people."

I knew then that my mother was crazy.

"An honor!" I gasped. "It took two days of work. I don't consider that an honor."

Mom laughed and patted my knee. "Someday you will," she said.

By the end of June, the potato fields needed to be weeded, so I set out every morning on the Honda 50 motorcycle. I felt a fierce joy that our crops were healthy, and I couldn't help noticing the sparse plants on neighboring fields. Although the entire valley continued to suffer drought conditions, the sprinkler pipe on the Ambrose farms provided consistent moisture for the thirsty crops. By August, the workers were struggling to carry the pipe through the wet thicket of knee-high potato plants.

After my chores were done, I saddled my horse and rode through the pastures. Singing in time to the cadence of Star's hooves on the road, I completed several verses of "We'll Sing in the Sunshine." The cadence increased as the horse approached the barn. When Star broke into a trot, I abandoned the jaunty song and clung to the saddle horn. My head barely cleared the barn door as the horse raced inside, eager to be free of the sweaty saddle and singing girl.

I brushed the white mare, fed her grain, and turned her loose. The horse rolled in the dirt, shook and snorted, then loped off for the green grass in the pasture. I headed for the house, hoping I wasn't late for dinner again. As I neared, I saw two figures in front of the house, so I quietly walked around to the edge of the porch to see who was there.

My father stood with his back to me talking to what looked at first like an old man. It was Chester Block, but his appearance startled me. His shoulders stooped, his rumpled clothes hung on his back, and one hand gripped the railing. His face revealed a haggard man on the verge of collapse. I crept closer to hear what he was saying.

"I need your help, Mr. Ambrose. I got nowhere to go." My father stood silently, waiting for the man to continue. "You know I lost the crop last year," Chester spoke as if concentrating on every word. "I owed everything to the bank. This year, I had to mortgage my farm to get my operating loan."

Dad remained silent.

"This damned drought." Chester's voice was so low that I strained to hear. "I had a contract with Simplot. They were going to buy all my potatoes. But they sent a guy out last week to check my crop. He says"—Chester's voice changed to a wail—"he says my potatoes aren't good enough. They won't honor the contract."

Dad took a long drag from his cigarette, the red glow piercing the twilight. He turned his head and blew out the smoke.

"Please, Mr. Ambrose, you got to help me. I don't have enough money to even dig the spuds out of the ground. The bank will foreclose on my property. I've got a wife and kids. Farming is all I know. Where will I go? What will I do?" The man broke into sobs that shook his entire body. He clutched the porch rail with both hands and bent his head.

"I'm sorry, I'm sorry," Chester muttered between sobs. "I haven't slept in a week."

When my father spoke, it was as a father addressing a troubled child.

"Get hold of yourself, Chester. I can help you."

Chester looked up, his eyes brimming. He wiped his nose on his sleeve, sniffed, and leaned forward.

"I know how you feel, Chester. I lost everything once to the bank. But only once," he said. "They're in business to make money, just like we are. The trick is never let them have too much."

Chester stood still, waiting to learn how Neal Ambrose could help him.

"I'll buy your farm, Chester. I'll pay you a fair price."

I thought Chester would fall onto his knees in gratitude, but he managed to hang on to the railing.

"You and your family can stay in the house, but you'll work for me. You can manage the property. We'll put sprinkler pipe on it next spring."

Chester grabbed my father's hand and clutched it with both hands. "Thank you, Mr. Ambrose," he whispered. "Thank you."

"We'll get my accountant, Bill Cooper, to draw up the papers in the morning," Dad said.

Chester backed away and hurried to his truck. As Dad turned to watch the truck disappear down the lane, his face revealed a small smile instead of his usual stern expression. I studied my father, realizing that his visionary plan was now underway. There were more desperate farmers out there just like Chester Block who owed their farms to the bank, and Neal Ambrose would help them out of their distressful situations. In the process, the poor boy from Gooding County soon owned land in three counties in Idaho and property in three other states.

Within a few years, the former sagebrush land produced a county record of 350 sacks of potatoes per acre with 83 percent "number one" quality. Ambrose Farms had doubled the potato production in the region.

Dad's empire continued to grow with the addition of a terminal in Troutdale, Oregon, and a truck yard near Sacramento, California. He remodeled the shop in Butte, Montana, to include sleeping quarters for the drivers, and purchased a furnished home in Butte.

While managing the trucking operation, he also controlled Ambrose Farms, a huge farming operation that included 30,000 acres of land, 1,000 head of cattle, and more than 4,000 pigs. There was equipment to maintain, contracts to sign, and employees to motivate. During this time, I attended school, worked on chores around the farm, and then stayed in my bedroom writing poetry and short stories and playing my records. In hindsight, I wish I had joined him on his nightly rounds driving around the farms. We could have learned a lot from each other.

~

Idaho Farm Girl

This vibrant land yields ample crops
and cradles coffins of the dead,
expanding to the mountain tops
and plunging to the canyon bed,
still clings to me on muddy feet
and tempts me not to leave so fast.

This family dirt is bittersweet;
the dust to dust of ages past.
With scratch of hoe on stubborn weed,
and boots on trails in search of space,
this sun-burned girl, the scattered seed,
returns to claim my resting place.

CHAPTER SIX

Waiting for the Harvest

It was late August, the day before school started, and I decided to enjoy one last chance to be alone in my favorite place. I rode the Honda 50 down a winding canyon road to Thousand Island State Park, a pristine public retreat located next to the Snake River. Hundreds of waterfalls leaked, fell, and sprayed from sheer canyon walls 350 feet above the river. The water came from the Snake River Aquifer, a pool of water that traveled underground more than one hundred miles and emptied into the river.

From there, I rode into Sand Springs Ranch, a famous 1,600-acre ranch that was the showplace of southern Idaho. My paternal grandmother had told me grand stories about the ranch.

"Your father used to hike through the ranch when he was a boy," she said. "He always said he would own it someday."

"Tell me more about the ranch," I asked.

"During the mid-1800s, ferry boats were used to cross the Snake River in the territory that would become Idaho. Long before the town of Wendell was established in 1909, ferry boats transported passengers and mail to a landing that would become part of Sand Springs Ranch," she said. "Your grandfather drove for the Overland Stage Company, and he heard stories of how the ferries were used to move the stage coaches. The ruins of the old stage stop remain on the property down by the river."

"What made Sand Springs Ranch so unique?"

My grandmother smiled, pushed back her wispy gray hair, and crossed her bare feet. She had always been a large woman, and during the summer she didn't wear shoes because of large bunions on her feet. I have inherited those from her. She knew the history of the area and had her own pioneer story. My grandfather Arthur Ambrose was a farmer and operated the Star Stage Line in southern Idaho. His wife died in the influenza epidemic of 1917, leaving him with five young children. He remembered the daughter of a friend back in Missouri, so he wrote and asked her to come to Idaho and take care of the family. She was a single schoolteacher, twenty years younger, and wrote back to say she wouldn't come unless he married her. He agreed and met her at the train station at Shoshone, Idaho. They married at the justice of the peace, and he took her to the farm near Wendell to meet her new family of four boys and one girl. They had three more children: Mac, Billie, and my father, Arthur Neal.

My grandfather became an alcoholic, and back in the 1950s alcoholics were sent to State Hospital, formerly known as the Idaho Insane Asylum, in Blackfoot, where he died. My grandmother never learned to drive and was a widow for more than forty years. A quiet, pious woman, she became the family historian and respected matriarch.

Grandma continued to share her memories about Sand Springs Ranch. "It was the dream of every poor farm boy and every rich visitor to own that ranch. From the banks of the river, it stretches over the rock walls to overlook the hundreds of natural springs that erupt from the canyon. The ranch includes almost two miles of a privately owned natural spring creek that meanders through the property. It became a dude ranch for rich people from back east who wanted to play cowboy for a week. They were given cowboy boots and hats and gentle horses to ride. The duck hunters received full hunting gear and private blinds. They even have blinds for the hunting dogs."

"Who were the owners?"

"Well, Indians used to live near the fresh springs. You can still find some arrow heads around there. The first documented owner was H.B. 'Hy' Berkowitz, the treasurer of the Old Mr. Boston distilleries. One of the most famous guests was former president Herbert Hoover. One documented news report revealed that the president was telling an animated story while fishing and fell into the creek. You were a little girl when the ranch was sold to C. P. Clare, a manufacturer from Chicago and an executive from New York City. I kept many newspaper clippings about the ranch."

Over twenty years, Clare remodeled and restored the property. The ranch featured elaborate landscaping details including long rows of huge rose bushes, a grape arbor with a waterfall spouting from a cement lion's head, and a working replica of the Mannekin Pis statue that sprayed water into the trout-filled creek that ran alongside the main house. The large house showed the latest in interior design: silk wallpaper from France, a granite fireplace from Italy, and hand-rubbed oak paneling. A working crew of employees ran the ranch and cared for the horses and cattle.

I rode the motorcycle through the property, and the old caretaker waved me through. I parked the bike and hiked down to the river, carrying a bag with my lunch, a notebook, and a pen. I stopped at the old grape arbor and picked some fresh green grapes, but the tart fruit puckered my mouth and I ate only a handful before spitting out the seeds. Hiking across the pasture to a meadow just above the river, I could see for miles down the canyon where the spray from the waterfalls created double rainbows in the sunlight.

I turned toward the remains of an old fruit orchard and several sagging, abandoned buildings clumped together at the corner of the pasture near the old stage stop. I picked through the briars to pull out plump, red raspberries and groaned happily at the sweet taste. The birds had eaten most of the fruit on the old cherry trees and there weren't many berries left on the bushes, but I managed to fill a small sack to tuck in my bag.

I always felt as if I were walking right into history as I neared the four deserted buildings that marked the site of a former ferry crossing. I knew the story so well that I could almost see how pioneers coming west on the Oregon Trail often took this alternate route that crossed the Snake River near Hagerman. After several wagons were lost in the wide, swirling river, one pioneer decided to stay and build a ferry, where he spent many years taking wagons and settlers across the river. He claimed the pasture as his own and built a wooden house and a large barn. Many of his passengers had no money so they paid him with seeds and plants. As a result, his fruit orchard became famous throughout the region and sustained him long after the ferry was no longer needed.

Now the weathered sides of the old buildings swayed under the weight of rotting roofs. Grass and weeds grew in the dirt floors, and the old barn sheltered a family of foxes and several owls. An overgrown orchard yielded only damaged fruit for the birds, and a fortress of briars smothered the berry thicket. My father rented the land to graze cattle, and four cows rested in the coolness of the rock stage stop.

Climbing the fence, I left the meadow and hiked back up a narrow path through the sagebrush on the south side of the property. I crossed over a rock plateau to the edge of the canyon and started back down, my tennis shoes gripping the lava rock as I made my way down the steep trail. A bald eagle and several hawks flew overhead, providing a private escort to the river. My descent ended at a pool known as Blue Heart Springs where the ice-cold water bubbled from an underground spring into a heart-shaped cove. Nestled in my favorite private retreat next to the pool I ate lunch, saving the fresh berries for last.

Beyond the sheltered springs, the river tumbled over several small rapids. I rested in the grass and watched as the water flowed past. Pulling out my notebook, I reread my latest story. It was about a girl who rides a magic bicycle up to the clouds to find a city of enchanted children who need her to take care of them. I studied the story, shook my head, and turned to a clean page. I wrote a poem for the river and titled it "Endless River."

Endless River

Beautiful river, where do you go?
That, perhaps, is for no one to know.
Endlessly you amble along
Quietly bathed in your gurgling song.
Day after day, you never sleep,
Passing valleys and mountains so steep.
Oh, river, why don't you cease?
Is going onward your only peace?
Venturing into worlds anew,
I guess that is exciting, too.
Cool, refreshing, and oh, so wise.
What do you see with your traveling eyes?
Faraway places with peaceful shores,
Each opening to you their doors.
Oh, river, going past to the sea,
Please, wait—wait for me.

Then I closed my notebook and lay back in the grass. I felt safe here, in a place no one could reach without considerable trouble. A flock of ducks flew overhead in perfect formation like sky-writers pointing toward the coming autumn. Soon the leaves on the aspen and scrub oak would turn the canyon into a patchwork quilt of red, orange, and yellow. The cattle and horses would grow bulky with winter hair as hundreds of noisy ducks arrived to take up winter residence on the ponds above the meadow. In town, the farmer's market already offered tempting displays loaded with fresh produce from surrounding gardens and farms. The constant rumble of machinery in the fields matched the heartbeat of the community. Autumn was an awesome time in the country.

A sudden breeze interrupted my daydream, so I got up and started to climb out of the canyon, stopping for a few more berries, and then rode the motorcycle over to my grandmother's house. Grandma Ambrose wanted news about the harvest, so I amused her with stories of awkward sprinkler pipe, drowned varmints, and the biggest potato plants in the county. My grandmother responded with stories of her youth. She remembered how she had to haul water from the well every morning for the family's cooking and bathing needs.

"I sure could have used a sprinkler pipe next to the kitchen!" she laughed.

"I think Dad can arrange that," I said.

"Oh, no. I was only kidding. I like plumbing in the house. What a luxury."

As twilight approached, I hugged her and rode home, savoring the last of summer and anticipating the excitement of tomorrow when another new chapter in my life would begin. I knew eighth grade was going to be my best year ever.

Wendell Junior High bustled with the noise of students fighting the urge to run outside and capture some fun in the sun yet eager to be with their friends again. For my friends and me, eighth grade meant being older and wiser than the seventh graders and almost big enough to go to high school. The new eight-room junior high building sat next to the high school, an old brick fortress built in 1940. Junior high students weren't allowed in the high school, and it loomed as a mysterious attraction full of teenagers who could drive, earn money, and hold hands.

I loved the first day of school. I wore new saddle shoes with white socks, a green jumper, and a long-sleeved white blouse. At lunch, Sandra, Jeneal, Sally, and I met to make plans for the coming school activities. The fathers of several of my friends now worked for my dad, but such private matters weren't discussed.

The second day of school brought an interesting assignment. Mrs. Coffman, the eighth grade English teacher, rapped her pencil on her desk and asked for attention. Cleo Callen responded by belching loudly and the class dissolved into snickers.

"Now, children," Mrs. Coffman said as she walked over and stood beside Cleo. "I have a project for you. I want you to write a poem."

The class groaned.

"Now, listen," she continued. "The *National High School Poetry Anthology* is publishing a book next spring. They want to select some poems to be included. We are not just country hicks out here and I know some of you can write quite well." She walked over and patted Annie Thompson on the head. Annie, the banker's daughter, responded with mock surprise.

"The assignment is due Monday morning," the teacher stated, tucking her red pencil behind her ear. "The best poems will be read to the class and then sent for consideration in the anthology."

Mrs. Coffman was known for her incredible use of red pencils. She had taught in Wendell for twenty years, and students estimated that she had gone through a million red pencils. Every returned assignment featured red circles, underlining, question marks, and scribbled notes in the corner. It became a contest to see who could get the most red marks.

The assignment pleased me. I wondered if Mrs. Coffman would like my poem about the singing frog or the one about the evil monster who bites the heads off live gingerbread men. My current collection depended a great deal on what mood I was in at the time I wrote each poem.

The next Monday, I handed in my poem about the endless river. I felt it would pass inspection. Jeneal's poem described her mother making the famous Jones' Candy; Sandra wrote about how sad a balloon looked as it slowly deflated. Cleo bragged that he didn't have to write poetry and no one could make him, so Mrs. Coffman kept him after class.

A few days later, Mrs. Coffman called the class to attention. She looked particularly pleased with herself.

"Good morning, class," she began, standing beside Cleo so he would stop hanging pencils from his nostrils. "Today we're going to hear the poem that will be submitted to the anthology. Annie, will you read for us?"

Annie tossed her long curls and strutted to the front of the class. She waited for silence then began reading.

"Every hour, I see the flower. The morning shower brought such power. I can't be sour when I see the flower. Oh, pretty flower."

I looked at Cleo and stuck my finger in my mouth. Cleo burst out laughing and Mrs. Coffman marched over and rapped him on the head with her pencil. Annie straightened her shoulders and continued.

"I take a chance and like the flower I dance. Like a wild horse I prance. Will there be romance?"

The students twisted uncomfortably in their seats. I studied the calluses on my hands and dared not look at my friends. I heard Sandy smothering a giggle, and I bit my tongue.

Annie finished and floated to her seat. Mrs. Coffman clapped alone.

"Many of you wrote interesting poems," she said. "I encourage you to continue writing."

Then she looked at me. "I'd like to see you after class," she said. I nodded as Cleo hit me with a spitball.

After the bell rang, I picked up my book and walked to Mrs. Coffman's desk. The teacher had my poem, "The Endless River." It was covered with red pencil marks.

"Elaine, this is a good start," the teacher said. "But you didn't capture the right tone or the mood I wanted."

"Was I supposed to capture your mood?" I asked, unsure of the criticism.

"You need to work on setting the tone. I can't explain it, just rewrite it for tomorrow."

I walked out the door, wadded up the poem, and threw it on the floor.

"Elaine," I heard someone call from down the hall. I turned to see Mrs. Petersen, my science teacher and, according to most of the students, the best teacher in the school district.

"What did you throw down?" Mrs. Petersen said as she reached for the paper.

"It's nothing. I'll throw it away in the garbage can," I said and reached for the paper.

Mrs. Petersen unfolded the crumpled paper and read the poem. I stood quietly as the teacher read the poem a second time.

"This is very good, Elaine," she said.

"Old Coffman doesn't think so," I responded, frustrated and sorry that I was so sensitive about my poetry.

"The teachers talked about the poetry anthology," said Mrs. Petersen. "I think you should enter this one."

"I don't want to," I said. The bell rang and I turned to go to class. I didn't care that Mrs. Petersen kept the poem. It wasn't important anymore.

I sat through my next class staring out the window. I watched the cars going back and forth, wondering what it would be like to drive away. Seven years of near-perfect attendance proved my love of school, but on this day I hated everything about it.

That Friday night, the entire town turned out for the high school football game. Tom played on the team, so George claimed a spot near the players' bench, eager to carry drinks to the team or run for end zone footballs. My mother saved a place on the bleachers for Dad, who had promised to make it there by half time. I joined my friends in the pep section, cheering for the team and singing the Wendell Fight Song.

Wendell lost the game, but the loyal fans had a good time anyway. High school sports events drew more people than any other activity in the community. When the Twin Falls newspaper featured a Wendell player, the article remained taped in store windows for weeks.

Dad left after the game, taking George with him while my mother and I waited in the family car for Tom. It usually took twenty minutes for the team to shower and receive a pep talk from the coach. Many of the players drove their own cars but Tom had the shame of being driven home by his mother. He had saved most of the money he earned for moving sprinkler pipe and his goal was to buy a car before his senior year.

I grew impatient waiting in the car so I got out and walked over to a group of students standing around the gymnasium waiting for the football players. Most of them were in high school, but they welcomed me anyway. The first player to come out and greet the crowd was a junior named Les. Years earlier, we had been in the same 4-H clubs.

"Hi," he said, winking at me.

I couldn't remember how to talk.

He moved closer and gave me a hug. I suddenly felt uncomfortable because he was a junior, and he was hugging an eighth grader in front of God and everyone else. I wanted him to keep on hugging me.

He stepped back and smiled at me.

"You've changed a bit this year," he said softly. "I think you're pretty."

Pretty! I prayed that my feet would stay flat on the ground and not go cavorting around the parking lot. No one had ever told me I was pretty. I still didn't believe it, but it was sure a nice thing to hear.

Just then a junior girl came over and pulled on Les's arm. "Come on," she said. "You promised we'd all go for a ride in the van."

Les winked again at me and left with half the crowd. They clambered into pickup trucks and drove off, ready to raise a mighty ruckus in the limited streets of Wendell. I stood in the moonlight, totally transfixed by the power of a few spoken words. One voice in my mind told me to ignore a silly remark from an older flirt. Another voice told me it felt great to be alive and I was the prettiest girl in the entire universe.

Tom came out of the gym, hot and tired, and we drove home in silence. I decided that night to stop wearing my hair in a ponytail every day.

By the end of September, the mood around the Ambrose house grew from eager anticipation to sheer joy. The abundant harvest surpassed expectations, and the word was out that Neal Ambrose was a genius. His potato plants were forty inches high and most of the potatoes weighed over two pounds each. A buyer came from Simplot's in Boise to inspect the crop and immediately bought the entire field. The potatoes would be hauled to Caldwell, near Boise, to be processed into French fries for a small but expanding hamburger chain known as McDonald's.

In turn, Dad used the advance on the crop to buy more land, and there was plenty of land available as other farmers struggled to settle their debts. Newcomb Irrigation in Twin Falls drew up plans to remodel its office as Dad tripled his orders for sprinkler pipe. The abundant harvest had been worth the wait.

On the Friday before the potato harvest started, I sat in class, eager for the bell to ring. My father wanted me to work at the weigh station taking the tickets from each potato truck after it left the field. This was an exciting responsibility, I liked talking to the drivers, and, best of all, I didn't have to ride on the back of the harvester.

Just before class ended, the principal's voice came over the speaker.

"Attention, students," the principal said, sounding like a general addressing his troops. "We know that harvest is underway and the faculty reminds all students to be careful when working in the field. School will be released early next week so you can help."

A collective cheer went up from the students in the room, especially from those who had no intention of working in the harvest.

"One more announcement," the principal continued. "A special congratulations to Elaine Ambrose. Her poem 'The Endless River' was selected for publication in the *National High School Poetry Anthology* next April. This is a real honor for Wendell Schools, particularly since Elaine is only in the eighth grade. Congratulations, Elaine."

The speaker on the wall went silent, and all eyes were on me. I stared at my hands and wanted to disappear. Finally, Jeneal spoke.

"That's neat, Elaine. I can't wait to tell my mom."

"Hey, how much did you have to pay them?" snorted Cleo.

"That's not fair," Sandy defended me. "She writes good poetry."

"They must have lost my poem," sniffed Annie.

The bell rang and I bolted for the door. I brushed past Mrs. Coffman, who glared at me from her classroom door. I headed outside for freedom, only to bump into Mrs. Petersen.

"Congratulations, Elaine," she said, resting her hands on my shoulders. "I hope you don't mind that I submitted your poem. It is well-written."

I relaxed. "I wish he hadn't said it over the speaker," I mumbled. "But, thanks, anyway. I'm glad it will be published."

We exchanged smiles and I rushed to the school bus. I wanted to be alone to steep in the warm feelings of my accomplishment.

The next morning, I hurried to get ready for work. Dad took me to the weigh station, where I remained until nightfall, watching as trucks loaded with potatoes rolled onto the scales to be weighed and recorded. Tom, almost fifteen, drove one of the trucks. He waved at me, proud to be in control of something. I worked at the station all month long as the heavy trucks lumbered out of the field, taking their precious cargo to be weighed and then transported either into cellars or directly to the processing plant.

The weeks flew by, and I enjoyed the commotion of the harvest activities. On the counter at the weigh station, I kept several odd-shaped potatoes that the drivers had given me. One had four knobs and resembled a turtle; another looked just like a duck. During slow times, I drew faces on the potatoes or made characters for a potato family play.

Each evening, I took a bag home for my mother. Mom had at least one hundred recipes for potatoes; a thick, hearty soup was one of the family favorites. She used fresh onions, mustard seeds, and sweet cream.

Our family ate mashed potatoes at least four times every week. The huge bowl of mashed potatoes always featured a slowly melting lump of butter that was a prize for the one lucky enough to claim it. Mom's homemade potato chips made a hearty snack. She cut potatoes, with the skin still on, into thin slices, brushed them with oil, salted them lightly, and then baked them for twenty minutes. My brothers usually burned their fingers in their eagerness to eat the chips.

The potato harvest motivated the community as men, women, and equipment worked day and night to gather the crops. All were on the verge of exhaustion when the harvest was finally completed at the end of October. My job ended on a sunny Saturday afternoon, and I went home to clean up and grab a snack.

After eating some fresh fruit and crackers, I took a long walk around the property and stopped on the hill that overlooked the fields. What had been lush green landscape was now barren dirt covered with tangled, dead potato vines. The crops were gone and the land emerged scarred and plundered.

Other crops, planted in a rotation so there was always at least one crop in the ground, surrounded the empty potato fields. It was time for the third cutting of hay, and then the winter wheat would be planted. It was a continuous cycle, working the ground, planting the crop, waiting for the harvest. I watched as a crew in the distance loaded the sprinkler pipe on a long wagon that would carry it to the shed to be stored for the winter.

My father's truck came down the road; he had begun his ritual of inspecting the land. The truck turned into the empty field and stopped. He noticed me and walked over. We stood there silently, looking over the land together.

"It's been a good harvest," he said finally.

"It sure beats last year," I answered.

"We've already received orders for next year's crop. And it's not in the ground yet."

"Are you going to buy more land?"

My father looked at me. "Of course," he said. "We'll soon have five thousand more acres."

I stepped back. "You're kidding!" I exclaimed. "Why?"

"Because it's there," came the reply.

We gazed at the fields, and for a brief moment I wanted to talk to him about the land but changed my mind. After the overwhelming enterprise of the harvest, this quiet interlude seemed a rare luxury. Finally, Dad turned to leave. "Don't be late for dinner," he said.

"Don't be early," I retorted.

He stopped and looked at me. I shrugged my shoulders and grinned sheepishly.

He laughed. "See you later, kid." He walked to his truck and drove off to view the rest of his property.

I stayed and surveyed the countryside. The lifeless potato fields stretched to the distant canyon, ready for a winter's rest. Clumps of lazy white clouds dotted the vast blue sky, nudged along by an autumn breeze. A v-shaped flock of geese honked farewell on its way south. Cattle dozed in the pasture, taking advantage of a warm Indian summer afternoon.

For a brief moment, I forgot my youthful anxiety and marveled at my abundant life. So much had happened. I was changing, I wasn't so awkward anymore, and a boy had said I was pretty. My poem would be published, and I had completed several notebooks full of short stories. Just as the water had nourished the thirsty crops, I was thriving because of my good fortune. I felt glorious.

Here, on the hill near the potato field, I rejoiced in the splendor of my existence. That's when I felt it. A calm sensation poured over me, stirred my very soul, and quietly released through unrestricted tears flowing down my cheeks. Through my blurred vision, I knew that this warm feeling was the peace I had read about in my grandmother's Bible. And it was a peace that passed all understanding.

My father continued to buy land. He allocated a third of the land to crops, including potatoes, sugar beets, and hay, and the rest for grazing. He bought a thousand head of black Angus beef cattle and continued to install pumps and sprinklers on the various properties. He still also managed the trucking company.

With the proceeds from the crops, he had enough money to purchase a Bonanza four-seat airplane so he could fly back and forth to Butte, Montana.

The closest airport to Wendell was twenty miles away in Gooding. When Dad flew back to Idaho, he would fly over our house and circle several times as a message to my mother. Then she ran to her car and drove to Gooding to get him. Sometimes she took a kid or two, and our job was to set the blocks under the wheels as Dad secured the airplane. On lucky days, we would stop at the Gooding Tastee-Freeze and get an ice cream cone. At the time, the experience seemed like a normal family outing.

The regular flying trips were curtailed after one serious event. My dad was thirty minutes outside of Butte, Montana, when he experienced an appendicitis attack. He radioed for help and in the course of landing, his appendix burst. He was rushed to the hospital and stayed in serious condition for several days. True to form, he survived to fly again. I didn't know how he was able to be so strong.

I was in awe of him, as well as being afraid of him. He never attended college but possessed extraordinary vision for successful businesses. My respect was tempered by the harsh reality of his strict punishments. I kept my eyes down when we were together. Once I heard my grandmother mention that my father had been bankrupt in 1951 and was a multimillionaire fourteen years later. Through the trucking company and the farms, he hired more than two hundred employees and one fourth of the town's adults called him sir. It was 1965, and he was only thirty-seven years old.

∼

CHAPTER SEVEN

Potatoes and Poetry

I felt free when riding my horse, Star. On her back, I reached my arms straight out and screamed with joy at the exhilarating feeling as she thundered over the ground, pounding the uncharted flight into wisps of frantic dust. Welded to the saddle by experience, my blue-jeaned knees hugging the sides of the big, white mare, I rode the hundred-acre pasture in triumphant conquest. With the reins looped securely over the saddle horn, we rode as one, the half-ton horse and the eighty-pound girl, relishing the last hot days of summer.

I loved the feeling of riding free and unrestricted as the horse jumped ditches and raced along the wooden fences. I felt the powerful muscles propel the horse in a steady rhythm that grew with intensity as the horse broke from a gallop into a full-blown runaway. I hollered with delight, twisted my fingers through the horse's coarse mane, put my head down near its neck, and surrendered all control to the massive animal as she jumped the fence into the next pasture. The thrill was worth the terror.

Quivering and snorting, the horse finally stopped at the edge of the pasture. Foamy sweat covered its neck and legs, and the eyes were wide, the nostrils flared. I let go of the mane and adjusted my long brown ponytail. I sat in the saddle and breathed in unison with the mare, enjoying a race well run. It was a ritual the two of us shared many times during that summer of 1963.

Before heading back to the barn, I rode my horse to a hill and surveyed the surrounding countryside. In silent appreciation, I gazed at the patchwork of rolling pastures and abundant fields that stretched to the uncluttered horizon. The land produced the crops, supported the homes, and cradled the coffins of the dead. It was a part of my heritage, and I felt a kinship with my great-grandparents who came west in 1890, destitute and driven, to claim forty acres of free homestead land in southern Idaho. I knew I would have done the same.

The white mare tossed her head impatiently, so I quit daydreaming. "OK, Star. Let's go home. We can't be late again tonight." I picked up the reins and turned the animal toward home. It would take a long time to brush the sweat out of the horse and I dreaded being late for dinner. I kicked the horse to a trot and left the pasture.

As usual, dinnertime at the Ambrose house was not pleasant. Each member of the family approached the table with an apprehension that only hunger could subdue. My father had grown weary of the frozen dinners, and he requested meat and potatoes. The warm food did little to remove the chill around the table. On evenings when we didn't have frozen TV dinners, my mother scurried about with heaping plates of pork chops, mashed potatoes, gravy, bread, and various bowls of vegetables. She believed that quantity made up for quality. Dinner was especially difficult because she never really knew when my dad would be home. But when he did arrive, dinner had to be ready.

The usual scenario occurred when my father arrived and sat at the head of the table. He would scan a magazine about agriculture, aviation, or news, and wait.

Mom, a foot shorter than her husband, wore her short brown hair done in the latest permanent. Her pride and joy was her flawless skin, still supple despite years of hard work in the fields when she was younger. Neither her appearance nor her wisdom and dedication to work were noticed or appreciated by her family. To her friends, she was charming, witty, and funny. But at home, especially when Dad appeared, Mom became quiet and on guard.

She would frantically bring in the dishes, admonishing her children to hurry to the table. Tom, the oldest, sat next to our father. George, the youngest, always tumbled in breathless and noisy to find his chair and then be quiet.

One time, I rushed through the kitchen door, puffing after running from the barn with my messy hair falling out of the ponytail and my clothes covered with dirt and horse sweat. I splashed my face and hands with water from the kitchen faucet and plopped in my chair. My brothers stared at me in the silent room.

"You're late," Dad said without looking up.

"You're early," I mumbled and reached for the pork chops. Sometimes the remark amused him, but not this time.

"What did you say?" My father had stopped eating. The room froze.

I closed my eyes. *Don't talk back now*, I told myself. *It's been a good day.* I knew my mother and brothers were silently pleading for the same thing. I opened my eyes, knowing I had the power to make this a good meal or a bad meal. I opted for a good one.

"I'm sorry, Dad. I'll try to be on time."

The apology worked and the tension broke. My mother remained nervous because she didn't want another ruined evening. Her mind scrambled to think of a topic. Then she said, "Tom, how do the spuds look?"

Tom knew the routine. He obliged because he pitied his mother. "The spuds on the south field are looking better," he said. "They're small but still the best in the county."

"They need more water," said my father. He could control everything but the weather. Idaho's warm days and cool nights provided optimum potato growing conditions, but the dry land ached for water.

It was late August; the harvest would begin in a month and continue through October. Harvest was always a time of hope and sweat. The corn and beets were dug first and then the potatoes. Farmers in Idaho worked with pride, knowing they produced 25 percent of the nation's potatoes.

A successful potato harvest required exact timing, hard work, and help from Mother Nature since the potatoes could be dug only after the vines died and before the first hard freeze. Farmers prayed for the weather to remain between 50 and 70 degrees. Hot weather meant soggy potatoes that bruised easily, and freezing weather damaged the skin and ruined the taste. When the right moment finally came, gigantic harvesters were driven methodically through the fields, gathering mounds of potatoes and carrying them on rattling conveyor belts into the trucks that drove alongside. The dead vines were discarded out the back of the harvester, a rough dressing for the wounded earth.

Everyone in the Ambrose family participated in the potato harvest. Tom drove one of the spud trucks, and George picked up the potatoes that were left by the harvesters at the ends of the rows. I worked with the hired women and migrant workers riding on the back of the harvesters picking out rocks and dirt clods. Mom prepared huge meals for breakfast and dinner and sent loaded boxes of sandwiches to the field. She also worked at the spud storage cellar, keeping track of each load brought in. One missed tally could mean the difference between profit and loss for the season. Dad orchestrated each day's activities like a military general responsible for bringing in the bounty for a starving world. He had a tireless energy in the autumn and seemed to thrive on the sounds and smells of the work.

Dinner was over when the last plate was clean and Dad stood up. "Elaine, we need those sunflowers out of the south forty-acre field," he said without looking at me. "They're almost six feet high."

"I'm weeding there in the morning," I replied. "I'll be done in a few weeks."

Dad patted George on the head as he went outside to climb into his pickup truck. Every evening he drove around each field, inspecting the crops, checking fences, watching the livestock. Sometimes he was gone for hours, and he preferred to go alone.

I helped my mother clear the table and wash the dishes as my brothers left to finish various chores. It bothered me that the males in the family never helped with dishes, but I learned the hard way not to complain. I remembered last Thanksgiving, when the women began to clean after an exhausting meal for forty relatives. I had loudly refused to help unless my boy cousins also volunteered. For my impudence, I was taken to my room, spanked with The Board, and made to finish the dishes by myself.

Punishment was something to be avoided and never discussed at the Ambrose house. Respect for authority was enforced with The Board, a foot-long, two-inch-thick piece of wood kept in the kitchen and used adeptly by either parent. Tom, the oldest, had learned not to anger our parents and had avoided The Board for several years. He quietly kept to himself and when not doing chores, retreated behind a book. George was more gregarious and often in trouble, but could usually reduce the number of strikes through clever negotiating.

I, though, was a regular candidate for a session with The Board. My instant retorts and stubborn independence created an ongoing clash of wills that brought out the ugliness in all of us. I defiantly refused to fear The Board or submit to its power. I never cried during spankings, and as the blows fell harder, the more resolved I became not to cry out. It was my only victory.

I received my last spanking when I was thirteen years old. I had said something sarcastic to my father so he dragged me into my bedroom and spanked me a few times on my rear. The rage and humiliation caused me to start a five-year-calendar to mark off the months until I was eighteen. Being hit by my father distorted my concept of a healthy relationship. A few years after I left home, the man I was with hit me hard enough to split my lip and knock me to the ground. My father was only thirty minutes away, but I didn't call him because I didn't want him to know.

After the dishes were done, I went to my room to play my records. I shared my father's love of orchestral music and often lay in the dark, imagining great dramatic scenes while listening to Henry Mancini's orchestra. My favorite, "Exodus," would play again and again, each time to a different passion play in my mind.

My room, a haven of simple pleasures, was also the guest room, so I had a double bed covered by a bright yellow and orange quilt made by my grandmother. Huge orange and white pillows were stacked in one corner under a bright floor lamp. A bookcase held a wealth of adventure with titles such as *National Velvet, Treasure Island, The Diary of Anne Frank*, and *Little Women*. In the other corner of the room stood a small vanity table, mirror, and seat that my mother had purchased with coupons known as Gold Strike Stamps. I never sat at the vanity but I liked the way it looked.

My closet held a disheveled array of jeans, T-shirts, boots, tennis shoes, and jackets. Skirts and dresses, most of them made by my mother or grandmother, filled half of the closet. Girls were not allowed to wear pants at school, a ruling that particularly annoyed me.

Hidden in the back corner of the closet, buried under stacks of clothes, a large boot box bulged with my original short stories and simple poems. I wrote my first story in the fourth grade about a girl named Nan who lived in an attic and watched the world from her tiny window. Since then, I had created other characters, but Nan was always there, nagging me for a new story.

My poetry touched on ordinary objects that turned into fantasy characters: jelly beans became dancing soldiers, a weather vane came to life at midnight and bemoaned its lofty perch, an old woman fell asleep in the meadow and emerged as a butterfly. My writing was my escape and I revered a new tablet of paper as a special treasure. Aunt Billie, my father's sister, the only family member who read my poetry, would send back the poems with handwritten notes that ranged from "Nice work. I like this one" to "Come now, it can't be that bad!"

After listening to my records and taking a quick bath, I slipped on a clean nightshirt and retrieved some clean sheets from the hall closet. One of my favorite pleasures was to sleep on sheets that had been dried outside on the clothesline. Smoothing the white sheets over my mattress and covering them with the quilt, I called, "Good night," to my mother, who was reading to George, and turned off the light. Then I snuggled up in the sheets, savoring the clean, sweet feel and smell of the cool cotton. The summer breeze rustled the curtains at my open window, and I fell asleep to the sounds of crickets and distant cattle.

The next day I packed an extra-large lunch because I intended to ride my horse, an activity that sustained me during summer days on the farm. After my chores were done, I usually raced to the barn to get the hackamore and reins to catch Star. She was a big white horse, over fourteen hands high (almost fifty-eight inches from the ground), and had been trained as a prize-winning barrel racer. My father had acquired the horse from a man who owed him money, and the horse was all he had to give. At ten years old, she was past her prime for the rodeo, but I didn't care. She was my passport to liberty, and I loved her.

I would catch her in the pasture, bring her to the barn, and put on her bridle and saddle. I would be gone all day, and no one ever checked on me. Probably, they were just as eager to have me out of the house as I was to leave. After every ride, I brushed Star's hide and fed her oats. Sometimes I brought her an apple or some sugar cubes. My brothers referred to her as an old gray mare, but to me, she was a gorgeous white horse who could run like the wind. And she was my best friend.

In junior high school, I joined a 4-H Club for horseback riders and practiced how to ride my horse as she raced around three barrels set in a dirt arena. She knew what to do, and all I did was hang on for dear life. She loved the full gallop after rounding the third barrel, and within weeks we were the fastest team in the Club.

"You should ride her at the barrel race at the Gooding County Fair and Rodeo," my 4-H leaders encouraged me. "She should do well, even though she's not so young anymore." Again, I resorted to theatrical pleading to receive my parents' permission. I also needed silver cowboy boots, a purple saddle blanket, and a purple vest to ride with the 4-H Club. That required extra days of working in the field at one dollar an hour to hoe beets and weed potatoes. Soon I had enough money, and I was ready for the Fair and Rodeo at the end of August.

Two weeks before the Fair and Rodeo, I used bleach and water in a bucket to comb through Star's long mane and tail to make them gleaming white. Then I saddled her for a solo practice in the pasture. Just as we were riding toward the first barrel, a flock of pheasants suddenly flew up in front of us. Star jumped to the side and I lost my grip. I flew through the air and landed on my right foot. I screamed as it broke.

Star trotted back to me and lowered her head. I knew there would be no "Lassie moment" because I couldn't tell her to go get help. My only choice was to get to the three-rail fence and try to climb back on the horse. I grabbed the loose reins and told her to back up. She understood my command and slowly backed to the fence, pulling me through the dirt. We finally reached the fence and I managed to pull myself up on my good foot. Then I climbed up and straddled the top rail.

"Come here, Star," I said. "Easy now." She pressed against the fence so I could fall across the saddle. Then I sat up, secured my left boot into the stirrup, and reached for the reins. That's when I noticed her mouth was bleeding because the bit had rubbed it raw while she was pulling me. That's the only time I cried.

We rode back to the barn and found one of the hired hands, a gnarly old guy named Smitty. He helped me off the horse and into his pickup truck. "I'll get you home and then take care of the horse," he said. "I have some ointment for her mouth." I was grateful.

Going to the doctor was an inconvenience for many farm families. It just wasn't done without considerable effort and reason. "Are you sure it hurts?" my father asked. "Maybe it's just sprained?" I went to bed and moaned most of the night. When I couldn't walk the next morning and the foot was swollen and purple, my mother decided to take me to town to see Dr. Scheel. The x-rays confirmed a broken bone, but I needed to wait for the swelling to subside before receiving a cast. I hobbled home on crutches until we could return the following day for the cold, messy cast to be applied from my foot to my knee.

"Stay off of it for six weeks," the doctor said, and the words echoed like a prison sentence.

"But I'm competing in the barrel race at the rodeo in two weeks," I said. My mother and the doctor laughed. I did not see any humor in the situation. "I'm riding," I said with all the conviction I could muster. The doctor handed me the crutches and patted my head. "Go home now, dearie, and get some rest," he said. That's when I knew I would ride.

The following day, I called Todd Webb, my 4-H leader, and explained the situation. He seemed reluctant to talk with my parents about the barrel racing competition. "I just need help getting on Star," I said. "She knows what to do. Please let me try."

Todd Webb approached my father that night and, after a few shots of Crown Royal, convinced him that all I had to do was sit on the horse. And basically, that was true. Somehow, my father agreed, and I was thrilled.

The day before the race, Todd Webb and several 4-H Club members came around with horse trailers to get the horses. By then, I only used one crutch and could maneuver quite well with my clunky cast. We drove to the stables at the fairgrounds and unloaded the horses, our gear, and extra bales of hay. Star seemed nervous, so I brushed her hide and sang my favorite songs from our lazy riding days. She stopped quivering.

The next day, we all arrived early to prepare for the race. The right leg of my jeans was split to cover the cast. The Club members assisted in hoisting the saddle onto Star, joking that I would need to split any prize money with them. Star's mouth had healed, but I decided to pull a hackamore without a bit over her head. I struggled onto the horse and took the reins. I felt comfortable, except the cast caused my leg to stick straight out and I knew it would hit the first barrel as Star galloped around it.

"Tie me down," I said to Todd Webb. He hesitated but then agreed. He used a small rope to secure my right leg to the stirrup. "Don't fall," he said. "Or we're both in trouble."

We trotted to the arena and joined the other riders. I supported my weight on my thighs and left boot as we rode in a slow lope around the arena. I could feel Star getting tense. She had owned this competition many years ago, and I knew she was eager to return. "Easy, Star," I murmured. "We can do it."

There were seven riders ahead of us in the race, and we were last. They all posted times between twenty and fifteen seconds.

Star's ears were rigid as we eased into the chute. I matched her breathing as we waited for the countdown. Suddenly the gate flew open and Star shot out in a fury of speed. She leaned around the first barrel and my cast rubbed the side, then she ran toward the second barrel and circled it so sharply that I could touch the ground. She sped toward the third barrel. We rounded it and headed toward home. Dirt flew, the crowd cheered, and my cast banged against the rope as I rode the relentless force of pure energy. I knew my magnificent horse was running to win. We crossed the finish line in fourteen seconds and the crowd went wild. The clumsy, problem child and the old horse were the improbable winners.

I don't remember all the details after that. I know I looked into the stands and saw my mother cheering for me. The $500 prize money, a fortune back then, was added to my savings account. Star and I never raced again. After that day, she became slower and less eager to run free. We still took regular rides, and she would pick up the pace as I sang, but we had nothing else to prove.

My foot healed, I entered high school, and I didn't have much time to ride. Star spent her last days roaming the fields, and every now and then she would raise her head, point her ears, and break into a full gallop. The last time I saw her she was jumping a ditch on the far side of the pasture.

My older brother, Tom, and I competed throughout high school. He was student body president and I became student body secretary. He was elected a state officer in Future Farmers of America, and I was elected a state officer in Future Homemakers of America. He was chosen for the American Legion Boy's State training and I went to the Girls' State weeklong session and was elected Speaker of the House. Finally, I couldn't compete when he was accepted to Harvard University, because females in my family didn't attend college. I also knew my father wouldn't pay such a high tuition and expenses for me.

I enjoyed high school, and my favorite classes were English, choir, band, and speech. I played alto saxophone in the pep band and sang soprano in choir. I continued to write poetry and short stories and was excited to write for the school newspaper. During my senior year, an English teacher named Miss Luke introduced me to rhythm, meter, and rhyme. My poem about the endless river didn't have exact meter, so I concentrated on writing future poetry in iambic tetrameter: the accent is on every other syllable and the line contains four accented beats. I used a rhyme scheme of ABCB—the last word of the second line rhymed with the last word of the fourth rhyme.

In the spring of my senior year, my fifteen-minute poem titled "Revenge" won superior ratings in regional and statewide declamation contests. I still recall the first two stanzas:

Revenge is repetition done
of unjust acts that slowly burn.
The soul but seeks one thing alone—
An act of vengeance in return.
The tongue is whetted with reprisal,
raging hot with maddening thirst
Until the cup of vengeance quenched and
proudly wronged who wrong her first.

I balanced the darkness of the poetry by writing humorous essays and short stories. After being named editor of the school newspaper and editor of the yearbook, I was invited to a high school journalism conference at the University of Idaho. That adventure left a huge impact, and I begged for the chance to go to the University of Idaho. Women in my family were expected to get married and find contentment at home, down on the farm. My father was skeptical, even thought he was paying for my brother's expensive tuition at Harvard. The conversation was not positive.

"Dad, here's a brochure about the University of Idaho. I want to go."

"Why?"

"I want to study journalism and be a writer."

"Why?"

"Because it's a job I can do."

"You write for a high school newspaper. Big deal."

"Dad, I'll work to earn money during the summer and on Christmas and spring breaks."

"Go paint the fence down at the pig barns and you can use the profit from the next sale of pigs. That will help cover a semester."

"Thanks, I'll do that," I answered. "And it will be a lot cheaper than what you're paying for Harvard."

"Your brother is male."

"Big deal."

"You're grounded."

"Big deal."

That went well. But after I received a small scholarship for leadership, my parents couldn't say no. I packed my best flannel jumpers, white blouses, and wire curlers into a blue metal trunk and marked the days until the eight-hour drive to the university.

No one talked as my parents drove me to college. I sat in the back seat of the sensible, reliable Buick Riviera and stared out the window as we left Wendell and passed lush fields of potatoes, corn, and sugar beets. Harvest would begin in two months, and for the first time, I wouldn't participate. The landscape turned to high desert and the only green vegetation fringed the Snake River as it cupped southern Idaho on its way to the Pacific Ocean. We traveled through Boise, the capital city, and I stretched my neck to see the tall buildings and the capitol. In 1969, the population of Boise, the state's largest city, was only 75,000. We followed Highway 55 north of Boise, and the two-lane road entered a scenic panorama through the Payette National Forest, a vast expansion of rugged timberland that spanned 2.3 million acres. The land was bordered by two of the deepest canyons in North America—the Salmon River Canyon and Hells Canyon. Our journey continued north as the road hugged the mountains along the tumbling Payette River and we climbed to 5,000 feet above sea level. I felt as if I were being born.

After five hours of driving, we stopped in the resort town of McCall and found a quaint restaurant. We were only three hours from our destination, and my anticipation was palpable. We sat in silence. I wanted to talk about moving away, but I didn't know what to say. Part of me wanted to jump up in the restaurant and holler "I'm free!" but I didn't want to blow my chances. Any disruption in proper protocol could cause my father to change his mind and take me back home, where I would remain grounded forever. Deviating from my normal behavior, I kept quiet.

We left McCall and passed a pristine alpine lake. I made a mental note to live on the lake someday. The late afternoon sun danced on the golden grain fields of the region known as The Palouse as we neared Moscow, the home of the University of Idaho. We found the new student dormitory, and some cheerful students rushed out to greet us. They took my blue trunk and I eagerly followed them into the building. I never looked back, and my parents drove away. My grand adventure had just begun.

I arrived at college prepared to experience life beyond my hometown of 1,000 people. I was naive in thinking everything would be perfect because finally I was away from home. For the first time, I was responsible for myself, and the freedom came with a smorgasbord of choices. My first taste of freedom involved Budweiser beer and a clumsy frat boy. I still blush with the memory. College during the 1970s introduced this farm girl to hippies, anti-war protestors, demonstrators, musicians, poets, and wide-eyed friends who were just as eager as I was to test our wings. We studied, partied, gained and lost lovers, and attended a few classes. I played the guitar, sang in the college jazz choir, wore my hair long and parted, and bought flower dresses from consignment shops.

This first experience with freedom changed my life, and I focused on one main goal: getting a job and supporting myself. The University of Idaho provided opportunities to learn and explore. I majored in journalism because I enjoyed writing and in high school had been the editor of the school newspaper and yearbook.

I was encouraged to go through Sorority Rush, even though I didn't know anything about it. As the first female in my family to graduate from college, I didn't have any sorority legacies to shepherd me through the weeklong popularity contest. In the fall of 1969, the university had nine sororities, all located on campus. I attended the selection parties wearing my best wool jumper, even though the temperatures were still warm.

I didn't know anyone at any of the sororities, so I tried to behave myself and observe the procedures. The members in each house presented daily skits and routines to attract the favorite new pledges. Each evening, the house members would discuss each potential pledge and remove those who didn't make the cut. Back at the dormitory, I joined the other applicants in following the same process of elimination to decide which houses we preferred and the ones we didn't like.

By the third day, I was weary of the game. The most popular houses were Gamma Phi Beta and Kappa Kappa Gamma. I endured their perfect, polished programs and made small talk until both houses dropped me. We were all relieved. I enjoyed laughing with the members of the Delta Gamma house and decided that was the one I wanted. On "Squeal Day" I received a bid from Delta Gamma and moved into the house where I would live during all four years of college. I met young women in my pledge class who became lifelong friends. Over the years, we shared important events that included weddings, births of children, and trips with and without families. Now we share news of grandchildren and various ailments as we endure divorces, remarriages, and the deaths of parents.

I've always loved to sing and tried out for the Vandaleers, the prestigious concert choir, even though I'd never had any formal voice training. I was delighted to be accepted in my freshman year, and the group changed my life. During my sophomore year, the choir toured Europe and sang in cathedrals throughout England, Germany, Luxembourg, France, and Holland.

Most of the choir members had never traveled far and some had never left Idaho. We sang in cathedrals more than five hundred years old, and the acoustics created such harmonic sounds that many of us cried through the performances. When the airplane took off from Heathrow Airport in London, I sobbed for an hour. I knew my life would never be the same and I vowed to see more of the world.

My first writing classes prompted me to write more poems and try short stories. One professor expressed a tolerance for my emphasis on metered rhymes but encouraged me to try free verse. One assignment was to write without stopping and the subject was, "What Haunts You?" I submitted this poem and received an A.

Beggar Madonna

She haunts me still.
The beggar woman,
with outstretched hand,
huddled in the shadow
of the Spanish Cathedral,
a ragged baby at her breast.

Inside, pure in cool and splendor,
the white Madonna on a pedestal
with outstretched hand
received my offering.
Lo siento, Madre.
I'm sorry, Mother.

The professor challenged me to write more free verse. Our next assignment was to write about our earliest memory or feeling. I wrote about the twin sister who never breathed.

Solitary Sibling

In the mysterious void of initial creation
I shared my mother's womb
with a growing mass of defective development.
She came first and was promptly discarded.
I emerged yelling
and the doctor was elated
at my ten fingers and ten toes.
I was worth keeping.
Now free and independent
I avoid darkness and cramped quarters.
Still, I acknowledge my first companion
and wonder
if the heartbeat I remember was my mother's
or hers.
Did I feel my sister's soul evaporate
as she lost her humanity?
Or did I absorb her essence?
That would explain my ambivalent beliefs
and excuse my sporadic loneliness.

My creative enlightenment was interrupted every summer when I returned home to work for my father. Sometimes I worked in the office as a bookkeeper to track the sale of gasoline for the Texaco station. Other times I worked in the potato or beet fields. In June between my sophomore and junior year in college, I announced that I didn't want to work at home anymore. I wanted my freedom. I packed my plastic blue Samsonite suitcase and hiked to the bus station in town. I had saved enough money to travel a hundred miles to Boise. From there, I hitchhiked to my friend's house in Caldwell. Her parents allowed me to stay as long as we both had paying jobs.

The only job we could find was at the Simplot potato processing plant working the night shift from midnight to 8:00 a.m. I wore a white smock and hairnet and stood in an assembly line cutting spots off of the potatoes as they moved along the conveyor belt. During lunch break, I chatted with older women who worked the night shift so they could care for their families during the day. The experience taught me to empathize with them and make good decisions about my future. One early morning on the line, I realized that the potatoes were coming from my father's farm in Wendell. I quit the job and moved back home, duly humbled. I often think of those women, knowing how hard they worked day and night for their families. I'll never forget them.

During the month I was away, my family never contacted or visited me. I think they were allowing me to experience important lessons I didn't learn in college.

I majored in journalism, and my favorite courses included writing, speech, and music. In one creative writing class, the professor posted a winter scene on the board and instructed us to write without stopping. I wrote a poem about a vivid memory from my childhood, and didn't know the poem would become the metaphor for a memoir I would finish almost fifty years later.

1964 Town Crier

Ragged, rhythmic clouds of breath escape
from my mouth
as I push my burdened bicycle over
the patches of frozen snow.
Frost fills my nostrils and hardens
wayward hair
poking beneath my knit hat like spikes of rigid spider
legs.
The only sounds on this dark
moonless morning
come from the rustle of my frozen pant legs
and my boots squeaking and crunching through
the crusty layers.
I know every house on my paper route,
so I keep my head down
in a futile attempt to ignore the bitter winds
that slice through my coat.
Take a newspaper from the bag, slap it into
a roll, stick it into the can, keep going.
I'm 12 years old, and I'm outside in the brutal
Idaho winter
at 5:30 am to deliver 70 newspapers.
Every day. By myself.
My fingers hurt. Snot freezes on my lip.
A dog growls but doesn't leave its shelter.
Crunch. Breathe. My bag becomes lighter as
a sliver of daylight emerges through the dark.
I arrive home, and my father sits to read the newspaper
while my mother hands me
hot cocoa with marshmallows happily bobbing and
melting on top.

My aching hands circle the mug, and I lean over so the
steam can warm my face.
Silent tears roll down red cheeks.
I am the Messenger. I am the Town Crier.

During the winter of my junior year, harsh storms dumped a record amount of snow on northern Idaho. My parents bought me an airplane ticket to fly from Lewiston to Twin Falls for the holidays, but I arrived in Lewiston and the airport was closed due to bad weather. I called Dad and he said to call back in thirty minutes. I called back and he said he had rerouted an eighteen-wheel truck from Missoula, Montana, to get me. A few hours later, a snow-covered Montana Express truck arrived at the airport. I hopped in and expressed my gratitude, but the two drivers were not in a jolly mood. The diversion added eight hours to their journey and the roads included the old Whitebird Hill, a switchblade, two-lane, dangerous route in a snowstorm at night in the middle of nowhere.

"This will be some adventure!" I said, trying to stay positive.

"We just drove through a blizzard on LoLo Pass," said Dub Brownlee, a driver I had known for fifteen years. "We could be home now, but we'll get you home in about twelve hours."

"I hope Dad rewards you," I said.

"Oh, he will!" came a voice from the sleeper. Because I was a passenger, the second driver needed to stay in the sleeper.

We drove through the snowstorm and finally reached the treacherous Whitebird Hill. At an elevation of 4,400 feet, the snow was thick and blinding. The windshield wipers barely kept the top layer of snow off the windshield. There were no other drivers on the road. As the big rig creeped along the switchblade turns, I could look out the window and occasionally see the edge of the road that disappeared over the sides into steep canyons. One slip of a back wheel, and we would be over the edge and not found until the spring thaw. Brownlee kept both hands on the wheel and leaned forward to keep the truck on the road. I didn't dare tell him I had to go to the bathroom. I held that urge for another hour.

We approached the bottom of the grade as the wind blew the snow sideways across the windshield. My hands ached from holding on to the seat.

"I'm getting too tired," moaned Brownlee. "If I fall asleep, just grab the wheel and ease onto the brake pedal."

I looked at him, eyes wide and mind terrified. Then he winked. He enjoyed a good ten minutes of laughter after that joke. I couldn't laugh because I would wet my pants.

We arrived in Wendell the next morning. Driving the 390-mile journey in a car on dry roads took eight hours, but this journey was unique. My dad handed the drivers a thick envelope I assumed was full of cash. Over the years, Brownlee would remind me of his valiant sacrifice to get me home. I replied that I enjoyed being his favorite cargo.

Dad continued to run Montana Express and Ambrose Farms, even though his health deteriorated. He was diagnosed with several illnesses, including liver disease, gout, diabetes, and heart disease. He almost died in 1973 and was in and out of hospitals for the next sixteen years. He often conducted businesses from his bedroom with only a telephone and a legal pad.

In the spring of 1973, I was the only senior living in the sorority house. My friends were married and living in tiny apartments. A few had moved into apartments as single women, going against the rules of the sorority. One had dropped out of school. I was feeling restless with only a few months remaining until graduation. I posted the lyrics from "Wand'rin' Star" in my room. The song came from the 1969 western musical *Paint Your Wagon*, and was sung by Lee Marvin. A favorite verse was,

Heaven is goodbye forever, it's time for me to go. My dream was to find a rewarding job and to travel the world.

When I graduated in 1973, my father, mother, and younger brother drove eight hours to the University of Idaho, sat through the two-hour ceremony, and then drove back. They didn't take me to lunch or have a celebration. As they drove away, I knew I was on my own. The reality was exhilarating.

∾

CHAPTER EIGHT

Unfinished Eulogy

I fumbled in the darkness of an unfamiliar room. Where was that ringing phone? I finally found the receiver and muttered in sleepy irritation, "What?"

"Your father died."

The telephone call came on June 15, 1989, while I was on a business trip to Chicago. I was a thirty-seven-year-old manager for Boise Cascade Corporation and scheduled to conduct an all-day training seminar for employees. I thanked my husband for calling with the message, and then went back to sleep.

Several hours later, I woke, showered, dressed in my dark suit, white shirt, and silk bow tie, and took a taxi to the office to complete the training. That evening I attended the musical production of *Les Misérables*. The following morning, I changed my airline ticket and flew home. Ten years later, I finally shed tears about my father's death.

The conflicting feelings emerged the first time I heard a popular song titled "The Living Years." After I listened to the phrase "I wasn't there that morning when my father passed away," I burst into tears and sobbed until I couldn't breathe. I cried for all the emotional and physical pain, the guilt, and the regret for the lost opportunities to salvage any kind of relationship. Maybe, if he and I had just tried harder, we could have tolerated and even liked each other. But it was too late and reconciliation would never happen.

Peace finally came when I visualized picking up a battered little girl and staring into my own eyes. I rocked her and sang a lullaby that imitated the soft, cooing sounds of the mourning doves I used to hear outside my bedroom window. She clung to me and then asked if we had lived a good life. I held her closer and whispered, "Yes. Beyond your most vivid imagination!"

The relationship with my father evolved as I established my own independence and had children of my own. I no longer felt anger because of the harsh punishment during my childhood but attempted to see him as an intense man who rose from poverty to create several successful businesses. I was grateful that I had benefited from his ability to provide me a better life.

My father was a genius, cut from the same cloth as two other successful men from Idaho, J.R. Simplot and Joe Albertson, born in 1906 and 1909. They lived to be ninety-nine and eighty-seven. Simplot was an eighth-grade dropout who built a $3.6-billion global agriculture business, and Albertson started a grocery chain that grew to six hundred stores across the nation. My father was born in 1928 but died at age sixty, and I wonder what more he could have done if he had lived longer.

He shared the same humble beginnings, tenacity, and vision for success as the other two men. My dad worked his way from poverty to owning a multimillion-dollar estate because he saw a need and found solutions. His various businesses included trucking, agriculture, and fuel. He did all this before the introduction of computers, keeping the facts and figures in his mind.

He also shared their desire to make charitable contributions to the community. In 1970, Dad donated eight acres of land for a recreation park for Wendell. He named it McGinnis Park in honor of a favorite high school teacher, Gertrude F. McGinnis. He also contributed funds and labor to help build the town's first swimming pool. The park received additional funding from a government grant and local fundraising events to construct baseball fields, a picnic area, a basketball court, and a parking lot.

In 1978, my father realized a lifelong dream when he sold enough land to purchase Sand Springs Ranch. He never lived on the ranch but used the main house for an office and personal retreat. His crews repaired sagging fences, repainted barns, and restored elaborate landscaping. Sand Springs Ranch became a showplace again. He donated use of the ranch for hunting groups and for Easter sunrise services for the local churches.

After dad's death, we learned of other donations he made without wanting recognition. He paid for people's homes, medical surgeries, college tuitions, and emergency expenses. He donated to all local school activities and hired people who begged for employment. He gave them an opportunity to improve their lives. He also started a scholarship at the local high school in honor of Gertrude McGinnis.

I was in college in the early 1970s when he began to get sick. Heavy smoking led to several heart attacks, and a taste for Crown Royal whiskey played havoc with his liver. He developed gout, eczema, and adult diabetes. The stress of owning and running several businesses meant he never took a vacation. He worked every day, including Christmas. Finally realizing he needed more help, he surrounded himself with smart, hard-working people who helped grow the company.

When he came home from work, we respected his privacy and weren't allowed to use the telephone in case a driver called and needed assistance. There were round-the-clock emergency messages about wrecks, damaged pallets, stolen loads, or mechanical problems. His drivers were not unionized, and several times they were intimidated and threatened by union thugs in California. I remember the telephone calls about slashed tires and drivers who were beaten. On one occasion, my father took some union officials to court and won.

I was grateful to have some of his tenacity. After graduating from college, I drove to KMVT-TV in Twin Falls and convinced them to hire me as the first female television news reporter and talk show hostess in Idaho. They didn't have a job opening, but I was brash enough to convince them to give me a chance. I loved the job, and also loved the guy who worked there. Against my parents' wishes, we were married less than three months after we met. My family refused to attend the wedding, and I announced my new name live on the air. Later I realized I should have waited to plan a proper wedding because we didn't own the necessary household items, such as sheets, towels, or dishes. Being impetuous and impudent isn't always admirable.

Seven years later, my broken relationship with my father resulted in the most painful experience of my life. December 1980 somberly arrived in a gray cloud of disappointment as I became the involuntary star in my own soap opera, a hapless heroine who faced the camera at the end of each day and asked, "Why?" as the scene faded to black. Short of being tied to a railroad track within the sound of an oncoming train, I found myself in a dire situation, wondering how my life had turned into such a calamity of sorry events. I was unemployed and had a two-year-old daughter, a six-week-old son, an unemployed husband who left the state looking for work, and a broken furnace with no money to fix it. To compound the issues, I lived in the same small Idaho town as my wealthy parents, and they refused to help. This scenario was more like *The Grapes of Wrath* than *The Sound of Music*.

After getting the children to bed, I would sit alone in my rocking chair and wonder what went wrong. I thought I had followed the correct path by having a college degree before marriage and then working four years before having children. My plan was to stay home with two children for five years and then return to a satisfying, lucrative career. But no, suddenly I was poor and didn't have money to feed the kids or buy them presents. I didn't even have enough money for a cheap bottle of wine. At least I was breast-feeding the baby, so that cut down on grocery bills. And my daughter thought macaroni and cheese was what everyone had every night for dinner. Sometimes I would add a wiggly gelatin concoction, and she would squeal with delight. Toddlers don't know or care if Mommy earned Phi Beta Kappa scholastic honors in college. They just want to squish Jell-O through their teeth.

The course of events that led to that December unfolded like a fateful temptation. I was twenty-six years old in 1978 and energetically working as an assistant director for the University of Utah in Salt Lake City. My husband had a professional job in an advertising agency, and we owned a modest but new home. After our daughter was born, we decided to move to my hometown of Wendell, Idaho, population 1,200, to help my father with his businesses. He owned thousands of acres of land, 1,000 head of cattle, and more than fifty eighteen-wheel diesel trucks. He had earned his vast fortune on his own, and his philosophy of life was to work hard and die, a goal he achieved at the young age of sixty.

Dad had been sick for years, and he wanted help with the businesses. I had quit working full time to stay home with Emily. My husband wanted a chance to help run a business, so we sold our home in Salt Lake and moved to Wendell. In hindsight, by moving back home I probably was trying to establish the warm relationship with my father that I had always wanted. I should have known better. My father was not into relationships, and even though he was incredibly successful in business, life at home was painfully cold. His rock house on the hill was his castle.

After moving back to the village of Wendell, life went from an adventure to tolerable and then tumbled into a scene out of *On the Waterfront*. As I watched my career hopes fade away under the stressful burden of survival, I often thought of my single, childless friends who were blazing trails and breaking glass ceilings as women earned better professional jobs. Adopting my favorite Marlon Brando accent, I would raise my fists and declare, "I coulda been a contender! I coulda been somebody, instead of a bum, which is what I am."

There were momentary lapses in sanity when I wondered if I should have been more like my mother. I grew up watching her dutifully scurry around as she desperately tried to serve and obey. My father demanded a hot dinner on the table every night, even though the time could vary as much as three hours. My mother would add milk to the gravy, cover the meat with tin foil (which she later washed and reused), and admonish her children to be patient. "Your father works so hard," she would say. "We will wait for him." I opted not to emulate most of her habits. She fit the role of her time, and I still admire her goodness.

My husband worked for my father six days a week, and we lived out in the country on the prestigious Sand Springs Ranch in one of my father's houses. Every morning for eighteen months, Emily and I would stand at the picture windows and watch the waterfalls that tumbled into the river below us. In warm weather, I carried her in a backpack up and down the paths around the property. We were best buddies, and we loved the ranch.

Unfortunately, the relationship between my father and my husband was contentious. One afternoon in August of 1980, they got into a verbal fight and my dad fired my husband. My brothers and mother defended my dad's decision, and there weren't any reconciliations offered from either side.

I was pregnant with our second child. We were instructed to move, and so we found a tiny house in town and then my husband left to look for work because jobs weren't all that plentiful in Wendell. Our son was born in October, weighing in at a healthy eleven pounds. The next month, we scraped together enough money to buy a turkey breast for Thanksgiving. By December, our meager savings were gone, and we had no income.

I was determined to celebrate Christmas. We found a scraggly tree and decorated it with handmade ornaments. My daughter and I made cookies and sang songs. I copied photographs of the kids in their pajamas and made calendars as gifts. This was before personal computers, so I drew the calendar pages, stapled them to cardboard covered with fabric, and glued red rickrack around the edges. It was all I have to give to my family and friends.

Just as my personal soap opera was about to be renewed for another season, my life started to change. One afternoon, about a week before Christmas, I received a call from one of my father's employees. He was "in the neighborhood" and heard that my furnace was broken. He fixed it for free and wished me a merry Christmas. I handed him a calendar and he pretended to be overjoyed. The next day the mother of a childhood friend arrived at my door with two of her chickens, plucked and packaged. She said they had extras to give away. Again, I humbly handed her a calendar. More little miracles occurred. A friend brought a box of baby clothes that her boy had outgrown and teased me about my infant son wearing his sister's hand-me-down, pink pajamas. Then another friend of my mother's arrived with wrapped toys to put under the tree. The doorbell continued to ring, and I received casseroles, offers to babysit, more presents, and a bouquet of fresh flowers. I ran out of calendars to give in return.

To this day, I weep every time I think of these simple but loving gestures. Christmas of 1980 was a pivotal time in my life, and I am grateful that I received the true gifts of the season. My precious daughter, so eager to be happy, was amazed at the wonderful sights around our tree. My infant son, a blessing of hope, smiled at me every morning and gave me the determination to switch off the melodrama in my mind. The day before Christmas my husband was offered a professional job at an advertising agency in Boise, and we leaped from despair to profound joy. On Christmas Eve, I rocked both babies in my lap and sang them to sleep in heavenly peace. They never noticed my tears falling upon their sweet cheeks.

We moved to Boise and I found a job at Boise Cascade Corporation. I was promoted to manager and enjoyed a hectic life managing my career, caring for two children, and trying to keep my marriage together. I existed on less than five hours of sleep each night, and there wasn't any time for romance. While working full time, I only earned two weeks of vacation each year. This was during the 1980s, flex-time wasn't available, and working mothers needed to prove they could do it all.

The relationship improved between my parents and my husband and me. We lived a hundred miles away so we visited several times a year. Our children enjoyed visiting the farms, and we never discussed the traumatic events of 1980. When we visited for one Thanksgiving meal, my father sat in surprised amazement as my uncle asked about my corporate job. I felt vindicated, even though we never discussed the fight or the eviction. "Talk about it" never happened in our family.

My father's health continued to deteriorate. Doctors determined he needed a liver and kidney transplant, so he was scheduled for tests at the Mayo Clinic in Rochester, Minnesota. He was admitted and my mother stayed at a nearby apartment. Boise Cascade had an office in Minneapolis, so in March of 1988 I scheduled a business trip to see them. After my meetings, I drove a rental car to Rochester and found my parents. We took a slow walk outside and discussed small talk. Suddenly an alarm sounded on my father's beeper, meaning organs were on the way.

Our eyes met, and that's the only time I detected fear. They rushed back into the hospital and I drove away to catch a plane back to Boise. That night he received a new liver and kidney from the victim of a motorcycle accident in California. Tragically, the doctors didn't detect a small cancer growing in the liver.

After the transplant, my father suffered for fifteen months. My dutiful mother measured his daily medications, keeping regular charts and notes.

In the morning, he had Quinaglute, cyclosporine, prednisone, a multivitamin, Lasix, zyloprim, micronase, Tylenol, and dolophine. At noon he took another antacid and quinaglute. Antacid, cyclosporine, Imuran, zyloprim, and iron. Additional drugs included amphojel, aldactone. fambocor, septra, lonoxin, and synkayvite. Their house resembled a pharmacy. Once a robust eater, he had no appetite. Often, he would wake in the middle of the night, ring the buzzer to my old bedroom, where my mom slept, and request a casserole. She would make the food, take it to him, and he could only eat one bite. I don't know why they didn't hire a nurse to assist them. He never indicated how sick he was, and I regret not spending more time with him.

The medications weren't working because the cancer was undetected. He was weak, but determined to work, so he pulled himself upstairs to his office by holding on to the bannister. After suffering for fourteen years from heart attacks, gout, liver damage, and other ailments, the final indignity was to buy organs for transplant and have one organ cause his death. The Mayo Clinic denied any responsibility because the cancer was too small to be detected before the transplant.

His death certificate lists the causes of death as ventricular standstill, hyperkalemia, renal failure, allograph rejection, cyclosporin toxicity, and adenocarcinoma metastatic to hepatic allograph. Ultimately, he died a painful death from liver cancer.

There was standing room only at his funeral. I wore a red and black dress, the colors he chose for his trucks and trailers. I gave the eulogy and recited the following poem:

To My Dad

I took a walk the other day,
Alone, about a mile or so;
That's when I heard the mourning dove,
And thought of home and long ago.
I saw a diesel truck you bought
Just over thirty years ago.
You drove the truck both day and night,
You swore you'd make the business go.
You added trucks and hired teams
And sent them out against the best.

Soon red and black and silver trucks
Rolled day and night throughout the West.
I saw a patch of sandy ground.
You added sprinklers, time, and sweat.
They said it couldn't grow a crop.
You shrugged and said, "Let's make a bet!"
And then I saw the thriving farms,
The endless crops, the healthy fields.
I knew the heavy harvest trucks
Would work all night to get their yields.

And next I saw the Sand Springs Ranch—
A haven owned by only two,
A refuge from the hectic pace,
A poor boy's dream at last come true.
I tasted water from the spring

And smelled the roses in the breeze
As cattle grazed on rolling hills
And hawks perched high on poplar trees.
I saw you walking in a field
Just gazing over barren land.

You had a plan, just one more time,
To grow a crop from sage and sand.
But then I heard the mourning dove,
Its melancholy sound was low.
It seemed to say it's time to rest,
The work is done, and you must go.
You turned and slowly disappeared.
You never saw me standing there.
And then I saw a single bird
Just soaring freely in the air,

A splendid spirit flying strong,
No limits on where it could go,
So full of warmth and free from pain,
Inspecting all its world below.
And as it mastered wind and sky,
I heard great music fill the air.
"Blue Danube Waltz" was loud and clear;
Then came a peace, beyond compare.
And then the bird began to leave
Toward the warm and rising sun

And all of heaven opened wide
And God Himself declared, "Well Done!"
Though I was left with memories,
There came a vision clear and true:
A lot was left to carry on,

Another day, with work to do.
Now when I hear a mourning dove
Or see a bird up in the sky,
I'll think of you, so far away.
Until we meet again—Goodbye.

~

CHAPTER NINE

How to Steal an Estate

My father thought he had secured the future of his com- plicated multimillion-dollar estate through an extensive plan that designated how his assets would be managed and dis- tributed. He named my mother as personal representative with the admonishment that his wishes should be followed under the supervision of his estate attorney and certified professional accountant. Unfortunately, none of his plans were followed because my older brother, an attorney, thought he knew better and was smarter than anyone else. His duplicitous actions threatened to tear the family apart.

The first meetings began a month after Dad's funeral. There were four of us to manage the companies: my mother; my older brother, Tom; my younger brother, George; and me. We met in the office of Norman Cooper, CPA, in Twin Falls. After wading through piles of files and listening to confusing terms about Trust C and management agreements, Cooper proceeded to describe a Qualified Terminable Interest Property Trust, or Q-TIP. I scribbled notes to study later about how the Q-TIP provided a legal method for the surviving spouse to transfer funds and other assets into the trust and when the surviving spouse dies, the trust would then be distributed to any heirs.

Then Cooper distributed a thick packet of financial figures. The final amount left me speechless. The value of assets in my father's estate, including property, livestock, equipment, and money, had an approximate fair market value between $15 and $20 million. After he became successful, my father purposely avoided any show of wealth. He wore inexpensive, baggy pants and owned a few favorite shirts that rotated weekly. His boots were well-worn and usually had flecks of mud and dust. He disliked a suit and tie and rarely dressed up for any occasion. But I'm convinced his humble demeanor and conservative spending contributed to his prosperity.

My mother wasn't aware of the total assets even though she signed the yearly tax statements. I suspect my brothers knew. George had worked for the companies since graduating from college, and after Dad's death he managed both the farming operation and the trucking company. He was only thirty-three but proved his ability to make wise decisions. Over the years, my father kept him on a short leash and George often rebelled. Once, George left and said he wasn't coming back. My father convinced him to return, and he did. Even though he was proficient at his job, George never completely escaped the label of "the boss's son."

Tom seemed acutely interested in Cooper's information and asked questions I didn't understand. I knew I had a lot to learn to keep pace with my brothers. Ironically, the three of us brought unique talents that could have helped the family business: George excelled at operations, Tom knew the legal and governmental regulations, and I was a professional with marketing and communications abilities. Yet those attributes weren't enough for us to cooperate; each one feared the other ones would receive a better deal. I agree with the statement that a person doesn't know another person until they share an inheritance.

During the summer of 1989, I drove a hundred miles from Boise to southern Idaho several times for various meetings. I continued to work full time for Boise Cascade and balance the busy lives of my eleven-year-old daughter and eight-year-old son. My husband was the vice president of a major advertising firm in Boise, and we often passed each other coming and going. I tried to keep up with the family business and monitor the well-being of my mother. She continued to live in the house in the country, but she had a wide network of friends.

Tom was employed at a law firm in Boise, but we never were close and rarely saw each other. His studious demeanor clashed with my extrovert commotion, and neither of us wanted to change. Younger brother George was affable, easy-going, and talented. Clearly, he was my parents' favorite child, and he deserved that designation. Tom and I had moved away and started careers while George moved home after college graduation and worked for Dad.

The family meetings continued in Wendell with just the four of us. Many times, the conversation turned rancorous as Tom and I disagreed on management decisions. George usually kept quiet while Mom cried. She often remarked that "Neal was the lucky one." Tom continued to impose his opinions and began to make changes to the management agreements. He decided the company would pay for us to have new vehicles. How could I resist? Soon I was driving a new Jeep Wagoneer. The seduction was underway.

Tom became more bitter and combative with every meeting. One day he announced that he was quitting his job with the law firm in Boise and "sacrificing his profession" to move back to Wendell to manage the farms. In December of 1991, he finagled a legal quit-claim deed from Mom giving him forty acres of land in a prime location overlooking the rolling fields and $350,000 in company funds to build a house. My younger brother and

I didn't see the agreement until after it was signed. Tom also included an agreement that the company would pay his expenses and property taxes. No lawyers or accountants were involved in these documents.

Tom proceeded to build a mini-mansion: a two-story house with more than 5,200 square feet featuring a twisting staircase, dark walnut cabinetry, an ornate formal dining room, and a cavernous entryway with a grand piano no one knew how to play. Their master bathroom even had a bidet. It was the first bidet in Wendell, Idaho!

A reporter came from the *Twin Falls Times-News* to publish a feature about the elaborate landscaping around the mini-mansion. The Japanese gardens featured iris, maples, ferns, Austrian pines, azaleas, rhododendrons, peonies, and flowering cherry trees. The gardens stretched to a tennis court no one used. I was never invited inside the house, but I read about the details from the newspaper article.

In 1989, we decided to buy a diner near the freeway exit ramp. The plain metal building didn't have windows nor design and was called Gerry's Diner. Mom wanted to own a restaurant, so the company purchased the property and we changed the name to FarmHouse Restaurant. A massive remodeling project added windows, a salad bar, new furniture, and a larger kitchen. Mom hired excellent employees and talented cooks. The chicken-fried steak became well-known, and FarmHouse was named Best Restaurant in the Country by a vote of long-haul truck drivers. The award was mentioned by news anchor Tom Brocaw on the *NBC Nightly News* from New York. The restaurant became a favorite attraction for travelers and local residents, and continued to be popular after Mom sold it.

I continued to drive to Wendell for family business meetings. I continued marketing and communications responsibilities through writing and publishing an employee newsletter, writing and producing a company brochure, and participating in financial dealings for the farms and distributing company. The tension between the four of us became unbearable.

"Stop coming," Tom said to me after one stressful meeting over finances. "You only cause trouble."

"I want to hire an outside accountant for the farms," I replied. "I don't know where all the money is going."

"You wouldn't understand," he retorted.

"Tom, please," Mom said. "Why are you so mean to her?"

"This meeting is over," Tom announced. He gathered his papers and walked out. Mom cried.

We managed to keep the businesses going, despite the acrimony. By 1990, Montana Express and Ambrose Farms had more than a hundred vehicles on the roads on any given day. George was managing Montana Express and supervised the fleet as the fifty-five trucks covered 600,000 miles each month. The trucks averaged about five miles per gallon, and the high cost of fuel cut into the profit margin. George ordered new Cummins engines that were seven hundred pounds lighter and increased the fuel efficiency. Twenty new trucks were ordered to comply with strict new emission standards that reduced air pollution. The older drivers were impressed with the new cabs.

"The dashboards look like control panels of a small aircraft," said Jack Packer. "I remember when we didn't have heaters or sleepers!"

"Now we can stand up in the sleeper compartment," exclaimed Ray Eberhard. "I don't need to go home!"

"I'll take the soft upholstery and adjustable seats," said Bessie Bowman, the female of the husband and wife team. "No more spilling my coffee on these gentle rides."

Montana Express established a terminal in Troutdale, Oregon, and purchased land near Sacramento, California, to install a ten-thousand-gallon diesel tank and truck stop, scale, and shower facilities for the drivers.

I continued to live in Boise but helped with marketing activities for the companies. In 1991, I served on the entertainment committee for the annual Boise River Festival. I arranged for Montana Express to haul twenty thousand pounds of giant rabbits, bears, and butterflies from a float company in California. The drivers enjoyed the assignment because animated bunnies were easier to unload than hundred-pound sacks of sugar. Montana Express hauled the floats every summer for several years. I recorded their adventures in the monthly employee newsletter I wrote and published titled "Ambrose Action."

George and his wife, Marti, lived in the main house on Sand Springs Ranch. He wanted to move the trucking operation thirty miles closer to Twin Falls for better access to roads going south.

The four of us continued to meet and attempt a business atmosphere, but the discussions always became hostile. In an attempt to stop the fighting, we signed an agreement in April of 1993 that named Tom as managing partner, transferred $1.8 million in Montana Express stock to George, and distributed the shares of the farms, known as Sand Springs Ranch, equally to Tom, George, and me. Mom remained the personal representative of the estate. My mother agreed to everything my brothers said because they were the men.

Tom was only beginning to control the business and its finances. He hired his father-in-law to run the gas station, his mother-in-law to do bookkeeping for the farms, and gave his in-laws land from Ambrose Farms for a new house. Tom acquired twenty acres of land next to the gas station and opened a mobile home business. Soon the in-laws had a new home in the country and high-paying jobs. Tom hired his stepson and gave him a company house. I was the only one who complained about the abuse of assets, but no one listened to me. In our family meetings, Tom's financial statements became more confusing, and I questioned several unauthorized expenditures.

"I'd like to see an accounting for how you received money to build your house," I said. "I think all four of us should have voted on that use of company funds."

"Mom agreed to the disbursement, so that makes two out of four. George isn't complaining," Tom said. "That puts you in the minority."

"What would Dad say to that?" I asked.

He reacted with anger and slammed his fist on the table.

"You didn't care about Dad," he retorted. "You always made him mad."

"Right now, I think he'd be in my minority corner," I countered.

George remained silent. Mom cried. This scene was repeated countless times for more than a year.

George grew discouraged with the scene in Wendell and decided to move Montana Express to Twin Falls. By 1994, the trucking company was operating sixty-five trucks traveling almost nine million miles each year through eleven western states. The annual payroll exceeded $3.3 million. George and Marti built a house in the country near Filer and moved away. He successfully operated the company and didn't participate in the operation of Ambrose Farms. For five consecutive years, his drivers won safety awards from the Idaho Motor Transport Association for driving millions of miles without a major accident.

During the summer of 1995, only six years after Dad's death, the financial statements were a mess. Tom had signed a multimillion-dollar contract for a company to build a state-of-the-art potato cellar south of town. The building could hold 280,000 sacks of potatoes and incorporated the latest technology with large pipes running beneath the potatoes and large fans to push air through the pipes to keep the spuds at a controlled temperature. I mentioned that the farms had done just fine with old-fashioned, in-ground cellars, but he wouldn't listen. Tom also ordered expensive new farm equipment and built a new scale house. My dad used to keep old equipment held together with wires and salvaged parts, but Tom was easily swayed by every equipment salesman who came through the door.

I discovered he had collateralized Sand Springs Ranch for more than $2 million in personal loans. I hired an independent certified public accountant from Boise to go through the financial records, but Tom wouldn't allow him into the office, so the CPA returned to Boise. Tom knew I would not be quiet and allow him to continue to take all the money from the company. In desperation, he devised a plan to manipulate our mother into giving him control and ownership over Ambrose Farms and Sand Springs Ranch. I never anticipated the immense power or tragic consequences of his unethical behavior.

He wrote documents that allowed Mom, through her official role as personal representative of the A. Neal Ambrose Estate, to break and destroy Dad's will and trust agreements. Tom gave her the documents when she was alone and she didn't have legal counsel or time to consult with anyone, including me.

In return for the deceitful acquisition of Ambrose Farms and Sand Springs Ranch, my brother offered two promissory notes. One note pledged to pay her $1.8 million at 8 percent interest with the final payment ten years later in 2005. The note was collateralized by two mortgages of land my father had owned in Elmore County.

The second promissory note offered $3 million, bearing no interest, that would be paid over 360 months beginning in 1997. This note allowed my brother to gain ownership of a multimillion-dollar estate in exchange for a promise to pay Mom $3 million, interest-free, for thirty years. The final payment would be due when she was one hundred years old. Tom assumed she wouldn't live that long so the debt would be erased. Mom signed the agreement.

My younger brother, George, signed a similar buy-out agreement that removed his ownership of the farms in exchange for ownership of Montana Express. Obviously, my brothers had formed the agreements without my knowledge or participation. I was not informed of the agreements until several days later, after it was too late to contest the transactions.

Tom then sent me a certified letter informing me that I was a minority partner in Ambrose Farms and that Mom and George had sold their ownership rights. Tom wrote that as an owner I would be partially responsible for the million-dollar debts on the farms unless I also sold out to him. I believed I had no choice. I accepted his offer to sell my interests in the family business in exchange for an interest-free annuity that paid monthly. Tom borrowed $1 million against Sand Springs Ranch and bought my annuity.

In breaking my father's trust and estate agreements, my older brother also voided the Management Agreement for Sand Springs Ranch and Company. In that document, my father had named my younger brother, George, to be the managing partner. Also, a percentage of ownership and proceeds was designated for my cousin, Ron Ambrose, and a loyal employee, Ed Gulliford. These two men had helped my father maintain the farm's profitable operations. Once Tom took over, George, Ron, and Ed were no longer part of the agreement.

My children had loved Sand Springs Ranch; Emily lived there as a baby and Adam was conceived there. We returned often to tour the property, fish, ride horses, and feed the fish. As a young teenager, Adam loved to bring his friends to camp near the freshwater spring at the back of the property. One evening, he arrived with friends and set up camp. Tom appeared and began screaming at them to get off his property. The boys packed up and drove a hundred miles home to Boise. Tom sent a scathing letter to my attorney demanding that my son (his only nephew) never set foot on the property again or he would be charged with criminal trespassing.

Tom's mismanagement of assets propelled the companies into bankruptcy. He had mortgaged our beautiful Sand Springs Ranch for more than $4 million, and in desperation to acquire money, he listed the ranch for sale. Sand Springs Ranch sold for $4.5 million plus Realtor's fees. Tom profited only $100,000 after the transactions were settled. Several years later, the ranch sold again for almost $9 million.

Tom's next move was to sell the company's valuable water rights that my father had purchased during the 1960s. Still desperate for money, he sold farm equipment. According to one reliable source, he traded $100,000 worth of equipment on the Mayfield property in Elmore County to settle a $20,000 debt. The hired help hadn't been paid, so they quit. Other ranchers stepped in to save 750 cattle that were stranded in the snow. The multimillion-dollar potato cellar sold for a tiny fraction of the original cost and loan. Tom then sold the rest of the fertile farm ground to large dairy operations. Ambrose Farms and Sand Springs Ranch were systematically destroyed. He also stopped paying on the $4.8 million in promissory notes he had given our mother. He begged her to allow him to have a year's reprieve on his regular payments to her, saying my annuity was in jeopardy. That was a lie to sway her because my annuity was insured.

The community turned on him as employees lost jobs and assets were sold to pay off debts. He sold his mansion to a dairy man, moved his family to Oregon, and purchased a million-dollar, 6,000-square-foot home in an exclusive area near Portland. His wife insisted on opening a restaurant in the resort town of Seaside, so he bought another home there and established a high-end steak house. The Ambrosia Restaurant went out of business in less than a year.

With the companies in ruins, Tom sought part-time work and found a position teaching two courses at Lewis and Clark Law School in Portland. Ironically, the courses were in family law. On his biography, he listed his experience in owning and operating a multimillion-dollar family agriculture business. The irony is bittersweet. He taught there only a few years.

The turmoil of the family business claimed another victim: my marriage. I had been consumed with the angst and stress of what was happening to my mother and the assets, and I tried to remove all the friction from my life. I filed for divorce in August of 1996 and my husband did not contest the divorce so we settled out of court. Our children were eighteen and fifteen.

In September of 1996, I turned forty-five. My daughter moved away to another state to begin her freshman year of college. My divorce was final. I was forced out of the family business but gained a regular income. My fifteen-year-old son lived with me and kept me laughing. I bought land next to an alpine lake in McCall, Idaho, and began to build a house to be my escape from family and personal drama. I had dreamed of such a place on the lake ever since my parents drove me to college in 1969.

In December 1996, Tom planned an elaborate Christmas celebration for all the employees of Ambrose Farms and Sand Springs Ranch. Some had known and adored my mother for more than forty years, and many had helped my father establish and work for his businesses. Mom and I were not invited to the party.

Mom realized that she had been swindled by her own son. In June of 1997, she typed a letter stating that the contract between Tom and her had been "signed under duress and that the facts were not explained." She wrote that he had threatened her if she didn't sign it. She added, "The only agreement I will ever sign with Tom will be in the presence of my attorney." She had the letter notarized and wanted to meet with our attorneys in Boise.

I took her to the offices of David McAnaney and we met with his assistant, Janice Lawson. We explained the details for almost an hour, and Lawson decided to call Tom and ask him a few questions. She informed him at the beginning of the conversation that he was on speakerphone. Mom and I listened as Janice and my brother reviewed legal terms in the documents, promissory notes, and various agreements. At one point, Lawson questioned why Tom didn't insist on legal representation for his mother during the process. Tom was exasperated and irritated.

"She's a stupid old woman!" he snarled and ended the call.

I watched as my mother slumped in her chair. Lawson was speechless and tried to regain her composure. The anger that had boiled inside me for years burst forth in a string of expletives. I put my arms around my mother and held her as she sobbed on my shoulder. This woman had given away millions of dollars in assets to her firstborn son, and he only had contempt for her in return.

After the meeting in Boise, Mom drove a hundred miles back to her home in Wendell. She turned at Mountain Home to drive through Camus Prairie to see the lilies in bloom. She got distracted and drove off the road, overcorrected, and plummeted into the sagebrush. Her car rolled several times, landing on its top and plowing through the dirt and brush until stopping in the rocks.

I received a telephone call about the wreck, grabbed the files that contained details about her health insurance, medical instructions, and Do Not Resuscitate form, and drove south on Interstate 84. At one point, I was driving a hundred miles per hour. I didn't have a mobile telephone, so I pulled over at a gas station near Mountain Home and called my brother George for the latest information. He said Mom was being flown by Life Flight helicopter to St. Alphonsus Hospital in Boise. I sped back on the north-bound lane to Boise and arrived as the helicopter was landing on the roof. In the first of multiple hospital scenes that would repeat over the following seventeen years, I showed the files to the emergency room attendants and was ushered inside.

"Oh, God," was all I could say when I saw my mother on a bloody gurney in the emergency room. Her face was swollen and turning black and blue. The top of her head was a mess of blood, sagebrush, and cut glass. Though unconscious, she uttered a moan from the depth of her gut. She was taken away for x-rays, a CAT scan, and surgery. I sat and waited.

I knew the attending minister at the hospital and called him for help. George arrived from southern Idaho, and we shared a brief reunion. The minister escorted us into a private room where we held hands and prayed. That was the only time I ever held my brother's hand and prayed with him. The doctors prepared us for the worst scenario: she was gravely injured and if she survived, she would probably suffer brain damage.

My older brother was notified but he never called.

The next few days became a blur as I cared for my two teenagers—Emily was home from college for the summer—and stayed at the hospital with my mother. On one visit, I assured my mother as a nurse gently clean broken glass from her scalp. She was in and out of consciousness and restless. I talked with her, reassuring her she needed to slow down and take less drastic measures to get a new car. Doctors and nurses visited regularly, checking her progress and updating the diagnosis. She resented the constant noises and intrusions.

"Concentrate, Leona," one doctor said. "If you can move your fingers together, we'll move you from the intensive care to your own room."

I watched as my mother struggled for an hour to will her fingers to meet together. She did it and was moved to a semi-private room. The swelling in her face diminished and she could open her eyes. She asked for a mirror. I lied and said I didn't have one. She looked horrible, but she was alive. Tom visited briefly, stared at her, and left. He probably was hoping she would die so he didn't need to pay the millions he owed her. She lived anyway.

After Mom was discharged, George brought a medical bed to my house in Boise and she moved in with me. I tried to keep a positive routine as I monitored the kids, took care of her, and arranged for physical therapists and nurses to come to the house. After a month, I moved her to the house I had finished building in McCall. The first night in the new home on the lake, Mom slept in my bed and I slept on a sleeper sofa. She continued to gain strength, and the view of the lake inspired her. We sat on the deck every evening, and the kids joined us. It was August 1997, a time to live again. By September she was well enough to move back to Wendell. I drove her home and a week later drove my daughter to college in Oregon. My son was a junior in high school, and his football games provided a welcome distraction.

By 2002, Tom had fallen $500,000 behind on payments owed on the $4.8 million promissory notes. My mother was hesitant, but I convinced her to take action to pursue what she was owed. Because of the complicated legal issues, our attorney recommended a larger legal firm and we obtained a new attorney named Richard Boardman of Perkins Coie. We began a two-year ordeal that included paperwork, investigations, claims and counterclaims, and depositions. Finally, our attorney called for a summary judgment and our case ended in an old courtroom in Mountain Home, Idaho.

The judge approved the motion for summary judgment after my mother wrote and signed the following statement:

AFFIDAVIT OF LEONA AMBROSE
IN SUPPORT OF MOTION
FOR SUMMARY JUDGMENT

7/28/2004

My late husband, Neal Ambrose, and I created, owned, operated and developed Ambrose Farms. At the time of Neal's untimely death in 1989, Ambrose Farms owned approximately 30,000 acres of land, owned over 1,000 head of cattle, employed 100 people, and made a net profit of over one million dollars a year. In 1995 and 1996, my older son, Tom Ambrose, gave me documents to sign. These documents known as promissory notes were dated January 1, 1995 and July 5, 1996. When I signed these documents, I regret that I had no attorney present and my other two children were not present. Now Ambrose Farms no longer exists. Tom sold most of the land, equipment and cattle. Our faithful employees lost their jobs. There is nothing left but unpaid promissory notes.

September Sonnet

(written in John Milton's Italian rhyming scheme)

I was born in the Season of Harvest,
when fertile acres of land can yield more
than a bushel and peck of food to store.
The farmers know to survive winter's test.
Diesel trucks carry crops on journeys west.
Drivers trade time while they dream of the shore
of distant rivers they long to explore.
We stock the pantry, make quilts for the nest.
The gray geese point south as harvesters roll.
An elephant's eye is tall as the corn.
My birthday comes again at harvest time.
To market, to market, fill every bowl.
With gratitude for the time I was born,
cornucopias full of life and rhyme.

CHAPTER TEN

Judgment Day

L eaves were falling on October 5, 2004, as my mother and I walked toward the old, imposing courthouse. Autumn always had been a favorite time for us; it was the season of harvest when farmers realized the fruits of their labors. Decades earlier, my grandmothers had gathered and gleaned the final bounties from their massive gardens to prepare assembly lines over boiling pots as they canned vegetables and fruits for the winter. Residents in the village of Wendell planned activities and parades for the high school homecoming football game, one of the biggest events of the year. Geese squawked overhead as they pointed their way south. Thick coats appeared on cattle and horses and their breath was visible during the chilly mornings. Farm equipment and machinery was cleaned, inspected, and greased and moved into sheds and barns until spring planting. Of all the seasons, we valued the fall most of all.

My mother believed the biblical scripture that there was a time for everything, but she never anticipated going to court at age seventy-seven because of a lawsuit with her firstborn child. Her shoulders sagged as we approached the door, and I moved my arm around her. She seemed fragile and frightened, and I feared she would float away.

The courthouse smelled of old wood and wax. We noted the schedule of trials, and Mom cringed when she read the notice: Plaintiff, Leona Ambrose. Defendant, Tom Ambrose, Sand Springs Ranch. The lawyer for the plaintiff, Leona Ambrose, was Richard C. Boardman from Perkins Coie in Boise. I was listed as the counterdefendant because my brother sued me in response to my mother's suit against him.

We found the waiting area outside the courtroom of District Court Judge Mike Wetherell as our attorney Richard Boardman joined us. He was tall and impressive in a tailored suit, and his presence brought comfort to my mother. He provided the male authority and assurance I could not give her.

We waited on a hard, wooden bench in the hall, and I fingered the ornate, curbed armrests worn smooth after decades of rubbing from the hands of anxious plaintiffs. Boardman sat next to Mom, speaking with a positive opinion that the case would go smoothly. My mother and I had never been to court before, and the experience was intimidating. I felt her hesitation; she seemed weak and tiny. For a moment, I considered taking her home to end the emotional pain, but I wanted justice for her. I was focused but reminded myself to behave in the courtroom and refrain from interrupting the defense attorney.

When our case was called, I held Mom's arm and maneuvered us inside the courtroom. The judge's bench occupied the entire corner of the room and loomed about two feet higher than the rest of the furnishings. In front of the judge's platform were two wooden tables, one for the plaintiff and one for the defense. The clerk and court reporter sat to the side of the podium and a few people I didn't know sat in the gallery. The defense attorney took a chair at his table, and that's when we realized my brother wasn't going to attend. I scoffed aloud and received a warning look from Boardman. A side door opened, an armed bailiff in uniform entered, and someone said, "All rise." I had to help my mother stand as the judge entered and took his seat. We dutifully sat, also. After preliminary remarks, he asked for our attorney to speak.

Boardman addressed the court and described how Tom had presented two promissory notes to his mother, Leona Ambrose, a few years after the death of our father, Neal Ambrose. One, dated January 1, 1995, was for $1,875,000 and required interest-only payments with a balloon settlement in ten years. The second promissory note was dated September 27, 1996, for $3 million and did not require payment of interest but involved monthly payments for thirty years. I smiled when I remembered that I once told my brother he clearly missed his calling as a consigliere for the mafia.

Boardman addressed the judge and explained the reason for the motion for summary judgment. By 2002 Tom Ambrose had been unable to maintain the payment schedule on the notes and the outstanding debt owed was approximately $500,000. For collateral on the notes, he had promised mortgages on land in Elmore County once owned by my father, so my mother wanted to foreclose on those mortgages and receive the balance promised in the notes.

I bit my tongue to keep from muttering as Boardman explained how my brother had filed a counterclaim against me and presented unsubstantiated allegations that I had illegally acquired funds and stolen property from the estate. He did not provide any signed documents to prove his false accusations. In my opinion, he sued me to punish and intimidate me for helping our mother. I didn't have his legal knowledge, but I had the conviction and tenacity to challenge him in court. He didn't appear for the summary judgment but left the frantic mud-slinging to his attorney.

The defense attorney then addressed the Court and gave a rambling oratory that filled thirty pages of the fifty-three-page transcript of the proceedings. Clearly unprepared but determined to throw miscellaneous and unrelated case studies at the judge, he vacillated between contrite defendant and animated advocate for his client. At one point, he gave the ridiculous excuse that the statute of limitations had passed, so the debt wasn't real anymore. Then he seriously debated the different between a promise and an agreement.

"That doesn't say promissory note, that says agreement," he said. "And that's going to become important in our argument, Your Honor."

Then he said Mom told Tom he didn't need to pay and could have a year's reprieve. The defense attorney admitted he didn't have any signed documents to prove Mom had agreed to waive the payments.

That's when my mother started to react. Boardman had told us before going to court that we should remain silent, but Oberrecht's lies were too much for my mother. She started shaking her head, mouthing "No!" and then she started to weep. The defense attorney continued to throw out contrived excuses. When he plowed into a question about the wording of "even date hereof," the judge interrupted.

"Who prepared the documents?" the judge asked.

The defense attorney stammered, "I don't know the answer to that, Your Honor. I think that—well, I just don't know the answer to the question."

Obviously, Judge Wetherell realized my brother, an attorney, had prepared the documents, so it was silly to now claim the promissory notes had been misworded.

The judge then asked, "Do we know whether the documents were prepared at the instruction of Mr. Ambrose or at the instruction of Ms. Ambrose?" The judge was making it clear that he suspected my mother did not ask to be robbed by her firstborn son.

The defense attorney again mumbled and replied: "I don't know the answer to that question." His starched white collar seemed too tight as his face reddened under an array of erupting splotches. With an ounce of pity, I assumed he didn't want to be known as the ruthless lawyer who wasn't prepared to defeat a weeping widow.

I thought about my older brother and pictured him during our childhood. He was almost two years older than I was but just a year ahead of me in school. We both were student body officers and members of the Honor Society. He was intelligent, studious, and constantly shocked at my independent behavior. Once I ran out of the house after a fight with my father. Tom had a cast on his leg from a recent ACL surgery, but he hobbled and followed me as I marched two miles into town. He caught up to me and convinced me to return home.

Another time, my father gave me a ride home from school after a game. As we neared the country road out of town, I glanced over and thought I saw my brother walking home. He waved at us but I was too afraid to be wrong so I didn't say anything to my father and we drove past him. Tom walked the two miles home, and when he arrived he wasn't too happy with me.

"Why didn't you stop?" he asked.

"I didn't see you," I lied. The fear of making a mistake in front of my father was stronger than my compassion to give a ride to my brother.

Somehow over the next few years, my older brother lost that passion to make everything right. He was accepted into Harvard University and moved into an apartment with students who lived on trust funds. After graduating from Harvard with a degree in economics, he obtained a law degree from Lewis & Clark Law School in Portland, Oregon. He married and had a son, and later divorced his wife to marry his secretary. Once a respected lawyer in Boise, after Dad's death he drastically changed to became a person who could manipulate millions of dollars from his mother and sue his sister.

The defense attorney was getting desperate and began to toss out random, unrelated court cases. He said there was an insufficient address on the document, and my mother's address was incorrect on the promissory notes. At that point, several people in the courtroom stifled laughs. My parents had been well-known throughout the area, and Leona Ambrose could be easily found and identified.

The judge raised his eyebrows but motioned for the defense to proceed. The defense attorney continued his weak case by taking a new tactic. My brother had given my mother a promissory note for $3 million, but he promised to pay it back in thirty years, so the current value, obviously, was not $3 million. I laughed out loud at that ridiculous remark but quickly recovered my composure so I wouldn't cause trouble.

The judge seemed irritated. "Did Mr. Ambrose file any tax returns in which there was imputed interest declared as income?"

"Don't know. Don't know that, Your Honor." The defense attorney looked deflated.

As a last-chance defense, the defense attorney stated that Tom attempted to make a payment of $49,999 on the past-due loans, but the check bounced. Tom claimed he didn't know money was not in his account. Again, I stifled a laugh. Boardman shot me another warning look.

The defense attorney noticed my scorn and decided to go after me. He mentioned that I had signed a "tolling agreement" admitting to my liability on an outdated financial document. The problem was, he could only produce an agreement that Tom had signed but I hadn't. In the transcripts, he asks the court to believe his client that there had been an agreement but it couldn't be found. Not even a first-year lawyer would attempt that implausible defense.

The judge looked frustrated. "Ms. Ambrose took a three-million-dollar note with no interest to be paid over time, and we are supposed to discount the amount that Ms. Ambrose has given to a current value from thirty years? Not a very good deal for her compared to everybody else, was it?"

At that point, the defense attorney made a motion to strike a paragraph from his client's affidavit. Apparently, the great legal mind had made a mistake when calculating discount interest payments. With that, the defense attorney sat down. I glared at him as my mother slumped beside me and quietly twisted the mother's ring on her finger. Years previously, my two brothers and I had pooled our money to buy it for her. She wore the ring until she died.

The ordeal had taken ninety minutes by the time Richard Boardman, our attorney, stood to speak to the judge. The defense attorney had fumbled for ninety minutes. Boardman methodically refuted his arguments in less than twenty.

"In terms of the alleged agreement by my client to forbear for one year on the payments under the 1995 and 1996 note, there is no written agreement to that effect; number one major point."

The judge took notes. Several people in the audience leaned forward, eager to hear from our counsel. Mom nervously fingered her pearls. She had worn her favorite blue-and-white polka-dot blouse and black knit pants because she wanted to make a good impression. Her eyes stopped watering as Boardman proceeded in dismantling Tom's affidavit in response to the summary judgment.

On the Idaho statue of frauds allegation, Boardman was precise. "Tom is an experienced attorney, has been out of law school a lot longer than me. He knows what a statute of frauds is. He failed to comply with it."

I enjoyed watching the defense attorney squirm. They never anticipated Mom's suit would proceed and the judge would hear the motion for summary judgment. Tom had wrongly assumed she would acquiesce to him because she never disagreed with the men in the family. He forgot I refused to adopt that discriminating family tradition.

Boardman then addressed the bounced check for almost $50,000, and the fact that he claimed he didn't know there were insufficient funds.

"Come on. I mean, above and beyond the man being an educated person, being an attorney, how many of us have accounts and float $50,000 on them and don't know that, oh, there might not be enough in that account to make good on that tender? Not unless you are a criminal you don't do that."

I suppressed the instant desire to jump and hug Boardman by the neck. I felt my blood pressure begin to drop, and I stopped clenching my fists. I patted Mom's knee. She was trembling. Boardman's next words shot like lasers.

"On the mutual mistake issue, this is truly an area where I believe Mr. Ambrose and the defendants have manufactured facts."

What an elegant way to declare my brother and his attorney were liars. I momentarily considered becoming a lawyer, but quickly decided I'd rather hire a good one such as Boardman.

Boardman criticized the defense's confusion about interest payments on a loan given without interest. "They want you to believe, Judge, that there was a mutual mistake on this three-million-dollar note that specifically says there was no interest. The defense attorney argues: 'Well, we don't know whether it was principal.' Well, I don't know what else it could be if it isn't interest."

Boardman continued to address the judge with measured points to prove the case.

"The defendants are trying to convince you to go outside of this note. In due respect, Judge, you can't do that. The note is not ambiguous. It is for $3 million. It is for the principal amount only. My client was nice enough to her son to not charge interest." The murmur from people in the gallery indicated others wondered how they could get $3 million interest-free from a sweet widow.

With efficient articulation, Boardman continued. He called the statute of limitations claim a red herring. He was incredulous that the defense claimed they couldn't find the correct address for Leona Ambrose, the defendant's own mother. And he adamantly questioned the unproven claim against me.

"Mr. Ambrose can't come up with a written tolling agreement. The defense attorney makes the argument that: 'Well, he attests to the fact that there was an agreement.' To my mind, that simply ignores Idaho law."

Boardman concluded his comments with a direct plea to the judge. "They have done a commendable job of throwing everything, shooting every arrow they can at us. But when you finally do roll up your sleeves and work through all these agreements and the mortgages and the factual circumstances, you will come to one conclusion, that is, the defendants are in default, the promissory notes are valid, the mortgages are valid, and it's time to foreclose. It's that simple, Judge."

At that moment, I expected the ghost of Perry Mason to burst into the courtroom with a film crew and declare victory for the plaintiff. But the defense attorney wanted the last word and asked to be heard. Boardman objected. The judge said he had heard a significant amount of argument and that any further information was contained in the briefing material. The defense attorney didn't agree and demanded to add comments that weren't argument.

"It's manufactured evidence … it's extremely serious."

We all leaned forward for this new revelation. It turned out he was making another claim against me, probably at my brother's instructions. The defense attorney adamantly said that just because I never signed a tolling agreement with Tom didn't mean I really didn't sign it, so "there is no countervailing affidavit that she didn't sign one." The argument wouldn't pass a high school debate quiz.

At this point, after two hours of legal wrestling, it came down to my brother's attempt to blame me for everything. My mother started to cry again. She had taken the lies against her, but she couldn't stand the continued assault on me. I grabbed her hand and whispered, "It's okay." That's when she trembled and looked horrified. I could tell by her expression and the faint odor she had wet her pants. My seventy-seven-year-old mother buried her face in her frail hands, and the sudden intensity of my rage frightened me. I scribbled a frantic note to our attorney, "Stop this!" He nodded, and when it was his turn to address the judge, he shortened his closing remarks to a brief but brilliant petition for justice. I watched as Judge Wetherell listened intently and glanced at my mother's anguished face. At that point, I knew the case could go either way, and I momentarily regretted convincing my mother to proceed with the lawsuit. What if we lost?

I closed my eyes and remembered an old black-and-white photograph of Tom and me sitting on the running board of our father's first eighteen-wheel truck. I was a toddler, and we were so cute. The truck had a refrigerated trailer full of frozen TV dinners. My dad had paused briefly to join us in the photograph and then shooed us into the yard so he could drive away. My father assumed his sacrifices and hard work would be rewarded with a better life for his family. I remembered the low rumble of the diesel engine as the truck drove away on another journey.

I opened my eyes when I heard the judge say there was no proof of manufactured evidence. Boardman motioned for dismissal, and the judge concluded the proceedings, saying he would respond with a ruling within a few days. I was emotionally drained and frustrated that I wasn't allowed to speak. I may not have had the intellect of my older brother, but I had words and the fearless power to use them.

I ushered my mother out of the courtroom to the restrooms. To add further indignity, the women's restroom was occupied and locked, so I took her into the men's room. At first, she objected, but I looked and convinced her no one was inside the restroom. She gasped at the row of urinals but escaped into the one stall. I stood at the door, ready to prevent anyone from entering. She cleaned up as best she could and washed her hands in the old sink. The unbearable pain of the moment was broken when she insisted on applying lipstick. This brave, good woman had just been attacked in district court by her son's attorney but she wanted her lipstick. So right there in the men's room, she smeared the ruby-red color on her lips, adjusted her smile, and walked out, carrying the courage and strength of all the warrior women who place one foot in front of the other in order to survive. I remain in awe of her resilience.

A few days later, Richard Boardman called with the verdict: We won the summary judgment. My mother was awarded $2 million plus our attorney fees of $60,000. The victory was bittersweet because the amount of my brother's promissory notes to her totaled more than $4.8 million. She would never receive the remaining $2.8 million, but at least she wasn't insolvent as he had left her. In my opinion, the entire experience exacerbated her declining health and ultimately led to her heartbreaking slide into dementia.

Tom eventually paid the money required but never again communicated with Mom or me. He never paid the remaining $2.8 million he owed her.

The summer after the courtroom drama, I convinced Mom to move away from the farm and buy a new home in Twin Falls.

She had lived in the house east of Wendell for forty-two years, the last sixteen as a widow by herself. We had a dumpster moved to the property as we sifted through items to keep, donate, or toss. She shed tears as we convinced her to part with unnecessary items: old magazines, my father's outdated medications, broken ornaments, half-finished craft projects, and dozens of cookbooks. By then, she was seventy-eight and hadn't cooked a large meal for several years.

She refused to part with her Bibles. There were more than a dozen books, from embossed leather-bound editions with gold-leaf pages to large-print paperbacks. She had read each several times and underlined favorite passages in red or black ink. Several of her favorite scriptures were highlighted with bold markers and scattered stickers. She had been a good and faithful witness.

The process took weeks, but we moved her into her new home as we continued to clear the old one. She paid cash for the house and felt a new energy as we decided on drapes, landscaping, and cabinets in the garage. My daughter and I decorated the interior with new furniture and planned an open house. Guests came from miles away, and her new home was full of laughter. I hadn't seen her that happy in years. She looked radiant in a new purple jacket, black pants, and sensible shoes.

Unfortunately, she was manipulated into one final unscrupulous real estate transaction, and she didn't consult an attorney or tell my younger brother or me. At age seventy-nine, she sold the unique castle and ten acres of land for $125,000, one-fourth of its value. To make it worse, the buyer's Realtor talked her into carrying the contract. She was almost eighty years old and would never live to see the final payment. After she named me her designated power of attorney over health care and finances, I wrote a stern letter to the buyers and suggested they pay off the note. I added that my father would not have been happy with their real estate coup against my mother. They finally paid, and the money was allocated for her future living expenses.

She lived alone in her new house for four years before the accidents started to happen. I noticed several new dents on her car and knew it was time to take away the keys. I finally had the opportunity after she drove her car into the back wall of her garage, slammed the car into reverse, and hit the closing garage door behind her. The car was damaged on both ends, so I had it taken to the shop for repairs. That was the last time she drove. I kept telling her we were still "waiting for parts."

In 2009, we moved her to an assisted living facility in Boise to be closer to my grown children, her grandchildren, and me. She became frail, often falling in her room, and there were numerous ambulance trips to the hospital. A broken hip resulted in six weeks in a rehabilitation facility. She returned to rehab the following year with a broken back. Other falls resulted in staples in her head, bruises, and cuts. We made the decision to bring a wheelchair, and she reluctantly agreed to use it. She began a slow descent into dementia, and soon she couldn't remember our names. Her older son never visited, and eventually she stopped asking about him.

I hoped to jog her memory by surrounding her with familiar friends and sights. I moved her back to the Wendell Manor in 2013. She seemed happy for a few months, but then became withdrawn. That's when she lost the quilt. I was a hundred miles away and couldn't check on her every day, so I moved her, with the quilt, back to Boise.

My mother never fully recovered from the humiliating, excruciating experience in the courtroom. Ten years after the summary judgment, as her health deteriorated, she finally stopped eating and fell into a coma. As her designated power of attorney for health care, I consulted with hospice staff and we decided to withhold artificial measures but to keep her comfortable in her transition. On November 1, 2014, my mother died at eighty-seven, frail, broken, and lost in dementia. The only fact that keeps me from screaming for vengeance is I believe she is laughing, dancing, and singing with angels in the glorious light of her Lord.

≈

CHAPTER ELEVEN

The Book of Leona

My mother was dying. Her breathing had changed over the past few days—irregular, pausing only to alarm us, then continuing with a raspy rattle. My daughter and I sat beside her bed and held her hand, limp and translucent, as Tennessee Ernie Ford sang about peace in the valley. Gentle hospice workers came silently during her last week to shift her body and dab a damp sponge on her lips. Though they didn't know her, they treated her with the dignity and grace she deserved.

Outside her room at the assisted living facility, other residents shuffled by, some with walkers, as silent sentinels in the last act of the drama of life. After eighty-seven years, my mother's body and mind were gone, except for her strong heart. We could do nothing but wait.

I met many wonderful people who worked at Mom's various homes and rehabilitation centers. They did the jobs others don't want to do: showered old people, changed adult diapers, fed the feeble ones. They became the family when the real family stopped visiting. Most of the facilities had regular activities and the residents enjoyed group outings, visits from entertainers, and craft projects. But many of them lived their last years in quiet and lonely resignation.

It's often easier to show compassion and charity to worthy causes that include children, pets, and natural disasters. It's not as appealing to help elderly people, but they are the old souls, the ones who worked to build our country, fought in World War II, and faced a steep learning curve as technology during their lifetimes introduced airplane flight, interstate highways, television, computers, and cell phones. In simpler times, they danced to jazz, Sinatra, and Glenn Miller. Now, they leave the light on in hopes their adult children will visit.

During my mother's last years, before she slipped into dementia, her once-busy calendar was reduced to simple entries: shower on Tuesday and Friday, hair appointment on Thursday, and church on Sunday. I watched the spark grow dim in her eyes, and I wept for the proud woman who once worked in the fields, held several jobs as she raised her children, and dutifully supported my father's ambitious businesses. When she no longer remembered my name, I added more family photographs on her tiny dresser. "Don't forget us," I whispered. But it was too late.

She stopped eating during the third week of October 2014. After decades of physical and mental suffering, she used her last bit of control to decide her destiny. She wanted to go home and find peace in the valley. After she refused to eat and became too weak to get out of bed, I consulted with the gentle people from hospice. As her designated power of attorney over health care, I followed Mom's wishes to withhold life-saving measures. She rested beneath her hand-stitched quilt as kind people swabbed her mouth with damp cloths, and we played her favorite spiritual music.

After several days, her breathing became raspy but her heart was too strong to stop. One afternoon my daughter, Emily, and I were sitting with her when we were visited by the senior minister from the Center for Spiritual Living, the church my daughter attended. She asked if we could pray together, and we agreed.

"She's refusing to go because she's still waiting for my older brother to come," I said. "He's not coming. He hasn't visited her in twenty years."

The minister motioned for me to follow her into the hall.

"Your mother senses your moods," she said. "She doesn't want you to remain angry."

At first, I resented her remark. She didn't know Mom or me, and our story was too complicated and painful to explain in the hallway as she was dying. But I was struck by her words: "She doesn't want you to remain angry." Of course, my mother would want me to be happy. So, I decided to lie to her.

We returned to her bedside, and I knelt to hold her. I said clearly, "This is Elaine. Everyone is happy. Tom is fine. George is doing well. Your grandkids and I are happy, and we love you so much. Now it's time to be with Dad. It's time to let go."

She passed away a few hours later, leaving a wound in my heart that will never heal. Someday I hope to see her presence again. I suspect she'll say, "I knew you were lying, but that's okay. Now, please get your hair out of your face." Then we'll laugh.

As Mom's designated power of attorney, I had the duty to make the final arrangements for her funeral. Her passing brought a wide range of feelings, from relief to sorrow, but I knew she would want to look her best for the last viewing.

"What do you want her to wear?" the gentle woman from hospice asked as she took notes.

"The nice robe," I answered. "With the pearl necklace."

The woman stopped writing and peered at me, unsure of what I had suggested. "You want her buried in a robe?"

So I told her why. In 1969, my father traveled to Japan on a business trip and brought back an elegant silk robe as a gift for my mother. They had been high school sweethearts; he was the gregarious student body president and she was the timid valedictorian. He wasn't one for giving gifts, and she wasn't comfortable accepting them.

Over the past forty-five years, I have asked her why she never wore the robe, and her answer always was the same: "It's too nice."

That's how she lived, protecting special objects in her life that she never felt worthy enough to enjoy. She never burned the fancy candles so they melted in storage. The good china dishes and silverware only came out at Thanksgiving and Christmas. And she saved and reread every birthday and holiday card she ever received. (I have inherited this trait, and it's a tough one to break.)

To arrange for her service, my to-do list was filled with complicated assignments. How do I get the headstone engraved? It's been waiting at my father's grave since 1989. How do I condense her amazing life into a three-hundred-word obituary? Should I request that in lieu of flowers, people can contribute to the scholarship she established at the University of Idaho? The donation would be nice, but she also would love the flowers. She'd say she didn't deserve them and they were too nice, but she would love flowers. The only easy decision I had to make was what she would wear for her final outfit. I had the robe professionally cleaned and ready.

She wore the nice robe for the first time at her funeral service. And she wore pearls. She always wore pearls, even with her favorite cozy sweatshirts ordered from the Country Living catalog. She was beautiful. At the end of the service, bright sunlight broke through the clouds and shined through stained glass windows she had commissioned for the church years earlier. Light filled the sanctuary, and we felt at peace.

My mother passed away on a cool but clear November morning. My children, her legacy, delivered her eulogy at the funeral. I continued to sort through all the articles she left behind, including several well-worn Bibles full of underlined passages and colorful stickers. Even in death, she made me smile.

After the funeral, the mortician handed me a small velvet pouch that contained my mother's jewelry: her favorite poinsettia earrings, a pearl necklace, and two rings. The first ring was a wedding ring my father gave her after she lost the original while working on the potato harvester. The second ring was the mother's ring from my brothers and me, which she wore for fifty years. She often fingered it with tears in her eyes.

My brothers and I gave her the ring decades ago when we were young, all lived at home, and still spoke to each other. I still have trouble breathing when I remember the years of strife and the painful courtroom scene. The judge ruled in her favor, but the damage was done. Our family was shattered beyond repair.

My older brother never visited our mother after losing the lawsuit, and he didn't attend her funeral. His birthday was in January, the first birthstone in the mother's ring. It's a cold month.

The velvet pouch sat on the buffet table in my kitchen for two months and remained there when twenty-four people joyfully arrived for Christmas Eve dinner. No one moved it, not even the children. The bag held the last personal belongings of our mother, grandmother, and great-grandmother, and it seemed almost irreverent to examine the only tangible things of value that remained after eighty-seven years of life.

After the new year, I finally opened the velvet bag and placed the rings in a container of jewelry cleaner. I left the necklace and earrings inside, tied the pouch, and placed it in a donation box. I hope someone will be pleased to wear the items.

The two rings have been professionally cleaned and are stored in jewelry boxes. I'm saving her wedding ring for my daughter and her daughter. As for the mother's ring, I hope to meet a woman who had babies in January, September, and

October, and I'll give it to her. This ring deserves and needs to be celebrated.

Mom was conservative and chose to support her church instead of buying lavish gifts for herself. Several years ago, she commissioned and helped design a two-story wall of stained glass windows for the new Living Waters Presbyterian Church in Wendell. A prominent member of the church objected to her chosen design because it included a rainbow and, as everyone knows, that could endorse the "gay rights agenda." My mother remarked, "The rainbow was good enough for Noah, so it's good enough for me."

The rainbow design was enlarged and the magnificent windows were carefully installed in the sanctuary. On certain hours of the morning, the sun shined through so brilliantly that some people in the congregation needed to wear sunglasses. The person who objected to the design moved away, but we hoped someday she could witness a spectacular rainbow and be humbled and thankful. No agenda would be necessary.

Mom didn't want or need to support or condemn the gay lifestyle or any lifestyle, for that matter. Instead, she chose to follow the teaching of Jesus and endorsed his commandment to "Love one another." Her worn-out Bibles were covered with underlined verses, mostly about love and grace. A favorite passage came from the book of Hebrews in the Old Testament: "Keep on loving one another as brothers and sisters." She followed that advice, often to her own peril as people took advantage of her generosity.

Holidays continued to be the most difficult times without my mother. To make Thanksgiving less painful, I decided to think of funny things she used to do before dementia took her away. Turkey pudding came to mind. My mother overcooked the Thanksgiving turkey for two days. For some reason, she thought she was a pilgrim doing a slow-roast over a pit behind the covered wagon so she set the bird in the oven before midnight on low heat and basted it every hour. As a result, she was tired by dinner the next day and the turkey had lost all its shape as the butterball morphed into turkey pudding hanging off the carcass.

I often accused Mom of sinking the gravy boat. Because the turkey took all the space in the oven, she cooked the green bean casserole, the potatoes, the gravy, and the stuffing on the stove—all at the same time. She wrapped bread rolls in tin foil and stuffed them around the turkey until they hardened into crusty dough balls. When the gravy was thick enough to stand on its own without a pan, it was time to eat.

Mom thought there should be a dessert per person, and death by sugar was an unfortunate side effect. If a dozen guests were coming for dinner, there would be at least four pies, four cakes, and four platters of fudge. Pants and belts were adjusted accordingly.

She required real whipped cream on the pies, so she would aggressively operate her trusty hand mixer like a frantic high-speed drill until the cream was two seconds shy of becoming real butter. She wore a festive, handmade apron over her best appliquéd sweatshirt, so she resembled a jolly, plump elf scurrying about the kitchen.

My mom loved my aunt's sweet potato pie and assumed it was a healthy dish because it used a vegetable, despite the butter, brown sugar, pecans, and marshmallow sauce. She would sneak a bowl for herself and hide it behind the pickles in the back of the refrigerator. She later grinned with delight about her sneaky accomplishment.

Like a dutiful drill sergeant, she organized the girls and women-folk to hand-wash all the dishes after the meal while the men meandered to the living room to pat their bellies and watch football. She took great pride in dividing leftovers into equal portions and filling Tupperware containers and Corningware dishes for guests to take home. To ensure her items were returned, she used fingernail polish to paint her initials on all the containers. I now have stacks of dishes sporting faded red initials "LA."

That first Thanksgiving without her, the family came together to toast the holiday and give thanks for our abundant blessings. Some things remained the same: commotion came from the children's table, the men wrestled for the last turkey leg, and I declared that red wine goes with turkey—and everything else. The most noticeable difference was the empty chair at the table. I toasted a happy Thanksgiving to Mom and promised to sneak a bowl of sweet potatoes for her.

We managed to survive the first year of other holidays without her. I deliberately walked past the festive displays of Mother's Day cards and ignored the advertisements for flowers, and I tuned out the hype and the obligatory admonishments to do something, anything, for Mother. Because she died.

Experience taught me that time erases the sadness. Sometimes I forget my father's birthday. After almost three decades, I don't remember the sound of his voice. On Father's Day, I send cards to my son and son-in-law and give a small present to my husband, and I'm grateful for my honored role as mother and grandmother. Now I have the new title of matriarch. The cycle of life isn't new; babies are born and people die. I accept that. But I don't know why some people suffer so much and others get to die peacefully in their sleep. Both my parents spent their last years in physical and mental pain, and I couldn't do anything to ease their transition. Because of the visions of my parents lying ashen and twisted in their beds, when I'm too feeble to live with dignity, I intend to have a grand party before I exit this life and explore what is beyond.

After a parent dies, there are the usual regrets from those still living. I should have visited Mom more often. Every time I got up to leave, she would clutch my hand and beg me to stay. I should have played her favorite music, opened her scrapbooks, and patiently listened as she attempted to say words she couldn't remember. I should have combed her hair again and brought her costume jewelry. I should have stayed longer.

The guilt consumes me every time I drive past her former assisted living facility. She lived in three rooms, progressing from resident to assisted living to terminal. Instead of a child passing onward to higher grades in school, she was going backward with every physical and mental collapse. I used to cry in my car before and after every visit. I should have stayed longer.

I saved a wreath from her funeral. The flowers were dried and brittle, but I took it to her grave on Mother's Day. I returned again a week later on her birthday. I won't forget the date. It's May 20.

The mailbox continued to bring memories of Mom years after she died as I tried to cancel her fifty-three magazine subscriptions. A few years before she died, I visited my mother in her assisted living facility. She was sitting in her wheelchair looking at a copy of *ESPN* magazine.

"Studying for the Super Bowl?" I asked.

"No," she responded. "I don't like sports."

I noticed the stack of magazines on her table. *Forbes. Men's Health. Ebony. Jet. Yoga Today. Elle.*

"Have you been taking your medications, Mom?" I asked, wondering about her sudden interest in all things young and masculine.

"I don't like those magazines," she answered. "I'm waiting for my prize."

She wheeled over to her dresser and pulled out a large envelope stuffed with "official" letters and postcards from the office of the senior vice president of a well-known clearing house announcing that she was in the Winners Circle! Yes, she only had a limited time to return the card with the Official Authorization

Code to be eligible to collect her millions in prizes! But the time-sensitive message was urgent!

"The next step is up to you!" screamed the bold text highlighted in bright yellow. "You could be just days away from winning! Respond today!" And, of course, Mom thought that it wouldn't hurt to subscribe to some of these magazines.

She had dutifully written notes on each and every letter: day received, amount of check enclosed, day check mailed. She already had subscribed to most of the women's magazines, including *Cooking* (she didn't have a kitchen) and *Oprah* (empowerment had never been part of her lifestyle). I tallied up the orders, and she had paid for fifty-three magazine subscriptions, some of them until 2016. And there was no Prize Patrol pounding on her door.

My mother wasn't stupid, just frail. She was a Depression-era woman who knew the value of a penny, and thirty years before she had helped my father manage several large businesses. In her defense, I know that she grew up in a time when women took oaths to "obey," and they believed every official-looking document they received. The evil hucksters disguised as clever marketers know how to manipulate these innocent people, but the fraud they're committing against the elderly should be labeled a criminal offense.

Canceling the subscriptions became almost as difficult as winning anything. Before she passed away, I considered staging an event to have some people show up at her door with balloons and a big (worthless) check. I really wanted her to get a prize.

Through my online blogs and speeches, I advised my middle-aged friends and associates who were acting as caregivers for their aging parents. I told them to monitor any spending on subscriptions, and gently suggest that it's OK to have a few magazines. If the parent was intent on submitting an entry in any contest, I reminded them to show the small print that says it's not necessary to buy more in order to qualify for any prizes. As a last resort, I suggested to mention how many trees are being wasted to make the publications.

Magazines continued to come long after my mother had passed away. The tractor catalog is still addressed to my mother in care of my parents' farming company that went out of business twenty years ago. Obviously, no one in my family needs any agriculture equipment to use for spring planting. I could have purchased a trowel to set some petunias, but that's all.

After Mom died, I spent years going though boxes of her possessions. She kept thousands of photographs, and I wanted to look at each one. I was intrigued by the grainy, black-and-white photographs from 1946, free from decades of bondage among hundreds of photos in my mother's leather albums. I picked up the images and stared at my parents and strained to imagine the young couple in love.

My father stood in his army fatigues in front of a row of tanks in Japan. While he served overseas after World War II, his wallet contained the photo of my mother in a swimming suit. My earliest images of her are quite different. I remember her in a large flowered dress, waving to me with plump arms while admonishing me to "be good" because my father was coming home from work. I'm amazed that she once was a charming young woman, smiling to her fiancé, wearing a bathing suit in front of a flower garden. I wish I had known her then.

Another photo from 1948 was a self-portrait, taken long before instant selfies were available on cellular telephones. Their young innocence intrigues me. I imagine my mother sewing linens for her hope chest while listening to the Glenn Miller Orchestra on the radio. I see my father coaxing an old tractor to complete one more row in the field before dark. They married on a cool day in late November 1948 with nothing but determination and grit. The years brought prosperity and heartache.

I never saw them hug and kiss. I guess the stress of several businesses and bad health depleted their romantic energy. For several years, my father lived in another state during the week, where he operated a trucking business. Every year, Dad would give me money to buy Mom presents for Christmas and other special occasions. She would always buy him a patio lounge chair for Father's Day. The fabric rotted, unused, in the sun.

Of all the faded photos I've examined, none were as profound as the ones of the young couple in love. That's how I chose to remember them. They were beautiful, before the trauma and drama of life cheated them out of growing old together. I wanted them to know their legacy was strong, and lived on through their amazing grandchildren and great-grandchildren.

My mother is never far from my thoughts. In the silent expectation of dawn, just before the first slice of silver reveals the horizon of a new day, a slight breeze moves through the pine trees in my yard. The brief rustle of branches releases a faint smell of long-past adventures in summer mountains and stirs the chimes that hang in the arbor. I look upward and smile at the memory of my mother, Leona Ambrose.

Her morning ritual remained the same for twenty years. She woke early, and slowly walked down the lane to retrieve the newspaper. Her breath came in puffs as she tugged her sweater closer against the chill and gazed at the stars before they faded behind the emerging sunlight. Back inside, she turned on her radio, sometimes she listened to the farm report or else to gentle sounds from the 1940s. She fixed some toast, sipped coffee, read the paper. She did this every morning by herself.

Widowed for two decades, she forgot how it sounded to be greeted every day, to feel the touch of someone else in the house, to hear her husband ask for more coffee. Even though her schedule was full of volunteer activities and various appointments, she never got used to the loneliness. Her regular companions were the ticking clock over the mantel, the cooing mourning doves outside the window, and the pleasant voice on the radio telling her to have a nice day.

I finally convinced her to move into an assisted living facility because she had endured too many serious falls, too many minor car accidents, and a growing number of health issues. On the last morning before the move, she lingered outside on her morning walk and noticed a warm breeze meandering through the trees, as if to say farewell. She nodded and went inside.

Years later, after moving six times to various assisted living facilities in Wendell and Boise and two rehabilitation hospitals in Meridian, she was too tired to get out of bed. Not even her favorite sweatshirts and pearls could tempt her to get dressed. Finally, she knew it was time to go and she stopped eating. She died in her bed beneath her favorite quilt. Outside her window, a sudden wind tossed the tree limbs, and the leaves floated to the ground.

Two weeks later, I woke earlier than usual, dressed, and stepped outside. The stars were still bright as I walked to get the newspaper. I turned to go back and a fresh gust of wind tickled the chimes. "Good morning, Mom," I said, beginning my own ritual of greeting her in the morning. "Let's have a nice day."

$\sim$

Southfork River Sonnet

A sliver of river now dappled with rain
embraces the melt from the snow-covered ridges,
dividing the meadows and mountain terrain
as it flows through the canyons,
beneath weathered bridges.
From cities they come on the warm summer days,
to bounce over rocks in their guided plump rafts.
When they value adventure, the river obeys,
and the air is resplendent with singing and laughs.
Too soon leaves turn gold and fly free from the trees,
while the river recedes, and the dark shadows grow.
The hairy, fat elk herds prepare for the freeze,
and the river awaits a soft blanket of snow.
Cold waters return as they have through the years.
The river responds with a song no one hears.

CHAPTER TWELVE

Finding Warmth

My first family consisted of parents and three siblings living together in Wendell. During my childhood, I knew we didn't qualify for the perfect home as described in my Sunday school classes, but I never imagined the family would be forever fractured through the suicidal destruction and demise of Ambrose Farms, Sand Springs Ranch, Ambrose Distributing, and Montana Express. The legacy and name of that family is one of loss and squandered inheritance, and what remains is useless as the mystery ingredients of those old TV dinners—cold, unwanted, and without value.

With my family in shambles and divorced, I charted a course for survival in 2008 and focused on writing. I sold my lake house for a substantial profit and moved back to Eagle, Idaho. I received a publishing contract from Adams Media to write *Menopause Sucks* and formed my own publishing company called Mill Park Publishing. I continued to write books and publish books for other women, producing fourteen books in five years.

Using proceeds from the sale of my McCall house, I built a cabin in Garden Valley, Idaho, and organized writers' retreats with faculty that included Pulitzer Prize winner Anthony Doerr and *New York Times* bestselling authors AK Turner and Jennifer Basye Sander. I immersed myself in the Boise writing community and became a founding member of the Idaho Writers Guild.

I fulfilled my childhood dream to travel and succeeded in finding myself. As a girl reading my grandparents' *National Geographic* magazines, I promised myself I would travel the world. I kept that promise and enjoyed the good fortune to visit thirty-two countries. The various travel adventures included the most splendid, inspirational, and heartbreaking experiences: I saw the Jade Buddha in Thailand, hiked across the Haleakala Crater in Maui, Hawaii, and cried at Dachau Concentration Camp in Germany.

I dined on the second floor of the Eiffel Tower in Paris, bought wooden shoes in Holland, cruised the Caribbean, watched a leopard drag a deer up a tree while on safari in South Africa, and climbed to the top of the dome at the Vatican in Rome. I wrote a poem in Ireland, ate bird's nest soup in Hong Kong, snorkeled at night off the British Virgin Islands, floundered on chocolate in Switzerland, photographed the ruins at Pompei, and drove with my daughter through Spain to the Mediterranean Coast. Favorite memories include standing in Mass at the Duomo in Florence, riding a zip line through the jungle in Costa Rica, and golfing at a remote resort overlooking the Sea of Cortez. Throughout the long and winding roads, I relished the journey but always returned home to Idaho.

My dreams of travel were interrupted as I worked full time, married, and had children. Finally, I jumped at the chance to return to Europe in 1995 as a chaperone for my daughter's high school trip to Europe. In my school days, a class trip meant we were going in an old school bus to Boise, the state capital. The following generation improved upon that goal as it raised funds to travel overseas. Much to my daughter's chagrin, I went, too.

We enjoyed adventures in Italy, Germany, Switzerland, Austria, England, and France. I received a reduced rate because I was a chaperone, and that planted an idea for how to continue to travel. I would find a way to help pay for each trip. After my children were grown and had moved away from home, I had more time to travel.

More traveling opportunities came when I served on the volunteer board of the University of Idaho Alumni Association. After being elected national president, I qualified to host alumni trips. I was more than pleased to entertain jolly groups of alums on excursions to Ireland and Spain. My transportation and accommodations were paid for by the educational group in charge of the tours.

Another less expensive way to travel was to join an organized tour. In the year 2000, I found an opportunity to join a tour that was circling the world and included a visit to the Taj Mahal in India. We flew out of Los Angeles, California, and landed eighteen hours later in Bangkok, Thailand. From there, we toured Hong Kong and Nepal, staying in a tented camp at Tiger Tops. On that trip, I sat cramped in a tiny, old airplane beside the Himalayan Mountains, rode in an ox cart across a river full of crocodiles, traveled on a camel in a street market, and rode on the back of a bull elephant and watched a tiger kill a water buffalo in Nepal. The trip continued to India, where I saw the Taj Mahal in Agra. We ended the round-the-world trip in a pub in London before flying back to the USA.

It was a childhood dream to see the pyramids, so in the spring of 2001, I signed up to go on a Vantage Tour of Egypt. It wasn't five-star, but I enjoyed the incredible experience of walking into tombs in the Valley of the Kings, floating on a barge down the Nile River to Abu Simbal, and touching the Great Pyramids of Giza. As we floated past the countryside, I remembered the poem I wrote decades before about the endless river. Never in my wildest dreams did I consider someday I would be on the Nile. The group toured the Luxor Temple, and I marveled at the carvings on walls that were more than four thousand years old. For souvenirs, I brought home scrolls of artwork painted on parchment.

I also discovered a joy for cooking, much to the frustration of my children, who grew up eating hamburgers and chicken nuggets. I found a company out of Washington State called A Cook's Tour, and signed up for a cooking tour of Tuscany. That trip remains one of the highlights of my life. The group stayed in an ancient villa near Verona and toured Cinque Terra, Sam Gimignano, Sienna, and Modena. We took classes from expert chefs and ate our meals outside on long tables set up in orchards. We found hidden wineries and sampled delicious wines served with crusty bread and cheese. We only spoke a few words of Italian, but we shared a universal love for good food and wine.

The second Cook's Tour excursion was to South Africa. We saw the cell on Robben Island, a rock quarry off the coast of Cape Town, where Nelson Mandela had been imprisoned for twenty-seven years. We enjoyed cooking classes with local chefs who taught us how to use spices to enhance a cuisine influenced by early traders traveling around the cape. We visited a shanty town where local women were making candle holders out of cut glass. Then we journeyed inland to a safari camp and stayed in a tent as armed guards patrolled the grounds.

A return trip to Italy took our tour group to Rome, Florence, and north to Bolzano and the Dolomites. We were in Portofino on September 11, 2001, and terrified by the attacks on the World Trade Center in New York. I purchased a carved statue of St. Christopher in Bolzano and carried it home two weeks later.

My mother had a dream to travel Canada by railcar, so she took her friend, my daughter, and me on a twelve-day excursion from Toronto to Vancouver. The views and camaraderie were wonderful, but my daughter and I agreed that a three-day trip would have been fine. She was twenty-two years old and loved her grandmother but was eager to see Vancouver come into view on the last day of the trip.

Mexico was another favorite destination, but I never stayed in dangerous areas and preferred the resorts in Cabo and Loreto. My daughter lived in Guanajuato on a student exchange in college, and I visited her once to enjoy the sights, the flower market, the Cathedral, and worry about her apartment because she didn't have a stove or refrigerator. We all survived.

My home state of Idaho offered abundant adventures. I've enjoyed a week-long float trip down the Middle Fork of the Salmon River, riding a snowmobile to the top of Scott Mountain near Garden Valley, waterskiing at Twin Lakes in Northern Idaho, and hiking in Harriman State Park in Eastern Idaho. As I neared my sixth decade of life, I was getting slower and preferred the comforts of home, but I continued to look through the next travel catalog. Freedom came with the next excursion.

By age fifty-seven, I was resolved to remain alone. I didn't consider dating until February 2009, when my neighbor asked me to go to dinner with her husband and their friend who was visiting from Texas. I liked to eat, so I agreed. I was introduced to Ken McKay, and the four of us drove to Chandlers, a high-end steak house in downtown Boise. Ken and I were immediately attracted to each other and were holding hands by dessert. The first time he visited my home, I dashed inside to remove a picture hanging on the wall. It was a copy of my "Endless River" poem with my age and the date it was published. He didn't know how old I was, and the information would have told him I was five years older. I had imagined him seeing the poem and muttering that it was time for him to go. We laughed about it later because it didn't matter.

We enjoyed a nine-month, long-distance relationship before he found a job and moved to Idaho that November. He became my rock, the yin to my yang, the one who understood me and still adored me anyway. We were married on the Greek Island of Paros and enjoyed an authentic ancient Greek wedding and reception, complete with a one-eyed musician playing a goat bladder. I remember laughing out loud with a joyful noise to celebrate a splendid new chance at happiness.

Ken and I were both born in September, so I organized fun birthday celebrations every year on the patio. One party featured a karaoke disc jockey with all the equipment necessary for raucous renditions of songs that never will be included on a nationwide talent show. At the end of the party, my children, Emily and Adam, took the microphone and sang my favorite tunes from Broadway musicals. I had never received a better birthday gift.

After the guests had gone home, Ken and I sat outside with our grown children to share a bottle of wine and talk about life.

"Did you hear from your older brother?" Emily asked.

"No, I haven't seen or talked with him for more than twenty years," I responded. "I mentally divorced him long ago."

"I felt so sorry for Grandma Sweetie," Emily said. "She still waited for him to visit."

"I'll never forget when he screamed at my friends and me for camping at Sand Springs Ranch," Adam said.

"Then he sent a formal letter to my attorney threatening to sue you for trespassing," I said. "Not exactly Uncle of the Year."

We laughed and moved to other, more important topics. After all the rancor and stress of my childhood family relationships, I was grateful my children were close. One, a liberal, and the other, a conservative, chose to set political differences aside to respect and love each other. Their families often planned activities together and traveled on summer vacations. I felt a need to pick up the little girl with her broken arm in a sling and tell her, "See. Your life was glorious beyond your wildest imagination."

Flashbacks of emotional pain occasionally intruded into my new and improved life when insecurities interrupted my positive attitude. In 2015, I traveled to a conference in Nashville to speak to a national gathering of women bloggers. I smiled with assurance and prepared to meet, greet, and tweet. Then I noticed the conference sponsor—a frozen food company introducing a new product—and my self-confidence disappeared. A small child stood in my place.

As this little girl, I felt the business clothes hang loosely on my youthful frame and my small feet wobble in the heeled shoes. I stared at the compact packages of frozen meals as the stage and podium turned into the cold dining room from my past. I fingered my hair to check for ragged bangs and tugged on my skirt so it wouldn't be too short. Again, I was a sad child in need of comfort food that never came.

I envisioned my childhood while eating frozen dinners on disposable aluminum trays that provided exact portions of mixed vegetables, a meat concoction, manufactured potatoes, and bland apple crisp or a meek cherry cobbler. I saw my father, the stern, successful workaholic who built a trucking empire hauling frozen food and TV dinners throughout the Northwest.

My mother dutifully heated and handed the aluminum trays to her children, and we ate in silence. As a stubborn girl, I defied the orderly presentation and pushed the wrinkled peas into the potatoes and plopped the dessert onto the meat. It all tasted the same, anyway. As we consumed our meal, I wondered how it would be to live in a place of warmth, peace, and laughter. I longed for a hearty homemade meal shared with a happy family, so I made it my mission to have that scenario.

My story began as a child sitting silently around a table in a cold room, chilled from within, following a predictable pattern that would repeat for years. As a young girl, I vowed to someday come in from the cold when I had a family of my own.

Decades later, I finally realized my childhood dream of living in a warm, loving home full of laughter. Challenges remained, as in all situations, but my table was covered with home-cooked food and surrounded by contented grown children and giggling grandkids.

After more than sixty years of growing up, falling down, and getting up, I finally learned some important life lessons that helped navigate beyond the cold childhood. I was not disposable. Just as the trays from frozen dinners were tossed into the garbage, I often felt unwanted during my childhood. After I left home and financially supported myself, I felt the first taste of freedom. I finally mattered, and my skills were worthy of a paycheck.

I started to create my own path. My adult journey often was treacherous as I took risks to find a better life. I stumbled, took several wrong turns, was financially cheated more than once by unscrupulous scoundrels, and had to start over many times. But I always stood, brushed off the dirt, and kept going because I knew what I didn't want and what I wanted. I worked at several jobs and found better ones. I attended cooking classes and registered for cooking tours to visit other cultures and learn how to make special dishes. I earned enough money to purchase quality plates, silverware, and glasses that weren't tossed into the garbage after every meal. I married, divorced, and finally found my forever love. My children survived many meager meals while they were young, but we survived together. After many years of trial and error, we finally got to enjoy dessert. And it was delicious.

My desire to provide and enjoy a warm home was fueled by the vision of a festive holiday table. Over the past few years, I've dined at such a table and thankfully watched my adult children and grandchildren laugh, tell stories, and barter for the last piece of pie. Then my husband would offer a toast, and we raised our glasses in celebration. This spontaneous merriment often led to multiple toasts. Through it all, we remembered to acknowledge the empty chairs at the table, and I wished our four parents could join us.

I finally gained a respect for my father. During my youth, I didn't get along with either of my parents, and we all rejoiced when I finally went away to college. Decades later, after I researched their history and read Mom's journals, I developed a new empathy for them. They did the best they could as they battled health, economic, and relationship issues. I regret not trying one more time to kindle a small spark that would have bonded us together. As their legacy, I will honor them with positive thoughts, not dwell on sad memories, and do the best I can.

While sorting my mother's possessions, I found my father's wallet. The wrinkled leather folder held his driver's license, medical cards, and other identification. In a back pocket there was an old photograph of me on my white horse. For some reason, he carried that image with him, and I never knew.

I discovered that acceptance is liberating. I had the maturity to appreciate the work my father did to advance his business success and support the family. But the wealth came with a price. Every mile he drove, he purposely placed distance between himself and his family. Even after he stopped driving and had accumulated the resources to buy more trucks and hire other drivers, the house remained cold. I used this experience to motivate my own search for emotional and physical nourishment.

Family mealtime is an important ritual that forms the basis of childhood memories. Successful dinners don't need to be cooked from scratch from original recipes. Frozen entrees are a handy substitute after a hectic day, and the family needs to eat before midnight. A home-cooked meal or a microwaved dinner can be the centerpiece of an abundant family feast; it all depends upon the warmth in the room, not just from the dish.

Back at the conference in Nashville, my wounded inner child held out my hands and accepted the offering of warm macaroni and cheese cups from the representative. The adult me smiled and said, "Thank you." After all, macaroni and cheese were the proven comfort foods. "Frozen Dinners" became a metaphor, my birthright, but not my legacy.

I became determined to avoid the health issues that plagued my family. My parents both suffered for years from physical ailments. My brother George developed a ten-pound tumor in 2010 and was forced to immediately close Montana Express and sell the trucks and trailers at auction. His health continued to decline, and his wife and he stopped visiting us for holiday meals. One of my bigger regrets is that I didn't visit him in southern Idaho and insist we get together more than once a year.

George was a gentle giant. Considered chubby throughout his childhood, he had a large frame and a larger zest for life. During high school, he drove a dune buggy around town while wearing an enormous cowboy hat and everyone called him Hoss. His friends elected him to leadership positions in high school and college, and he also sang with the University of Idaho Vandaleer Concert Choir. He married a kind woman named Marti and they were married almost thirty years. Every December for her birthday, he filled the house with dozens of bright poinsettia plants and then gave the flowers as Christmas gifts to his employees at Montana Express. He was humble, funny, dedicated, a talented artist, and irreplaceable.

On May 28, 2017, Ken and I traveled to Wendell to place flowers on my parents' graves for Memorial Day and drove to Twin Falls to see George. We met on the patio of Elevation 486, an upscale restaurant and bistro located on the edge of the Snake River canyon. The panoramic view focused on the Perrine Bridge to the east, 1,500-feet long and 486 feet above the Snake River. The winding river flowed to the west, past Sand Spring Ranch. We could see the steep Blue Lakes Grade, the road our paternal grandfather traversed while driving rickety stagecoaches eighty years earlier for the Star Stage Line.

Ken and I were seated and had ordered drinks. I heard George walk up behind me and stood to hug him. I caught my breath at the shock of his appearance. His hair was completely white, and his clothes were baggy on his diminished frame. I will never forget his eyes. They looked beyond me, across the canyon, as he reached out for a brief hug. His eyes were iridescent and luminous, and I couldn't stop staring as he sat across from us.

We stammered pleasantries and asked about his health. He took a labored breath and talked in short phrases about a failed chemotherapy treatment that had formed a sack around his heart that needed to be drained. The damage couldn't be repaired.

"When did this happen?" I asked.

"In January. I didn't want to tell anyone."

"That was four months ago!" I said, shaking my head. "I would have been here. I could have brought you meals and told stories and made you laugh."

I never understood why we were so distant. George and I had similar personalities and a robust sense of humor. He was more reserved than I was, but so was everyone else. The waitress appeared and George ordered a glass of the house merlot.

"You can order premium wine," I joked, trying to lighten the mood. I had no idea that would be his last glass of wine.

"Let's plan a family reunion this summer," I said, knowing he hadn't seen my children or grandchildren for more than a year. We only lived a hundred miles away, but I couldn't remember the last time I saw him.

"That would be fun," he said. "Maybe in July."

He sipped the wine and started to tell stories and jokes. He told a tall tale about an Italian man riding on a train. The joke took several minutes, and he paused often to catch his breath. His eyes continued to shine. He told a few shorter stories and mentioned that his friend had taken him on an airplane ride that morning. George was an accomplished pilot and had owned his own small airplane.

"Wasn't that hard on your health?" I asked.

"It was worth it," he answered. He seemed at peace.

He was getting tired and said he had to go home. He didn't have any more stories to make me laugh. We took one last look at the Snake River flowing below us, and I wiped tears from my eyes. We begged to drive him but he refused so Ken took his keys and went to bring his pickup truck to the front of the restaurant. I walked with George down the sidewalk. He stopped several times, once to rest his head on his arms on a ledge on the wall. I was screaming inside and didn't know what to do. Why didn't I support him? Why didn't I put my arms around him? Why were we so damn afraid to show affection? I will regret that moment the rest of my life.

We helped him into the truck and he drove off. I don't know how he drove ten miles to his home. We drove back to Eagle and Marti called later with the tragic news that he died in his chair, only four hours after leaving us. I believed by the aura of the light in his eyes that he was transitioning at the restaurant, and I was humbled and honored that he wanted to see me before he died. At his request, there was no funeral or memorial service. He was gone.

FarmHouse Restaurant, the nationally acclaimed truck stop restaurant that my mother had owned for several years in Wendell, burned down a few months later. My family history was dying.

The Ambrose line from my paternal relatives ended for my immediate first family. My older brother had one son, but that son doesn't have any children. My younger brother chose to not have children. I retained my maiden name and have a son and a daughter, but their last names are Nielsen. The legacy of my father's success lives on through my children and grandchildren, but the Ambrose name for this lineage only will be preserved on the covers of my books.

My adult children—Emily and her husband, John, and Adam and his wife, Danielle—are happily married, live nearby, and have their own adorable children and step-children. Ken's older son, Malcolm, also lives in Boise, and his younger son, Cameron, lives in Texas. We often come together for boisterous family celebrations, and brother George and his wife, Marti, used to join us before he got sick. I've helped my children own their own homes, and that goal alleviates most of the pain of being kicked off Sand Springs Ranch when I was seven months' pregnant. As much as I've come to grips with the traumas of childhood and gained a strong respect for my parents, the hurt remains from August 1980, when we were forced to leave the ranch.

The past five decades have been as if I were living in a constantly revolving kaleidoscope of drama, trauma, glory, and adventure. The tragic times have been offset by the splendid opportunities and victories that continue to bloom in my path. My children are happy and healthy. I'm sharing my home and my life with an amazing man, and apparently, he enjoys it, too. I look forward to the journeys ahead.

On weekends, we escape to our cabin in the mountains of Idaho, and from our deck, we watch elk, deer, wolves, foxes, and wild turkeys. Several eagles perch in the trees in the back yard, and I affectionately refer to one as my Emotional Support Eagle. We watch the turbulent south fork of the Payette River tumble through the valley, and plan summer float trips through the canyon.

The river provides two of the most famous whitewater rafting locations in the country and features a forty-foot waterfall, a narrow gorge filled with natural hot springs, and the famous Staircase Rapids, a challenging Class IV run, before dumping into the mighty Snake River on a journey to the Pacific Ocean. My endless river came full circle and brought me home.

I continue to seek adventures. In the spring of 2018, at age sixty-six, I traveled to Ireland to lead a journal-writing class with a group of women on an excursion through an organization called Wayfinding Women. The title of my workshop was "Your Journey Is Your Story." I also returned to the University of Idaho to help inaugurate the Ambrose Storytelling Endowment, a program I funded in honor of my brother George. The endowment provided an annual workshop, a faculty award, and a student scholarship. I told students that storytelling was one of the first and most important forms of human communication and to embrace and write about their own unique experiences.

In my travels, I often pass eighteen-wheel trucks. I recognize the refrigerated trailers and wonder what groceries and products are being hauled to warehouses throughout the region. Maybe one of the drivers is an ambitious young man who grew up in poverty and dreams of riches and success. If that driver has a daughter, I hope he'll call her and say he misses her. He should remind her they'll spend time together. They'll enjoy a warm meal and celebrate life before she leaves on her own journey. My dad used to say, "Time is money," and maybe he was correct all along. Time is valuable, and can be spent on important treasures: family, friends, feasts, and adventures.

I finally understand why my mother, even in dementia, was so desperate to find her quilt. The patchwork pieces of our past are reminders of the frayed, personal fabric of our lives but they also offer comforting, familiar proof of the happiness that occurred and the enduring strength necessary to hold it all together. Now the heirloom quilt is my shield against the cold, contaminated legacy of frozen dinners.

∿

Acknowledgments

This memoir first percolated in my mind more than twenty years ago, and I adjusted the intensity of my writing for several years, often jumping into the mess of words only to quit and relinquish everything to the back burner. How do I, as a humor writer, rip open the scars to inspect the painful drama of the past? I couldn't finish it, so I sporadically wrote additional chapters for the manuscript while working on humorous books, including *Menopause Sucks*, *Midlife Cabernet*, and *Midlife Happy Hour*.

My mother's death in 2014, followed three years later by the death of my younger brother, George, convinced me to complete the book.

I want to thank my husband, Ken McKay, for editing advice and moral support, and I thank my children, Emily Nielsen and Adam Nielsen, for surviving the chaos during their childhood and encouraging my writing. They were my motivation to be a better parent.

Thanks to Jennifer Basye Sander for coaching me through the process and suggesting the title.

I thank Ross Patty for astute editing and Jeanne Core of DesignWorks Creative in Boise for designing the cover and interior. Ward Hooper contributed to the original artwork on the front cover.

I am grateful for the hundreds of employees of Montana Express, Ambrose Distributing, Ambrose Farms, and FarmHouse Restaurant for helping my parents establish and operate several successful businesses. Many people are mentioned in the book, but I want to add another note of gratitude for my uncle Muncie Mink, my uncle Henry Winterholler, my cousin Ron Ambrose, and our agriculture expert, Keith Wert, for their contributions to the businesses and loyalty to my parents.

Finally, I want to acknowledge my father, Neal Ambrose. Writing the memoir has softened my resentment toward him and introduced a profound level of admiration and respect. I acknowledge my mother, Leona Ambrose, as the person who suffered enormous physical and emotional pain but continued to leave smiley-face stickers in her Bibles. And to my younger brother, George, I regret that we didn't laugh together more. My childhood family is gone, but I recognize the best traits of my parents and George in my children and grandchildren. The long-haul journey isn't over yet.

~

About the Author

Elaine Ambrose is the award-winning, bestselling author of eight books. *Midlife Cabernet* won two national humor awards; *Publishers Weekly* reviewed it as "laugh-out-loud funny!"; and *Foreword Reviews* wrote that the book was "an argument for joy" similar to Erma Bombeck. *Midlife Happy Hour* was a Foreword INDIES Book of the Year finalist and won first place in Aging/Midlife from the Independent Press Awards in 2017. *Gators & Taters* won an award in Childrens–Fiction from the 2018 Independent Press Awards. Her bilingual children's book, *The Magic Potato / La Papa Mágica*, was selected by the Idaho State Board of Education for the statewide curriculum. Ambrose's award-winning syndicated blog posts are published on several websites, and one humorous post became one of the most-read posts in the history of the *Huffington Post*. Elaine lives with her patient husband in Eagle, Idaho. Find her books, blogs, and speaking events at ElaineAmbrose.com.

Photos

Ambrose Trucking Service, 1952

*Dad, Tom and me
with Dad's first truck, 1952*

*Tom and me
with Dad's truck, 1955.*

Me on my horse, 1965.

George and me, 1957.

*Montana Express brochure
(above) and truck lot
(below), 1980.*

Sprinklers on pivots in front of the house, 1970.

Dad and me, 1972.

Mom, 2000.

Family before Mom and George died.

Our wedding on the Greek island of Paros, 2011.

MANAGEMENT REWIRED

MANAGEMENT REWIRED

*Why Feedback Doesn't Work
and Other Surprising Lessons
from the Latest Brain Science*

CHARLES S. JACOBS

PORTFOLIO

PORTFOLIO
Published by the Penguin Group
Penguin Group (USA) Inc., 375 Hudson Street, New York, New York 10014, U.S.A.
Penguin Group (Canada), 90 Eglinton Avenue East, Suite 700, Toronto,
Ontario, Canada M4P 2Y3 (a division of Pearson Penguin Canada Inc.)
Penguin Books Ltd, 80 Strand, London WC2R 0RL, England
Penguin Ireland, 25 St. Stephen's Green, Dublin 2, Ireland (a division of Penguin Books Ltd)
Penguin Books Australia Ltd, 250 Camberwell Road, Camberwell, Victoria 3124, Australia
(a division of Pearson Australia Group Pty Ltd)
Penguin Books India Pvt Ltd, 11 Community Centre, Panchsheel Park,
New Delhi—110 017, India
Penguin Group (NZ), 67 Apollo Drive, Rosedale, North Shore 0632, New Zealand
(a division of Pearson New Zealand Ltd)
Penguin Books (South Africa) (Pty) Ltd, 24 Sturdee Avenue, Rosebank,
Johannesburg 2196, South Africa

Penguin Books Ltd, Registered Offices: 80 Strand, London WC2R 0RL, England

First published in 2009 by Portfolio, a member of Penguin Group (USA) Inc.

1 3 5 7 9 10 8 6 4 2

Copyright © Charles S. Jacobs, 2009
All rights reserved

LIBRARY OF CONGRESS CATALOGING-IN-PUBLICATION DATA
Jacobs, Charles S.
Management rewired : why feedback doesn't work and other surprising
lessons from the latest brain science / Charles S. Jacobs.
p. cm.
Includes bibliographical references and index.
ISBN 978-1-59184-262-0
1. Psychology, Industrial.   2. Interpersonal relations—Psychological aspects.
3. Personnel management—Psychological aspects.   4. Organizational behavior.
5. Management.   I. Title.
HF5548.8.J24 2009
658.001'9—dc22   2009001724

Printed in the United States of America
Set in Scala   •   Designed by Jaime Putorti

*To Jonas, the teacher who taught me the value of ideas,
and to my daughters, Julia and Emma,
who will only listen to stories*

CONTENTS

INTRODUCTION

I t turns out that most of what we thought we knew about management is probably wrong. New research shows that our emotions lead to better business decisions than our logic. Positive and negative feedback not only don't improve performance, they tend to make it worse. The quantifiable objectives that are a critical part of our strategic plans cause us to focus on the short term at the expense of the long term. Many of the management practices we've taken for granted are not only ineffective, they actually produce the opposite of what we intend.

At the same time, new approaches that have been proven to produce superior performance can't help but strike us as unreasonable. It's been demonstrated that smaller rewards tend to be more motivational than larger ones, that being competitive is often the best way to encourage cooperation, and that the managers who produce the best results are the ones who do the least managing.

The latest developments in brain science are teaching us a better way to manage, but they also challenge our common sense. Using functional magnetic resonance imaging, or the *f*MRI as it's known in the field, scientists are now able to watch the brain at work, and what they're learning is mind-boggling. Not only have they located the areas of the brain that are responsible for our emotions, our reason, and even our moral character; they've also discovered what makes us empathetic, able to learn, and take pleasure in our work. They've even figured out why teenagers drive their parents so crazy.

But perhaps the most surprising discovery has come from mapping the path information travels from our sense organs to our awareness of the world we live in. Not only are the perceptual areas of the brain involved, so are the areas responsible for our memories, our feelings, our beliefs, and our aspirations. Our minds aren't objectively recording our experience of the world; they're creating it, and that creation is influenced by everything else going on in the brain. Each of us lives in a mental world of our own making.

This isn't just some abstract, philosophical issue. It has enormous practical ramifications for how we live and work. The world we know is only what we think it to be, and we can't assume other people will think the same way we do. In fact, we know they won't. Since our customers, employees, peers, and bosses all see things differently than we do, the way we act toward them doesn't necessarily produce the results we expect or want.

While most of us accept that others see the world differently than we do, we trust in our objective, logical reasoning to resolve conflicting perceptions. But the *f*MRI also shows us that objective reasoning has nothing to do with the way we solve problems, make decisions, and plan for the future. At best, logic is just a way to justify conclusions we have already reached unconsciously.

This new understanding of how the mind works needs to be incorporated into all of our thinking about business. The resulting management practices may seem illogical, but they'll produce better performance. Our organizations will be more focused and efficient, and our strategies more effective at creating a sustainable advantage. We'll also be able to meaningfully transform businesses rapidly, and our leadership will bring out the best in people. The improvement in the bottom line will not just be incremental, but a quantum leap.

Any manager who's been around for a while has heard bold claims like this before only to end up disappointed by the latest and greatest initiative that doesn't live up to its promise. But brain science's transformation of management isn't just about another new technique or model. It's about shifting our paradigm to incorporate the hard data of science and fundamentally changing the way we think about business. When we do, we're able to gain access to an integrated set of management practices that really do deliver on the promise of superior performance.

With such enormous potential, why hasn't there been more interest in applying the insights of brain science to management? The reason is that our logical thinking excels at dividing things up and categorizing them. While this enables us to organize vast amounts of knowledge, it also separates what we know into specialties with their own unique language and ways of thinking. It's a daunting task for a layperson to come to grips with the complex Latinate terms of neuroscience. Businesspeople and brain scientists living in their own worlds have difficulty communicating and appreciating one another's concerns.

But this problem is an opportunity for those in business who are able to bridge the gap. It immediately gives them a leg up on the competitors who don't appreciate how the findings of brain science can be applied to their businesses. Nor is the application difficult once the implications of the basic discoveries are understood. There are no complicated algorithms or complex processes to master. With a just subtle shift of perspective it becomes clear what approaches don't work and how to generate ones that do. All you need to do is use the mind the way we now know it naturally works.

This book explains what the latest discoveries mean and how they transform our understanding of the way people think and behave. For each key area of management, from strategy to leadership, it shows the limitations of our current practices and details the new, often counterintuitive approaches that are in line with how the mind actually works. It then demonstrates specifically what managers can do in each area to improve the performance of their businesses. Implementing these new approaches is surprisingly easy. The biggest challenge is for managers to stop doing most of what they're doing now.

While the goal is a healthier bottom line, management based on the insights of brain science brings other benefits as well. When a manager's actions aren't producing the opposite of what they intend, management becomes easier, less stressful, and more fun. When people are managed in a way that encourages their natural inclinations, they find their work more rewarding. It's good for the business, for the manager, and for the people.

Leaving aside the practical benefits, the latest discoveries of brain science are fascinating in their own right, and the path we'll travel in applying them to business is full of interesting twists and turns. Along the way, we'll meet a hero who taught the world the best strategists are consummate liars. We'll watch a student whose inability to understand an idea has made the jobs of managers so frustrating. We'll see children whose IQs rise dramatically only because their teacher was deceived into believing they would, and a dolphin that learns to shift paradigms. While it's a unique and at times strange story, the end point is the best way to quickly improve business results.

I am out in the corporate world every day, and I see intelligent, well-meaning managers imprisoned by the conventional wisdom and frustrated by their inability to get an organization of people to do what they need them to do. I watch as the endless parade of new corporate initiatives produce disappointing results. At the same time, I know from experience that virtually every company can be more successful and that the success can be achieved far more easily and far more quickly than most believe is possible.

Understanding the recent discoveries of neuroscience can't help but change the way people think, and when their application to business is demonstrated, managers realize ways to improve performance that, while often counterintuitive, produce better results with less effort. With a perspective informed by science and a set of tools proven effective in the business world, managers will know what they need to do, not just for the bottom line, but for the people whose efforts are measured by that bottom line.

ONE

BRAIN SCIENCE

We assume that our minds, to a greater or lesser extent, faithfully record our experience of the world. While we'll acknowledge that our view of individual events is subjective, we don't question for a minute that there is a world that exists independently of us. In fact, one of the basic assumptions of science is that we can have objective knowledge of the world and everything that's in it.

But according to the latest research in neuroscience, such knowledge is impossible. The only world we can know is the mental one produced by the firing of our neurons, and it is purely subjective. While information from our senses may be input, it is assembled, edited, and assigned significance according to everything else going on in the brain. We don't record our experience of the world as much as we create it. Neuroscience doesn't deny that there's a world out there, it simply says that all we can know is our *version* of it.

Scientists call these different versions *paradigms*, and they view them as frameworks for making sense of our experience. The historian of science Thomas Kuhn saw the swapping of one paradigm for

another as a kind of cognitive revolution, causing not just an incremental increase in the knowledge we have, but a quantum leap to
a different, more comprehensive kind of knowledge. Because paradigms drive the way we think and the way we act, it's difficult to
overestimate the far-reaching effects of embracing a new one.

The classic example is the transformation of our view of the universe during the Renaissance. Until the sixteenth century, both the
conventional wisdom and science held that the earth was at the center,
and the sun, planets, and stars revolved around it. This earth-centric
paradigm was already beginning to break down because the planets
weren't always where it predicted them to be. Epicycles were added
to orbits, and numerous other adjustments were made to account for
the deviations. The paradigm grew increasingly complex, but it still
didn't fit the facts.

Then Copernicus realized that the conventional wisdom had
it inside out. The planets didn't revolve around the earth; rather,
the earth and the other planets revolved around the sun. This new,
greatly simplified paradigm was a much better fit with the observable data.

The discoveries of neuroscience have shifted the paradigm
of how the mind works, and as a result, they are challenging our
beliefs about the very nature of the world we know and how best to
think about it. When it comes to business, the effect is nothing short
of revolutionary. This isn't just about making use of a new management technique, model, or practice. The latest research goes right
at the way we think about management, highlighting fundamental flaws in our current approaches and offering in their place others that challenge everything we take for granted about how best to
manage.

THE MATTER OF MIND

The appearance of the brain doesn't offer us many clues about what it does. When we open up the skull and look at the brain, all we see is a grayish mass with a jello-like consistency. There is nothing we can observe to indicate the organ's function or purpose or suggest that this three pounds of flesh is the most complex system on the planet. When Aristotle looked at the brain, it seemed to him to be some sort of radiator to cool the blood. He thought the heart was the seat of the mind.

As scientists began studying the brain, they were able to make out different structures. By correlating structural damage caused by disease or injury with the loss of mental functions, they created maps identifying where various mental faculties were believed to reside. These maps have grown quite complex over time, and making sense of them is complicated by the Latin terms used to identify the different structures and their locations. It also doesn't help that not all neuroscientists slice and dice the brain in the same way.

But even a quick overview of the anatomy of the brain provides some interesting clues to how our minds work. There are specific areas dedicated to the processing of sense data, the maintenance of attention, the storing and recall of memory, and the higher-order thought that we believe is unique to humans and a few other primates. Our brains register our experience of the external world, select aspects of it to attend to, perform operations on these aspects, and save the results in memory, all not unlike what a computer is capable of.

But very much unlike a computer, an area of the brain known as the amygdala generates feelings that can direct, color, and transform the brain's cognitive operations. Perhaps we could think of it as a laptop with an attitude that changes moment to moment, but even that doesn't quite capture it. For the way the brain works determines both who we are and what kind of world we operate in, and neither of these two is anything at all like the way we thought them to be. This becomes strikingly clear when we look at how we make decisions.

THE HEART HAS REASONS

The way we think in the business world is supposed to be objective and logical. We quantify everything we can and guard against any emotions that might hijack our reasoning. While we often acknowledge gut feelings, no manager interested in continuing employment would make a serious financial decision without having the numbers and the logic to back it up. But according to the neurologist Antonio Damasio, the seat of our conscious thought, the prefrontal cortex, has a reciprocal connection with the emotion-generating amygdala, ensuring that we don't make our decisions with objective logic, despite our belief that we do. In fact, he conducted an ingenious experiment proving that if we did, we'd make bad decisions.

A subject is given $2,000 of play money to make wagers on the results of turning over a card from one of four decks labeled A, B, C, and D. The subject is not told how long the game will last, but each card will either result in earning or losing money. The given payoffs or costs are disclosed only after the turn of the card. The cards in decks A and B either win $100 or lose as much as $1,250. Those in decks B and C pay $50, but lose only up to $100.

Normal players sample all four decks and early on show an initial preference for A and B and their larger payoffs. After a while, however, they shift to C and D, apparently recognizing the high risk of the A and B decks. However, patients with lesions in the ventromedial area of the prefrontal cortex showed a sustained preference for the high risk A and B decks, even as their losses bankrupted them.

Damasio hypothesizes that the patients with the lesions had lost the ability to anticipate and plan for the future. Instead, they were ruled by the now. This ability to plan for the future has to do with what Damasio calls somatic markers. After trial and error, normal patients learned to associate a selection from decks A and B with a *feeling* of "badness." This feeling biased them away from choosing those two decks. The ventromedial area is, as you might expect, connected to the amygdala.

In a follow-up experiment, the game was played with subjects who had their skin conductive response measured, as in a lie detector test. Prior to the selection of the deck, normal patients experienced an increase in the magnitude of the response, and the magnitude continued to grow as the game continued. In other words, the prediction of "badness" from decks A and B was made unconsciously *before* the conscious decision of which deck to select was made. Emotions drove the prediction.

These findings explain how we actually make decisions. Our past experiences carry an emotional charge that is encoded in memories. When we encounter a situation similar enough to summon up those past experiences, along with their associated emotions, our prospective choices are marked by those emotions. We then are motivated to choose the ones that are "good" versus the ones that are "bad." This means that the more we attempt to strip out feelings and create an objective decision-making process, the more we lose access to what we have learned from past experiences.

Damasio's experiment raises questions about how much "I" am really in control. While the conventional wisdom holds that I consciously solve problems and make decisions, the results of the experiment suggest otherwise: I become aware of the solution or the decision when it has already been arrived at through processes that are not conscious. Perhaps even more counterintuitive is that emotions, not logic, drive the decision-making process. The ideal of decision making in the corporate world—rigorous objectivity—virtually ensures the loss of what's been learned through experience. It appears that it isn't the pressure from Wall Street for quarterly results that prevents an adequate long-term perspective, but our preference for supposedly objective thinking.

The results of Damasio's experiment make it clear that we're not reasoning the way we think we are. Mental processes we're not conscious of drive our decision making, while the kind of logical reasoning we believe our thinking should aspire to is really no more than a way to justify decisions we've already made. But it's not just our own thinking that is at issue. If we use logic to influence people unconsciously driven by emotion, we probably aren't going to be very successful in getting them to embrace our point of view.

While we've learned from mapping the anatomy of the brain that our minds operate differently than we thought, the mapping has also misled us into thinking that different mental functions reside in discrete areas of the brain. When we look at how information moves through the brain in real time, though, we realize that the way the brain works is a function of the relationships between the different areas, and that leads to some very strange happenings.

MIND OVER MATTER

At first glance, it's hard to make out what's taking place. On the screen is an image of the brain with different areas in different colors. The image is constantly changing, almost resembling a kaleidoscope, as the colors show us which areas of the brain are activated. As the functional magnetic resonance image (fMRI) records the heightened neural activity, what we are seeing is tangible evidence of those intangible thought processes that make up our minds, and what it tells us is stunning.

Before the invention of the fMRI, the inability to see the brain in action held back the progress of neuroscience. Although the electro-encephalogram (EEG) became available early in the twentieth century, it measures only the gross electrical energy given off by the brain. But the fMRI enables us to get a much more detailed view. By tracking the flow of blood carrying glucose and oxygen to regions of the brain that are active, it effectively provides a moving picture of the brain at work. Seeing the flow of information through the brain has taught us that many of the functions formerly believed to reside in one area are actually a product of the interaction between different areas. From perception to thought, things are not quite as simple as we believed them to be.

Our sense data of the outside world is represented in the digital on/off firing of nerve cells in an area of the brain known as the sensory cortex. This pattern of firing is then compared to memories of similar patterns, allowing us to recognize what we have perceived. This is straightforward enough. But the fMRI shows us that as the sense data is registered, the areas of the brain responsible for emotions, goals, and high-level ideas are also activated. Only then do we find activity in the prefrontal cortex, the seat of consciousness. What we finally become aware of is a re-creation of the world shaped by everything else going on in the mind, from our feelings to our aspirations.

Our most dominant sense, vision, is the best example of how our experience of the world is processed by the brain. The commonsense view is that an image is projected on the retina by light bouncing off an object and entering the eye. The image then travels up the optic nerve into the brain and we "see." But the *f*MRI shows us that this is not what happens. An image projected on the retina doesn't travel as an intact whole, as if through a pipe, into the brain.

Rather than responding to the part of the image projected on it, the cells of the retina are quite specialized and fire only in response to specific aspects of the image, such as color and contrast. In addition, there is a blind spot right in the middle of the retina where the optic nerve is attached, and it has to be filled in. The image projected on each retina is broken down into 127 million discrete bits of information that travel up the optic nerve to the brain's primary visual cortex as a pattern of electrical signals.

Once there, they are processed by over a billion neurons in two dozen different areas. Some of these neurons respond just to orientation, others to direction, and still others to color. As the information moves out of the primary visual cortex, it is broken down into two further streams for processing, one for motion and one for the recognition of objects. Finally, these different aspects of vision are reassembled into a coherent perception.

Scientists call the areas where the reassembly takes place *convergence zones,* and they identify a hierarchy of them. At one level, all of the visual data converges. At another, higher level, the data from all of the senses comes together to form an image of the outside world. Our sight of a baseball game, the noise of the crowd, and the smell of peanuts and beer all converge to create our experience of the game.

But it's not just sense data that converge. In order for us to recognize an object, the information from our senses must be compared with previous experience encoded in our memories. Once that happens and the image is finally structured and recognized, we become conscious that we are seeing. However, what we see is not a mirror image of the outside world. It is made up of bits of information reassembled, in the view of one neuroscientist, "according to a person's memories, past experiences, and possibly even wishes."

Because we construct our reality but don't believe we do, our view of a situation will inevitably be subjective, and so will everyone else's. With all of us unwittingly operating off of our personal versions of reality, conflicts are inevitable. Employees and managers will see things differently, and so will customers and suppliers. We can't assume that our actions and words will be interpreted the way we mean them, nor can we assume that we're correctly interpreting the actions and words of others.

THE WIRING OF IDEAS

Fortunately, neuroscience also teaches us how to be more effective in the world we work and live in, regardless of its nature. Like every organ of the body, the brain is made up of cells, approximately 100 billion of them. Unlike the cells of other organs, though, neurons connect to one another and transmit signals in potentially 40 quadrillion different ways. To appreciate a number this large, consider that it would take more than 125 million years to count all of the connections. On average, each neuron is connected to one thousand other cells. It is these connections that are responsible for the brain's enormous complexity.

Neurons make up the wiring of the brain. Information travels from one end of the neuron to the other in the form of an electrical charge. The real action, though, is not in the individual cells, but in the connections between them. Most neurons are not linked directly together. Instead, there is a small, fluid-filled gap separating them called a synapse. When the electrical charge reaches the synapse at the end of the neuron, chemicals known as neurotransmitters are released and travel across the gap to the neuron receiving the signal.

Anything that affects the production and action of neurotransmitters alters the way the brain works. We've long known that this is the case with substances such as alcohol, caffeine, and antidepressants like Prozac, but now we're discovering that everything from exercise to mood has the potential to change how we think. If we're happy, our brains operate differently than if we are sad. Stress, pain, and sexual arousal will not only affect how input is processed, but how it will be associated with other perceptions and thoughts. We can affect the quality of our thinking in profound ways by consciously altering our mood or physical state, which in turn will also change the nature of our reality.

Because of the synapses and neurotransmitters, the wiring of the brain is constantly changing, and so are the mental processes it produces. Older synapses are dying off, new ones are being created, and existing ones are either strengthening or weakening. Neuroscientists are fond of describing the cause of synaptic death as a case of "use it or lose it," and the creation of new connections as "neurons that fire together, wire together." Altering synapses is how the brain rewires itself in response to what's going on in the environment, increasing the chances of a fit between the capabilities of our minds and the changing demands of the world we find ourselves in. Rewiring is how we learn.

On a practical level, the more a mental process is used, the stronger it becomes. The more I practice the violin, the more I reinforce the neural pathways required for violin playing. The more I use certain thought processes, the more habitual they become. The more I think a given idea, the more it shapes the environment of the mind. In his study of sea snail neurons, Nobel laureate Eric Kandel found that just one instance of firing changes the chemistry of the synapse and lowers the threshold for subsequent firing, but the effect quickly dissipates. After five instances of firing, though, structural changes occur that create a long-term memory. Even at a cellular level, practice makes perfect.

The chemistry of the synapse explains why repetition is important to master a skill or to ensure that facts are retained in memory, and it explains why we can become prisoners of habitual patterns of thinking. It also suggests that exposure to different kinds of stimuli can create new neural networks that broaden our thinking.

Because the world you know is essentially just a network of ideas created by electrical charges and chemical reactions, it can be affected by the electrical charges and chemical reactions of other networks. These networks are organized hierarchically in what Damasio describes as a "supersystem of systems." Higher-level networks with a large number of connections key the firing of those at lower levels.

The ideas represented in those high-level networks, such as values and deeply held beliefs, will drive both ideas and behavior at lower levels that are in harmony with them. If I believe in the idea of equality, I will see other people as equals and behave toward them accordingly. Recent data suggests that changes driven by high-level networks are longer lasting and more comprehensive than those that originate at a lower level. Using cognitive therapy to treat mental illness by changing how patients think has proven more effective than the use of either drugs to reset synapses or behavior modification techniques. In practical terms, if we get the big ideas right, everything else will follow.

This runs up against common practice in the business world, where the focus is on managing behavior. According to neuroscience, such an approach will be much less effective than using ideas to change the thinking that drives the behavior. If you want to improve customer service, you're better off stressing its importance and linking it to an employee's values than prescribing a set of behaviors that will probably be executed with indifference or contempt. Behavioral approaches are more suited to those animals that don't live in mental worlds of their own making.

SWAPPING PARADIGMS

We can think of our versions of reality as movies, and they don't just differ in small, nuanced ways. Although we believe we're viewing the same event, you may actually be watching the Disney version, while mine is by Alfred Hitchcock. The different movies drive different thoughts and actions. Yours may be humorous and prompt happy thoughts and laughter. Mine may be threatening and key my autonomic nervous system to ready my body for defense.

Our movies must always make sense to us. If anything occurs that doesn't fit the story line, our internal editor goes to work. Without our being aware of it, our editor determines what stays in the final version and what is cut or changed, resolving any conflicts between dissonant pieces of information.

Cognitive neuroscientist Michael Gazzaniga believes that the internal editor is our reason and is probably resident in the left hemisphere. He illustrates how the editorial process works when he describes a visit to a patient at Memorial Sloan-Kettering Hospital in New York City. This woman had suffered a lesion to the area of the brain responsible for spatial location, but testing had established that all of her other brain functions were normal. When he first met her, she was lying in bed reading the *New York Times*.

During the course of an interview in her hospital room, Gazzaniga asked the woman where she was. She replied that she was in her house in Freeport, Maine. When he asked how she could explain the bank of elevators outside her door, she answered, "Doctor, do you know how much those cost to have installed?" She wasn't joking. In her version of reality, she really was at home with her bank of elevators. To us, she's "making it up as she goes along." To neuroscientists, that's just the point. We all make it up as we go along.

Not all versions of reality are created equal. Some are a better fit with our experience than others, so they lead to more effective actions. If Gazzaniga's patient had attempted to leave the hospital and navigate through New York City as if it were Freeport, Maine, she would have been in for a series of very rude awakenings. What we've realized from tracing the path of information through the brain is that the paradigm, or theoretical framework, we've been using to understand how the mind works and how humans interact with one another isn't a very good fit. As a result, the actions we take based on that paradigm don't produce the results we intend; often they produce exactly the opposite.

The biggest hurdle to understanding and utilizing the discoveries of neuroscience is the self-perpetuating nature of paradigms. Although they are just our *versions* of reality, we mistake them for reality itself, and have a hard time believing that they're not the same as everyone else's. This makes it difficult for us to appreciate their effect, let alone entertain the notion that we could shift from one to another. While the idea that our minds create our reality has been with us for thousands of years, it is only within the last decade or so that neuroscience has made available the kind of hard data our logical minds accept as proof.

At some level, all of us know about paradigms or at the very least have experienced their effect. Our different political, social, and religious positions are the result of different paradigms. Conflicting paradigms are often the cause of our frustration with our spouses and children, or their frustration with us. At work, such conflicts are what makes it difficult for manufacturing to get what marketing is saying, and vice versa. While we may believe those we disagree with lack the breadth of vision and reasoning capability we have, it's more likely that they're just assembling the world in a different way.

But our experience of conflicting paradigms leads us to underestimate the significance of neuroscience's discoveries. It's not just on the level of our belief system, or our role in a family, or our professional orientation that paradigms operate. They structure our basic experience of reality: literally what we see and believe about the very nature of the world we inhabit. Because these kinds of paradigms operate at a very deep level, they drive not just different thoughts, but different ways of thinking.

The *objective* paradigm that is responsible for our common sense and logical thinking probably evolved from our early experience of the physical world. It works just fine when we're dealing with inanimate objects like rocks, stones, or clumps of dirt. But when we're dealing with animate beings, it doesn't work quite as well, and when it comes to people with minds like our own, it fails miserably. Our anticipation of how others will respond to our actions doesn't take into account our previous experience with them, their internal motivations, or their personal versions of reality—that is, if we even bother to think about their response at all when we act.

Twenty-first century managers know that their strategies must anticipate responses, that they must account for differing customer perceptions, and that their employees don't always see things the same way they do. But given the pace of business, they rarely have the luxury or opportunity to self-reflect. Our logical thinking is on automatic, and it's the default mode we use whenever we think about anything. Without being aware of it, we ignore interdependencies, past history, and conflicting points of view. It's simply the way our minds have evolved to work.

The adverse consequences of seeing people as inanimate objects and ignoring the way they interpret events aren't limited to human resource management. Every aspect of business, no matter how much our objective paradigm discounts it, involves thinking, self-determining people. Strategies are formulated by people, implemented by people, and responded to by people we call customers and competitors. Organizations are designed and staffed by people. Changing a business is about changing people. And lest we forget, companies are run by people we call managers.

Neuroscience offers us a paradigm for human interaction that recognizes humans as thinking beings capable of self-directed action. How they decide to behave is a function of the environment they find themselves in, their relationships with others, and their personal versions of reality. This *cognitive* paradigm gives us a better way of thinking about the complexity of human activity, by calling our attention to the dynamics of human relationships and the role of the mind.

It only makes sense for us to supplement our logic with a mode of thinking that accounts for what is so unique about human beings. When we do, our actions lead to much better results. Strategies that anticipate the challenges of being implemented by people and the responses of customers and competitors are going to reap a substantial competitive advantage. Organizations designed to implement strategies *and* to facilitate how people naturally work drive cost savings right to the bottom line. When management, in the words of Peter Drucker, stops "making it difficult for people to do their work," every hard measure of performance will rise dramatically.

Perhaps one of the most counterintuitive conclusions of the latest research is the way scientists believe the mind naturally makes sense out of the world. In spite of science's preference for fact over fiction, stories are seen not only as the way the mind works but as a better fit with human activity. Different points of view, relationships, and motivations are built into the structure of stories, so they do a better job of capturing the complexity of human interaction. Because stories as a way of thinking predate logic in the evolution of our culture and in the development of the mental abilities of children, we find them immediately accessible.

While logic and science have been responsible for the incredible improvement in the material quality of our lives, it has not been without a cost. The bias of our objective paradigm against stories is, as we shall see, responsible for the loss of valuable mental abilities, but neuroscience is helping us rediscover them. Besides, if objectivity is just an illusion, as neuroscience maintains, a story is as valid a way of making sense of our experience as a scientific theory. Both are just paradigms.

THE POWER OF IDEAS

Tracking the flow of information through the brain demonstrates that the world we inhabit is just a figment of the imagination. Playing a game of chance with four decks of cards shows that our emotions lead to better decisions than our reason. Understanding how a signal moves from one nerve cell to another teaches us that ideas can quite literally change the world. Our brief survey of the findings of neuroscience has demolished our reality, our reason, and our identity. But it has also taught us how really powerful ideas can be.

So much of what we've taken for granted turns out to be the opposite of what we thought it was. I don't produce thoughts; my thoughts produce me. The world isn't physical; it's mental. Objective logic isn't the best way to make decisions; incorporating our feelings is. It's not physical force that makes things happen; it's the power of ideas. The world neuroscience gives us is a very different place than we thought it was, and it demands different ways of thinking and acting.

Virtually everything we do now has to be seen through the lens of what we've learned about the mind. When it comes to how we approach business, we need to rethink everything we thought we knew about management. This isn't just about a new model for measuring a business, reengineering its operations, or motivating its people. This is about the nature of the world being different than we thought it was and about the need for a fundamentally different paradigm to drive the way we think and act.

From a world that exists only in our minds to a reasoning process that is only a justification for decisions we've already made, the world according to neuroscience does take some getting used to. But when we come right down to it, the fundamental lesson is quite simple. The power is in ideas. They can change the world and they can transform a business. All we need to do is open our minds and let them in. They'll do the rest.

TWO

FROM BRAIN TO MIND

The new owners of the ski area located on the edge of a small New England town wanted to build vacation condominiums, arguing that the resort would only be financially viable if they could ensure a large enough number of skiers would use it on a regular basis. This pristine village, virtually unchanged from colonial days, was now evenly split over the proposal and the discussions had grown heated. One side welcomed the jobs the proposed development would bring, but the other side resisted the idea of a housing development so out of keeping with the character of the town. Since the plan required a variance under the current zoning regulations, a town meeting was convened to vote on the request.

After the meeting was called to order, the developers were up first to present their case. Nicely bound handouts with the details of their proposal were stacked on the table in front of them, and attractive architectural drawings of the housing development were prominently displayed on easels on both sides of the stage. The condominiums were cleverly designed and landscaped to blend in with the surrounding woodlands. One couldn't help thinking that the developers had been in this situation before and had come to this meeting well prepared.

Everything about their presentation was professional and polished. Dressed in jackets and ties, they spoke persuasively and with compelling logic about how important the resort was to the economy of the town, and what would happen should it go bankrupt. They explained how many people currently used the resort, how many were needed to turn a profit, and how many the new condominium development would bring in. Detailed financial statements established both the necessity of the development for the economic health of the resort and the huge benefit it would bring to the town.

By the time the presentation was over, those opposed to the condominiums were feeling overwhelmed. They had nowhere near the resources of the developers to call upon, and it seemed as if every possible argument they had intended to make against the development had been preempted. Their major concern was that the character of the town would be irreversibly damaged by the increase in population and traffic, but it was difficult to marshal hard data to support the contention that the town would "feel" different and the quality of life would suffer.

When the moderator called for comments on the developers' presentation, the hall grew silent except for the sound of chairs scraping on the hardwood floor and a cough echoing through the room. No one was eager to stand up and speak for what looked like a lost cause. But then an old Yankee rose slowly to his feet. Dressed in a faded plaid shirt, worn corduroy pants, and a navy down vest, he moved so tentatively that he appeared incapable of mounting a credible challenge to what had just been presented. Sensing that if this was their only opposition, victory was inevitable, the resort owners settled more comfortably into their chairs.

Deliberately choosing each word, the old man started to speak. "I don't understand much about all these numbers," he said, "and you fellas do seem like nice people. But your argument for the condominiums reminds me of the man that just had to have a pickle to eat with his sandwich. He would take a bite of the sandwich and then a bite of that pickle. Another bite of the sandwich, and then another bite of the pickle followed. His lunch was the sandwich, and that should have been enough for him, but it wasn't. He always had to have that pickle to make what he called a 'complete' meal. Gentlemen, you're asking for one hell of a big pickle."

With that, he slowly sat back down again. The room was still and everyone seemed a bit puzzled by what had been said. Then a little bit of nervous laughter could be heard in the back of the room. Steadily it grew louder and louder and more widespread until finally becoming a roar that echoed through the room as people got the gist of what the old man had said. Although he hadn't countered any of the arguments the resort owners had put forth for the development, he had effectively changed the terms of the debate. The condominiums were no longer a financial necessity, they were one hell of a pickle that nobody really needed.

The comparison transformed how people saw the development. While there is nothing humorous about high-density housing, a pickle is kind of a silly food, and that probably occasioned a bit of the laughter. The word "pickle" also can denote a difficult situation, and that was picked up on as well. There was nothing logical about what the Yankee said—clearly the proposed condominiums didn't have anything in common with a kosher dill or a gherkin—so there was no rebuttal possible. The resort owners couldn't very well say the obvious, that the condominiums were not a pickle, because the old man had never asserted that they were. But from that moment on, the condominiums were referred to as "one hell of a big pickle."

They were never built, and the ski resort closed several years later. The owners, with all of their polish and formidable resources, had been defeated by a metaphor.

THE MIND ON METAPHOR

Being done in by a simple little rhetorical device like a metaphor would seem more fantastic if we didn't know from neuroscience how the mind works. After data from our senses is processed in the sensory cortex, it is compared to similar patterns of neural firing stored in memory, allowing us to recognize the new perception by its resemblance to others we have experienced before. The memory structures the perception, directing our attention to certain aspects of it and away from others.

A metaphor operates essentially the same way, comparing what we don't know to what we do. Perhaps the best known metaphor is Robert Burns's "My love is like a red, red rose." This metaphor asks us to understand the poet's "love," which we don't know, by thinking about it as something we do know, a "rose." The way we do this is to consider the attributes of the known rose and then look for correspondences in the unknown love. What immediately comes to mind is the stunning beauty and delicacy of the rose. By correlation, the poet's love can be understood as stunningly beautiful and delicate.

Metaphors also add a dimension that wasn't there before. Even though we can't personally know Burns's love, we are able to experience something similar because metaphors bring our senses into play. Because we don't just think the metaphor, but feel it, more mental processes are engaged than when we're just reasoning logically. Given Damasio's experiment on decision making, we can see why the "pickle" could have such persuasive power.

Both roses and pickles can change the way we see things, what we think about them, and how we act as a result. But there are also metaphors that operate on a much deeper level and have a more profound effect. Such metaphors determine the very nature of reality and how we think about it. Cognitive linguists George Lakoff and Mark Johnson contend that "our everyday reality," and "the way we think, what we experience, and what we do every day is very much a matter of metaphor." Even when we think we are using plain language and viewing our reality as it really is, these deeply embedded "conceptual metaphors" are structuring our perceptions and our thoughts.

According to historian of science Theodore Brown, the source of these conceptual metaphors that shape both our scientific thinking and our common sense is "our most ubiquitous physical experiences." Because we were animals living in a physical world before we developed consciousness, the physical we were familiar with became the source of the metaphors we used to make sense of our experience. This works fine as long as we're thinking about the physical world, but when we turn our thoughts to experiences that are not physical, our metaphors don't fit them. We distort our experience, use a mode of thinking that isn't appropriate, and then take actions that are ineffective.

While we can expect objects in the physical world to respond to our manipulation in straightforward and predictable ways, people with minds are capable of all kinds of machinations. They don't just react. They think about their experience and make decisions about how best to respond. They can lead us to believe they're doing one thing and do something completely different. They can strike an agreement with us one minute and go back on it the next. Or they can just leave us guessing about what they're going to do.

Since the world we inhabit is mental, according to neuroscience, ways of thinking and acting geared to the physical world are bound to fail, particularly when it comes to our interactions with other people. At the same time, other ways of thinking and acting that are effective in a mental world are never considered because we mistakenly believe we inhabit a physical world. As a result, much of what we do as managers is either suboptimal or self-defeating. We can become much more effective if we recognize this mismatch and ensure that our perceptions, thoughts, and actions fit the nature of the world we're operating in. The place to start is an understanding of the differences between the objective and cognitive paradigms and the worlds they create.

LIVING IN THE MATERIAL WORLD

The physical world was all early people knew, so of course it shaped their thinking. Whether they were reflecting on other people or their own mental processes, they saw them the same way they saw rocks, clumps of dirt, and trees. Interaction in this world of inanimate objects follows the model of one billiard ball colliding with another. The first billiard ball imparts force to the second, causing the second to move in a predictable way. With Newton's three laws of motion and relatively simple mathematics, I can even accurately predict where the ball will move. We needn't concern ourselves with the environment (beyond the surface of the billiard table,) or with the past relationship of the balls. After the initial impact, they no longer have an effect on one another.

This view of the world parallels the thinking of the Greek philosopher Aristotle. He believed that since the world was made up of separate objects, the right way to reason was to break things up into their component parts. By understanding the parts, we would then understand the whole. In Aristotle's world, "what you see and reason about is pretty much what you get." So we can also assume that we have no effect on what we are observing and our view is objective.

In the twentieth century, the objective billiard ball paradigm produced behavioral science, and it quickly came to dominate psychology. Because what you see is what you get, what goes on in the mind was not deemed suitable or necessary to be concerned with. When it came to motivating people, external force in the form of the stick or the carrot was all that was required. There was no need to consider intrinsic motivation, relationships, or the nature of the environment. Since it was such a simple model and advocated direct action, it appealed to pragmatic business managers. Behavioral science shaped, and continues to shape, management practice in the corporate world.

Of course, we've moved far beyond such a simple view. We know that people are more than just objects, that they have minds, and that their behavior is driven by their psychology. But metaphors are tricky things, and it's easy to fall victim to them. The physical world is our default source of metaphors and it continues to shape our perceptions of the world. If it didn't, the view neuroscience gives us wouldn't be so disconcerting.

IT'S ALL IN THE MIND

In the world we know, according to neuroscience, there are no things, only ideas. Physical objects interact according to Newton's laws of motion, but ideas without mass don't. Nor apparently do they obey Aristotle's laws of logic. In Damasio's experiment, the decision to choose from the lower-risk decks is made not as the result of syllogistic reasoning but because it feels like the best fit with the experience of past trials.

The biological anthropologist Robert Aunger sees this process of *fit* as the way the mind reasons about virtually everything. In contrast to Aristotelian logic, "our nonrandom, 'designed' solutions to problems are the result of a multistage mental tournament in which there is selection among blindly created variants for the strongest option, given the environment of thought at the time." Ideas vie with one another and the one that fits best with the situation under consideration, relative to the others, is the one we become conscious of.

We see this process of competition for *fit* everywhere in nature. Charles Darwin called it natural selection and believed it was how the natural world evolved. According to his theory, there are many more organisms in nature than there are resources to support them, so there is a competition among them to *fit* the demands of the environment. Those organisms that win the competition are *selected* to survive and pass their genes on to future generations.

Natural selection is not a static process. As a result of random mutations or recombination in sexual reproduction, genes evolve and produce organisms with different traits. If those traits enable the organisms to fit the demands of the environment better, their genes are passed on to subsequent generations. The environment also changes, selecting out different traits. Who we are today is simply the result of the chance mutations of our genes, selected because they enabled us to survive and procreate.

It's not surprising that the brain should operate the same way as natural selection, for even though mental activity may seem different, it is just a natural process. Our ideas are the products of the metabolic processes of living cells, and because these ideas create the mental world human beings inhabit, that mental world also operates through natural selection. In place of the inanimate objects that make up the physical world, we have animate beings with minds that move of their own volition.

This is what neuroscience's revolution is all about. The physical world is recognized to be mental, and the objective "billiard ball" paradigm is replaced by the cognitive "natural selection" paradigm. Rather than attend to objects and forces, we need to focus on relationships and the environment.

To think about this world, we're better served by the dialectical reasoning of Plato than the objective logic of Aristotle. While for Aristotle, it was the physical world that was ultimately real, for Plato it was the world of ideas. Because much of Plato's thinking anticipated the discoveries of neuroscience, he offers us a better way of reasoning for the world we inhabit, one that dovetails nicely with the way the mind actually works.

Plato was convinced that humans are inevitably subjective. When everybody has their own verson of reality, the best way to determine what's true is to play one person's point of view off of another's. The process of doing this is called a dialectic, and it is essentially a competition of ideas to arrive at a more comprehensive one that encompasses both. As we move from idea to idea, we rise up a hierarchy to the biggest idea of them all. Variously called "the good" or "the truth," it then informs all of our other reasoning and ensures that it is valid.

The dialectic fits perfectly with a brain that works through natural selection. There's Aungur's competition, a hierarchical organization, and a high-level idea at the top creating a mental environment that selects out other ideas in harmony with it. Instead of following an artificial method for reasoning that excludes what emotion and other unconscious processes can teach us, we just let the mind work naturally. When we need to solve a problem or make a decision, we specify the criteria for the outcome, freely generate options through brainstorming ideas that compete against one another, and then select the idea or ideas that fit our criteria.

Leaving aside the way we reason, comparing Aristotle and Plato as representatives of the physical and mental worlds gives us a sense of the kind of interaction with other people that works best in each. Both attempted to convince others of their ideas, and that's essentially what we do when we want other people to support us in the accomplishment of our goals. Aristotle made no effort to persuade because he assumed that reasonable men would be convinced by the superior force of his logic.

In contrast, Plato used questions to encourage people to reach their own conclusions, though he did subtly shape the mental environment that determined what those conclusions would be. While this is not the direct control that we think we have in the physical world, it is probably the most effective way of "moving" people.

Thinking and acting in line with the nature of the world we live in doesn't require learning a new set of algorithms to replace the logical ones we've grown up with. That's the beauty of the way the brain works. All we need to do is think about the cognitive paradigm and it becomes embedded in a neural network. Our minds will then randomly generate ideas and actions that fit with it. In fact, what we've done in the last few pages is create such a neural network. Now we just need to let our minds work the way they naturally do.

A PARADIGM IN TIME

Increasingly, a wide range of cognitive scientists building on the discoveries of neuroscience have concluded that the human mind really works through stories. As cognitive scientist Mark Turner puts it, "Story is a basic principle of mind. Most of our experience, our knowledge, and our thinking is organized as stories." Much like the importance of ideas and the hierarchical arrangement of the mind, this is a notion dating back to the ancient Greeks and only now, over two millennia later, being substantiated by science. Stories were the preferred mode of making sense of the world before Aristotle and others "invented" logic.

Even today, stories are so pervasive in our culture that their presence is not always recognized. We don't necessarily notice that our nightly news is in the form of stories or that there's inevitably a story behind a sporting event or one or more of its key players. We have story stocks, corporate stories, and the conflicting stories opposing lawyers spin around a given set of facts. We have the stories our kids tell about why their homework wasn't done, and we have the stories our elected officials tell us about why a given foreign or domestic policy is necessary. For a culture that values fact over fiction and sees logic as the right way to think, we tell a lot of stories.

Or according to the philosopher Daniel Dennett, it's the other way around. "Our tales are spun, but for the most part we don't spin them; they spin us." Rather than telling stories, it's as if we are handed a script and must act the role that it defines for us. Because of this, when we encounter a story, we almost immediately identify with the main character, internalize his or her worldview, and move toward taking it as our own. This gives stories much greater power to shape the way we think than a logical argument. They structure our experience, determine how we think, and drive the way we act. As "moving picture paradigms," they select what we attend to and what we ignore, so that our perceptions conform to the story and it becomes our reality.

Even beyond their impact, stories as a way of making sense out of the world have advantages over logic and are much better suited to the mental world we inhabit. Because they are another's perspective on the world, we are forced to acknowledge that others have different perceptions than we do, preventing us from falling into the trap of thinking that we're just objectively recording what's going on. Attention to the environment and relationships are also inherent in the structure of a story. The setting frames the action, which is driven by the conflict between the characters.

Just like metaphors, stories don't claim to be true, so they don't elicit attempts to logically refute them. They ask only that we entertain them as a way of organizing our experience of the world.

USING STORIES

Given the effect stories have on us, they are one of the most useful tools one can have in a mental world, replacing the carrot and stick of the physical world. We can use them both to understand and to shape how others think and behave. There's even evidence from neuroscience that empathy and storytelling are two sides of the same coin. Those afflicted with the physiological disorder known as dysnarrativia, an inability to tell stories, lose "the ability to read other minds, to tell what others might have been thinking, feeling, even seeing. Sufferers seem to have lost not only a sense of self but also a sense of other."

If we can tap into the story that someone else is telling, we can learn enough about them to anticipate how they'll behave. Just as when we perceive something by attending to a few clues and filling in the rest, so too are we able to infer from a minimum amount of information the stories others are telling. This is because, as H. Porter Abbott suggests, there are a limited number of "masterplots" that appear repeatedly in a given culture and help to define it. One prominent example is the Horatio Alger story, "a variation of the quest masterplot that speaks directly to cherished values in broad swathes of U.S. culture." In Horatio Alger's novels, by dint of hard work and good character, the young man overcomes obstacles and makes good. When we encounter elements of this plot, we're quick to fill in the rest of the story.

In addition to poor boy makes good, we have other masterplots, like bad man gets his just desserts, good man succumbs to tragic flaw, and boy meets girl and does or doesn't win her. But in the stories we're most likely to identify with, the hero is a good man or woman who does triumph in the end. It is the romance with the happy ending that sparks our interest, and the greater the achievement, the more power it has for us.

Just as with masterplots, we can identify different stock characters that appear repeatedly. "People of a particular character are expected to inhabit similar roles in different stories. We can develop a categorization of kinds of character—generous, selfish, brave, submissive, and so on." When we encounter some of the traits, we make an assumption about the character and their story and fill in the rest. Not too long ago, the *New York Times* ran a story suggesting that a new masterplot of our culture is "the rogue CEO." Martha Stewart and Ken Lay were named as the representative stock characters.

If we want to know how someone else is experiencing the world, we can try out different stories from our culture's stock and find the one that seems to fit the best with what we observe about their behavior, the way they speak, what they say, and anything else that might be available. If it's someone we're familiar with, we'll have even more information about them. We may know their family, their background, and even perhaps their hopes and dreams. We can then induce from this information a masterplot and character type. This will facilitate our empathy and understanding, and enable us to figure out how to motivate them to take the action we desire.

But it's not only others who can be viewed through stories. We, too, are defined by the masterplots of our culture. So we believe that if we work hard like one of Horatio Alger's heroes, we will be successful, and the masterplot guides our actions. While identifying the story that's defining us increases our self-awareness, we're not at the mercy of it. We can tell ourselves a different story that will change the way we think and behave.

Like any of our ideas or perceptions, stories are the mental products of neural networks with lowered thresholds for firing. The more we tell the story, the more the network is reinforced through structural changes in the synapses. If we stop telling a story, natural synaptic death will eventually weaken the network. If we tell ourselves a new story repeatedly, we'll create a new network with a lowered threshold for firing. It's really no different than learning a new skill through practice. The more the network is reinforced, the more the story becomes our reality.

The same is true for the stories of others as well. Although we've seen that we can't move ideas around in our minds as we do objects in the physical world, we can affect the environment of thought by telling a different story to embed a new neural network. Because of our shared masterplots and characters, the subtle use of just the right details is enough to change the stories people tell themselves. Mention the honest and hardworking man or woman, and people will fill in the rest of the Horatio Alger story.

Beyond their role in empathy, self-definition, and change, stories can also serve as examples or illustrations. Just like the metaphor of the man who wanted a pickle to go with his sandwich, we tell the story and let the audience draw their own conclusion, a conclusion we determine by the way we tell the story. Because of the natural tendency to identify with the character in the story, the moral will be felt as well as thought. Because everyone enjoys hearing good stories, there's a better chance that we'll have more of an opportunity to finish the story without interruption than we would with a logical argument.

But the use of stories shouldn't just be restricted to "people issues." Although logic encourages us to strip out feelings and focus on hard objective data, the kind of thinking the business world favors, Damasio's experiment made it clear such an approach is neither possible nor desirable. Business is not a purely objective pursuit—it is a human activity. When we analyze a business only in terms of what appears on an income statement or balance sheet, we're going to miss a lot. If we can figure out the story people are telling themselves, we'll know what's behind the numbers and be in a better position to take corrective action. The way to do that is to embed a new neural network by repeatedly asking yourself what story other people are telling.

A CAUTIONARY TALE

During the dotcom boom, I was asked by a client to assess a company they had acquired. Before the deal had closed, they had high expectations for this company. Although it operated in a small regional market, it had a solid staff and a loyal customer base. The thinking was that if the company sold and delivered the consulting services my client had pioneered, their growth would take off exponentially. Unfortunately, after the acquisition was completed, there was just one disappointment after another.

The consulting services my client had pioneered were so attractive that the company was growing by leaps and bounds. As the company got bigger, the board decided it was time to hire a new CEO to take them to the next level. She had a reputation as a financial wizard and was said to be able to accurately assess the potential of a company with just a quick look at the balance sheet and income statement. The board gave her a mandate to improve profitability and grow the business. She immediately set about "tightening the belt" and getting costs under control, and then she bumped up the marketing effort. Costs came down and demand increased. Rewarded by a healthy increase in the stock price for her efforts at improving profitability, she went shopping for acquisitions.

Within a quarter, she had her first candidate. Although the largely unknown regional player looked like a perfect fit, the CEO was a bit concerned about the "quirky" culture of the company. It was located in the southeastern part of the country and seemed to sponsor an unusually large number of parties for the slightest of reasons. She sensed a little belt tightening wouldn't hurt there as well. It was agreed that new managers would be brought in from the parent and the owners would leave as soon as the deal was done.

Expectations were high as the new managers were installed and the company shifted over to sell and deliver the new services. Even when the profit forecast for the next quarter was missed, there wasn't much concern. There were inevitably glitches when companies were merged. But the following quarter saw a dip in not just profit, but revenues as well. The CEO quickly took corrective action, sending a no-nonsense "fixer" down from headquarters to get things on track.

But revenues and profits weren't any better the following quarter, and it appeared that the downward trend was accelerating. Perhaps most worrisome was that the backlog of orders was shrinking dramatically. This defied all logic. Due diligence prior to the acquisition had established that there was a healthy customer base, and with the parent company's service offering, demand should have increased exponentially. Instead, it seemed as if the opposite was happening.

The CEO replaced the sales manager and sent down a team of the parent company's best marketers to address the falling demand. A large investment was made in a new ad campaign for the region and extensive training sessions for the salespeople. But it was all to no avail. At the end of the quarter, every significant indicator was on a downward trend. Worse yet, the marketers from the parent reported that the acquisition's sales and marketing teams were largely unresponsive. They would just sit in meetings and not say anything.

When it finally got to the point that the acquisition's results were hurting the parent company's performance and stock price, I was asked to pay a visit to the company. It was expected that I would study the company for a couple of weeks or so and then recommend whatever changes might be needed. Instead, after just one day, I found the cause of the performance problems. It was the parent company's hot new service offering.

The managers of the parent company were doing precisely what they had been trained to do. They looked at the key metrics of the business, and when they saw the downward trend, they instituted the logical corrective action. When overall results weren't what they should've been, a fixer was brought in who would not shy away from taking action, no matter how unpopular it might be. When the demand still wasn't there for the offering, they replaced the sales manager and increased the marketing effort. But without the backstory, my client never had a good handle on why the results were slipping. So they were not only just treating symptoms, they were doing it in a way that actually made matters worse.

I attended a sales and marketing meeting during my first day at the acquisition that was a case in point. A marketer from the parent company running the meeting spent the entire time in "Aristotelian mode," telling people what they needed to do. If anybody raised a concern, it was met with a recital of how wonderful the new service offering was and how successful the parent had become because of it. It wasn't long before no concerns were raised. When I asked one of the acquisition's salespeople if he'd ever been asked why results were down, his answer was no.

The staff from the acquisition prided themselves on working for a plucky little company. It was part of their culture to balance work and play, and as the saying in the company went, "there's always a reason to have a celebration." They had no interest in being stars, and the story they told themselves was about being good workers, good parents, and good citizens. They saw themselves as salt-of-the-earth people who worked hard but knew how to have a good time. The parent company was the conqueror from the cold and far too serious north. They put a stop to everything that had made working at the acquisition fun, and their confidence bordered on arrogance.

If the acquisition raised an issue about the appropriateness of what the parent company was telling them to do, it was quickly dismissed in a way that made people feel inferior. Soon, everyone started to resent the visitors from the parent company, and they weren't about to offer anything that might be helpful. Some joked that it was like the old television program about POWs, *Hogan's Heroes*. They might be conquered, but they were going to make it as difficult for the conquerors as they could. They were never asked, so they never offered to explain what was responsible for the company's problems. After a while, they just became passive.

The Aristotelian logic of the parent company obscured the real cause of the acquisition's poor performance. The hot new service offering was only hot in a given *environment* in *relationship* to a set of competitors. The parent company sold almost exclusively to Fortune 1000 companies, competing against large, established firms that weren't nimble enough to match the offering quickly. But the acquisition was in a region with no Fortune 1000 companies, and the smaller companies that were their market had no interest in the service. Besides, their regional competitors were quick to match any competitive offering. Since the acquisition had been instructed to sell the parent company's offering in place of their traditional services, they couldn't sell what people wanted and nobody wanted what they could sell.

After I presented what I had learned, the fixer and the marketers packed up and went home. The acquisition regrouped and went back to selling the services that had brought them success in the past. Eventually, the results improved, but there was never the big boost that had been anticipated when the deal was first done. After this hiccup, the parent company again continued to post enviable growth rates every quarter and to pursue acquisitions. Not much later, I was dispatched to Switzerland. Apparently, there were some cultural issues with the company's first international acquisition.

PARADIGMS AND THE POWER OF STORIES

Although we might see metaphors as just rhetorical ornamentation, they are fundamentally how the mind works. The sense data that are disassembled and reassembled in the brain are only meaningful when compared to something we are already familiar with. At the deepest level of the mind, conceptual metaphors act as paradigms and structure our experience of the world, determining what we see, how we think, and how we act. Perhaps because it was the experience we were familiar with before the development of our conscious minds, the inanimate physical world became the metaphor we use for how our minds work and people interact.

The common sense entailed by the objective paradigm distorts the world, leading to actions that are self-defeating, while obscuring others that would prove more effective. When we look at the way the mind actually works, we see that it operates just like Darwin's natural selection. Options are generated randomly and the mental environment selects out the fittest. Because the world we live in is mental, the cognitive paradigm is a better fit with how we think and act. Rather than use force to get people to do our bidding, we'll be better served creating a mental environment that will select out what we need them to do.

Stories are the way our minds naturally work, and they preceded the invention of logic as a way of making sense of the world. The stories we tell ourselves determine the way we view the world, the way we think, and the way we act. We can use stories both to understand people and to change their minds, and we can use stories as a framework to analyze a business, going beyond the numbers to the reasons for the numbers. In almost every situation we find ourselves in, stories give us a much deeper appreciation for the forces at work and how we need to address them.

WORKING RELATIONSHIPS

Two prisoners are accused of a crime and held in separate cells. The police don't have enough evidence to convict them, so they go to each prisoner separately and offer a deal. If the prisoner confesses and implicates the other, he will go free. If he doesn't confess, but the other prisoner does, he will get ten years in jail. If both prisoners confess, they will each get three years in jail. If neither prisoner confesses, they both will go free.

This is the setup for Prisoners' Dilemma, a favorite of game theorists and a staple of psychological research on relationships. It captures two essential truths about human beings. The first is that when we are involved in an interaction with another person, our behavior is interdependent. Actions we take will affect, and be affected by, the actions of the other. So any decision we make about what we do must take into account how the other person will likely respond, and vice versa. The second is that all of us are, first and foremost, looking out for our own interests.

From a logical point of view, each prisoner's decision about what

to do is a straightforward calculation of the relative costs and benefits. If the first prisoner confesses and the second doesn't, the first
prisoner will go free. If the first prisoner confesses and the second
does too, both will get three years. So the choice to confess yields
either three years or freedom.

If, on the other hand, the first prisoner doesn't confess and the
second doesn't as well, both will go free. But if the first prisoner
doesn't confess and the second does, the first prisoner will get ten
years. So the choice not to confess yields either ten years or freedom. Because neither prisoner knows what the other is going to do,
the safe, rational choice is to confess. An outcome of three years in
jail or freedom is a better deal than an outcome of ten years in jail
or freedom. But because a confession by one prisoner puts the other
prisoner at a disadvantage, their interests are in conflict.

This is not unlike many relationships we find ourselves in at work,
where cooperation with our peers will improve the performance of
our group and benefit us in the long term but where we are also in
competition for promotions and incentive compensation. While we
may keep the good of the enterprise in mind and desire a cooperative
relationship, we can't just blindly trust that our peers will be thinking
the same way. Nor can they trust that we will want to cooperate.

In Prisoners' Dilemma, with no way to communicate with one
another and with just one decision to be made, there is no logical way
for either prisoner to forge a cooperative relationship that benefits
both and beats the game. But in real life, there is almost always an
opportunity to communicate, and the relationship is rarely "one-off."
Usually, there are repeated interactions over time.

To mirror this more realistic situation, researchers have come
up with an iterated version of the game with multiple rounds. Each
prisoner's decisions for any given round can then take into account
the decisions made in previous rounds and those that will be made

in subsequent rounds. At the same time, the prisoners' decisions can be used to communicate how they intend to play the game. With multiple rounds and the ability to signal intent, it becomes possible to turn the competitive relationship into a cooperative one.

So how should the iterated version of the game be played? Because the rational choice is to confess, the challenge for either prisoner is to figure out how to change the other's decision from "confess" to "don't confess." Let's say the first prisoner confesses. If the second prisoner then confesses as well, both are locked in a competitive downward spiral. If, on the other hand, the second prisoner doesn't confess, it simply reinforces the first prisoner's decision to confess. This is the dilemma.

The solution is for either prisoner to start out not confessing, in order to send the message that the two should cooperate. Given the rational calculation, this is counterintuitive. If the other prisoner gets the message and doesn't confess in the next round, then the relationship has been changed into a cooperative one. If, however, the other prisoner still insists on confessing, then the prisoner who didn't confess now confesses to send the message that there will be consequences for the competitive behavior. This is also counterintuitive because the prisoner is competing to become cooperative. In the following round, though, he goes back to not confessing to signal the intent to cooperate.

Political scientist Robert Axelrod solicited computer programs from game theorists to play an iterated version of Prisoners' Dilemma. After running close to two hundred rounds, the program that did the best employed precisely this strategy. Called tit for tat, it aims for cooperation but matches competition with competition so you can't be taken advantage of. To always compete locks you into the disadvantageous downward spiral. To always cooperate just complements and reinforces the competitive behavior of others.

The game demonstrates that either party in a relationship has the ability to change it from competitive to cooperative. In the world created by the objective paradigm, the tit-for-tat strategy will strike us as illogical because we tend to see ourselves as separate individuals and our actions as unrelated to those that come before and those that follow. But in the world structured by the cognitive paradigm, our focus is on relationships between people over time, so such counterintuitive strategies come readily to mind.

But our story isn't over just yet. In a twist on the original setup, researchers divided people who were to play the game into two groups. One heard a news story about a clergyman who donated a kidney and the other heard a news story about a clergyman who committed a murder. When they then played the game, those that heard the story about the donation of the kidney were much more willing to cooperate. In the physical world, hearing such a story couldn't possibly change the logic of how to play the game. In the mental world, an idea can change everything.

RELATIONSHIP EFFECTS

In keeping with the goal of being objective and unemotional when it comes to reasoning, the corporate world tends to use its Aristotelian logic to separate the people from the business issues. The relative importance of each is signaled by the bias in the terms that are often used to contrast them. Plants and equipment are "hard" assets, while people are "soft" assets. Financial, strategic, and operational skills are "hard," but those used in dealing with people are "soft."

In most organizations, the soft, people issues are stripped out of the business and become the province of the Human Resources function, with its correspondingly lower status and compensation scale. This supposedly frees line managers to spend their time on the more important business issues. When I ran Training and Development for a large corporation early in my career, I was complimented by one line manager for being "not bad for a human resources guy."

Yet for the more than two decades that I have consulted on the formulation and implementation of strategy, people problems have been behind the majority of the issues I've been called upon to address. I was hired by a large Midwestern bank to help them reformulate their strategy and redesign their organization, but the impetus to bring in a consultant, I later found out, was a running battle between the CFO and CEO. My work developing the management skills of physicians at a leading HMO was driven by the CEO's struggle to manage his relationship with the president. The redesign of a generic pharmaceutical company's R & D process was necessitated by the manager's inability to relate to his diverse and highly educated staff.

The importance of the people issues and managers' discomfort with them was really brought home to me when the highly skilled head of a successful high-technology company retained me because he "wasn't very good at dealing with people." This man was a brilliant strategist, a talented operator, and genuinely beloved by all of his people. Yet he bought 25 percent of my time for three years to be on call just in case his relationship with any of his managers soured. He felt just fine handling every aspect of a very complex business, but when it came to people, he wanted a backup available.

No matter how we might deny it, relationship issues are the most difficult problems we face in business. Most neuroscientists now agree that our oversize brains evolved as an adaptation to help us function in a social environment. In fact, among primates there is a direct correlation between the relative size of the brain and the average size of their social groups. Contrasting how our two paradigms drive the way we think about the interaction of animate beings shows why.

In the physical world, I hit one billiard ball with my cue stick, and it hits a second ball, imparting force and, we assume, causing the second ball to move. According to systems theorist Ervin Laszlo, this Newtonian view is then carried over to the world of living beings "so that when we speak of the 'response' of a living thing to an 'external stimulus,' we seem to be talking about something like what happens to a billiard ball when it is hit by another." But, of course, this isn't the way relationships work between thinking, animate beings.

Let's say I'm walking down a path in the woods when I encounter a snarling dog blocking my way. With my best logic, I determine that a swift kick with sufficient force will move the dog a reasonable distance out of my way. But this reasoning doesn't account for how my relationship with the dog at the present moment is affected by our previous interactions and the way both of us think. It isn't just the Newtonian force of my kick that causes the dog to move, it's how the dog's mind interprets my kick and uses its own energy to respond. The immediate goal of my kick may have been to get the growling dog out of my way, but its effect goes beyond my immediate goal.

When it's kicked, the dog might be frightened and run away, or it might be angered enough to turn and attack. If it bares its teeth at me as a warning to quickly vacate the area, I will then respond, depending on how I interpret the bared teeth and my own tolerance for pain. Perhaps I'll charge the dog and then stop, attempting to frighten it away. Maybe the dog will run away at that point, or maybe it will conclude that it wants to engage in battle and attack. In either case, I have decisions to make based on the dog's behavior, and it has decisions to make based on mine.

It makes no sense to view the parties to this interaction as independent, for the actions of one are based on the actions of the other. After the first billiard ball hits the second, we can pretty well conclude that they are done with each other. But my relationship with the dog is a circuit of repeated interactions, with each one affected by the previous ones and affecting those still to come. These interactions can lead to a competitive escalation of the battle until both man and dog are bloodied. Or they can fall into a complementary pattern where my aggressiveness and the dog's deference (or vice versa) reinforce each other.

This view of the interaction adds critical insights obscured by logic. We recognize that how each of us act is a function of the relationship, so before we decide on a course of action, we need to anticipate what the response of the other will be and then decide what we will do. We also see that what happens at a given moment in time is not an isolated event, but is a product of the past and will have effects in the future. We appreciate that the current state of a relationship is the result of the interaction of its parties, and that a change on the part of one will be compensated for by a change on the part of the other.

Relationship effects are quite understandable when seen through the lens of the cognitive paradigm, but they often surprise the logical mind as unintended consequences. Applying sufficient force to the dog with a good, solid kick should send it on its way, but it's a relationship effect when it comes back snarling in response. Appreciating such effects enables us to anticipate how animate beings will respond to our actions and to gain an advantage by leveraging them.

When the interaction is between people, it gets even more complex. Now we have to take into account those high-level ideas that drive decisions on how to act. Maybe the person I'm interacting with has just heard a news story about a clergyman donating a kidney, or maybe they've just been dressed down by their boss and are looking for a target for their aggression. Either way, logic isn't going to help me figure out what to do, but the kind of thinking entailed by the cognitive paradigm will.

Early in my career, I was invited to give a presentation of my company's capabilities to a division of Citigroup. This was an opportunity to sign up an extremely desirable client. It was *the* bank at the time, with a reputation for being far more aggressive and cutting-edge than other banks. There was also a touch of arrogance that went along with their success, and they were known for being tough people to do business with. But my work with them would not only be lucrative, it would be a great reference to use with other prospects. I must admit that I was both nervous and a little awed when I entered the division's posh offices on Park Avenue.

As I was waiting in a reception area while the staff attended to other business, I spent the time going over my presentation. I wanted it to be as crisp and polished as possible. I had worked hard to make sure the materials were the best they could be, and I'd invested a lot of time practicing it to ensure that I would come across just the way I wanted to. Finally, after what seemed an eternity, I was invited into their conference room.

Even before I had a chance to sit down, one of the executives expressed his conviction that I couldn't possibly be of any use to their division. He asked what kind of experience I could have that would be of value to a business as complex as theirs. But I never had a chance to answer that question, or any others for that matter. It didn't seem to make much of a difference because the questions were just rhetorical, and nobody seemed interested in what I had to say about anything. They were much more interested in what they had to say, and most of it had to do with how inexperienced and incompetent I was.

Every time I tried to get a word in, I was interrupted. The copies of my carefully produced presentation sat in front of me, never used. The abuse just went on and on, until finally there was a pause when they appeared to have run out of steam. It was now my turn, but given the relationship effects, I knew that I'd get nowhere arguing against them. Thinking back to Prisoners' Dilemma, I wondered if it wouldn't be better to do the opposite of what they expected and agree with them.

So I began with, "Gentlemen, if you'll give me a minute, I'll explain why you're right and I'm absolutely not the person to do this work for you." As soon as the words were out of my mouth, they were on me again. Only this time, they were arguing that I was the one they needed to do the work for them, and they were no less insistent than they had been before.

Perhaps they were enjoying a game of Pick on the Consultant, or maybe they just wanted someone to take their frustration out on. Whatever the cause, they were ready to counter anything I was going to come up with. Because I acted counterintuitively and cooperated rather than competed, I leveraged the relationship effect, and they ended up making my argument for me. It didn't hurt that their self-images demanded that everyone had to be seen as eager to work with them. It marked the beginning of a long and lucrative relationship.

THE THEORY OF MIND

Doing business seems much more complicated in the world according to brain science. In the world of logic and common sense, I can just do what I want with no more concern for relationships and mind-sets than a billiard ball has. But now science teaches me that my actions are constrained by the relationships I find myself in and that I have to account for how others think. Thankfully, though, my brain is naturally configured to work just the way neuroscience tells me it must.

There are a special kind of nerve cells in the brain called mirror neurons. They are one of the most recent discoveries of neuroscience, and they're generating a lot of excitement because they explain everything from our acquisition of language to how we learn new skills. They were first discovered in macaque monkeys when it was observed that the same premotor neurons fired whether a monkey performed an action or just observed others doing it. Mirror neurons have since been discovered in human beings, but there are subtle differences in our version of them.

In monkeys, the action must be goal-directed, but in human beings that's not necessary for the mirror neurons to fire. In humans, the prefrontal cortex is also involved, and it enables us to copy more complex actions and capture intention. Activity in our brains not only mirrors someone moving across the room, it mirrors how the person moves—dancing steps of the tango for instance—and it mirrors the intent—to teach the steps. We not only mimic the action in our minds, we mimic the mental state that leads to the action. It appears that there are mirror neurons for emotions as well. Because they are absent in children with autism, researchers believe that they are key to the development of social skills.

The discovery of mirror neurons provides a biological basis for what is known as the theory of mind. First identified in the late seventies, this is our ability to appreciate that other people have minds, just as we do. We are not only able to recognize that their intentions, desires, and goals may be quite different from ours, but to accurately predict what they are. The theory of mind appears to develop in children by age four, and it, too, is missing in people with autism. However, it is not flawless. We tend to apply it to our pets, other animals, and even to geometric shapes that appear to move intentionally.

We call what mirror neurons and the theory of mind enable us to do empathy. More than any other species, we have evolved the ability to step into others' shoes and see and feel the world from their perspective. It's easy to see how this would grease the skids of social interaction and enable us to more effectively negotiate the world we live in. It's also easy to see how, if we make use of this talent, we can be more successful in managing our business relationships.

We don't have to struggle to try to understand the perspective of others, because our brains automatically mimic the firing patterns of their brains. We don't have to worry about what story they're telling, because our brains are automatically producing the same story. We don't have to guess what action we need to take to get the response we desire, because our response will be theirs. All we have to do is just let the mind work naturally. However, there are a couple of hitches in the system.

It's been said that before you can step into another's shoes, you have to take your own off first. We have a tendency to get stuck in our own perspective and project it on other people. This inability to suppress our own perspective leads to errors in understanding others, and the errors seem to be greater the more different other people are from us. While there are lots of reasons for our failure to suppress our view, there is an easy fix.

Experiments have shown that we are capable of using our conscious minds to reappraise an emotion and change the way we feel. When subjects were shown a picture of a woman crying, they initially experienced negative emotions, but when they were told that she was crying tears of joy after her wedding, brain scans showed decreased activity in those regions of the brain responsible for emotion. This is the result of the prefrontal cortex releasing the neurotransmitter serotonin that dampens the activity of the amygdala.

This same kind of reassessment can enable us to suppress our perspective. If we believe that it's important, we can consciously shift our attention to focus on the perspective of another person. However, because ideas change the processing in our minds, learning about mirror neurons and the theory of mind will itself dispose our minds to unconsciously suppress our own perspective for that of another.

Reappraising a situation also requires seeing it as something other than it currently is, and it is our imaginations that enable us to do that. In the Aristotelian universe, what you see is what you get, and imagination is neither prized nor cultivated. But in the mental world, things become what we imagine them to be, and imagination is given free rein. When we accept the validity of the cognitive paradigm, it becomes easier to consciously shift our attention and make use of our imaginations.

THE CONSTELLATION OF RELATIONSHIPS

Although our brain has evolved so that we're well equipped to empathize, in order to benefit fully from our mirror neurons and innate theory of mind, we have to believe that it's important to manage our relationships. In the conventional view, there is one managerial relationship, and it is with employees. But if managers are going to be successful, they also need to proactively manage their relationships with customers, suppliers, peers, and their bosses. Asking questions can help us learn more about other people's views, and stories can help us to manage our relationship with them.

While a well-designed product or service, efficient operations, and skilled management are all nice to have, they are of no value without paying customers. But if you have customers, you can get everything else you need. Although it's just reasonable that you should do everything you can to satisfy them, there's a built-in conflict between customers and suppliers. Customers want as much as they can get for as little money as possible, while suppliers want to give as little as possible for as much money as they can get. Add the fact that customers often seem to be an intrusion into an organization and an interruption of the important work we do, and reasonable behavior goes out the window.

So we need to consciously put aside our perspective, adopt theirs, and then treat them the way we want to be treated as customers. It may seem simplistic, but the key to satisfying customers is to ask them what they want and then give it to them. At the same time, we need to guard against doing things that might increase our profit in the short term, but cost a customer in the long term. L.L. Bean is legendary for accepting any item for return, including a set of snow tires that weren't even bought at the store, and desk clerks at the Ritz-Carlton have the authority to significantly reduce bills for dissatisfied customers. But my cell phone carrier locked me into a contract I didn't need and then didn't stand behind the phone they sold me when it failed. Who don't I do business with anymore?

Just as Damasio's subjects used emotion rather than reason to make their decision on what decks of cards to choose from, so too do emotions drive our purchasing decisions. We don't necessarily buy a car because it's the most cost-effective and reliable transportation. We buy it because it satisfies our desire for status, because we like its styling, or because we enjoy the thrill of going fast. The same way ideas can lead to an emotional reappraisal, they can change our view of a product or service, and they are most powerful in the form of a narrative. Once we've empathized with our customer, we can fit our product or service into their narrative or create a new, more attractive one.

When we're dealing with customers, all of us have the ability to go beyond what is required or to deliver less than the customer needs. It might be advice, technical support, timeliness, or payment terms that are within our discretion, and we exercise it based at least somewhat on how we feel about the customer. Our suppliers are in the same position. Rather than take them for granted or repeatedly try to beat them down in price, it makes sense for us to build a relationship in which they use their discretion for our benefit.

Since I'm in the business of delivering a professional service, I have a lot of discretion over what my customers receive. I always strive to do the best I can, but I do have decisions to make. When it's two in the morning and I'm exhausted, do I put in that extra hour of work, or do I call it a night? Do I make that seven-hour plane trip for a two-hour meeting my client wants me at, or do I conveniently have a scheduling conflict? Does my client get me so turned on about their business that neurotransmitters are released that speed up my mental processing and enable me to do better work?

The most successful CEOs I've ever worked with have gone out of their way to build a satisfying relationship with me. I'm usually offered something to drink when I meet with them in their offices, and more often than not, they are the ones who go and get it. They ask me about how my business is going and seem generally concerned. While they are careful to manage the budget for my work, not one has ever tried to force me to reduce my price. Perhaps most important, they convey a narrative about what they're trying to do with their business that gets me as excited as they are.

In any customer-supplier relationship, there is always the potential for the kind of dynamics we saw in Prisoners' Dilemma, and one of my clients did a brilliant job of managing them. About two months after I called on him, he phoned me up and told me that he'd decided to give my firm all of the company's consulting work. I was pleasantly surprised, but I asked him how he could know that we'd do a good job since he hadn't checked any references. He answered that he was sure we would, and if any problems occurred, the two of us would work together to solve them. I then protested that he didn't even know how much we charged. His response was that he was certain I would be fair. Maybe my mirror neurons started firing, but I couldn't help but return his trust in kind. I worked to do the best job I could for him, and I charged him the lowest fee possible. We worked together for almost fifteen years.

When it comes to peers, things get a bit dicier. Sometimes they're our customers, while at other times they're our suppliers. Even when they're neither, a comment dropped to the boss can hurt us or help us, and in the future they may become our boss or our employee. Still, the approach is the same as in any relationship. We want to empathize and use questions to ensure the perspective we assume is accurate. We want to understand their story and convey our own in a way that enlists their support. But we can't ignore the potential for Prisoners' Dilemma dynamics.

One of my peers on a project team once kindly volunteered to put the finishing touches on a report of our findings and recommendations. But when he gave the presentation at a meeting with our sponsor, he ignored what the team had come up with and presented his view as if it were ours. When our sponsor raised some of the same concerns I had raised, the peer replied that he too had the same concerns but had been overruled by the team! Naively, I had trusted him not to confess.

Axelrod's research concluded that we should start out trusting, and it does set a cooperative tone that hopefully the mirror neurons will mimic. But we can't be so trusting that we're taken advantage of. I'm sure my peer was telling himself a story that provided a moral justification for his dishonesty. My mistake was not to have built in any insurance. I still start out trusting, but I've learned to always be on guard against the inevitable pull of our selfishness.

Perhaps the most counterintuitive relationship to think about managing is the one with the boss, because the conventional wisdom holds that managing the relationship is their job. In the early 1980s, John Gabarro and John Kotter wrote an article for the *Harvard Business Review* entitled "Managing Your Boss." In it, they recommended asking the boss a series of questions about their needs, goals, and preferred working style, so that the boss could be managed like a customer. It was simple and brilliant. Ask what bosses want and then give it to them. While many employees feared that the approach might seem a bit presumptuous, handing an article to the boss with the imprimatur of the *Harvard Business Review* on it beforehand made it acceptable. Besides, all managers would love an employee who wants to make them successful.

Proactively managing relationships just makes it easier to get the job done, and the tools we need to do it are hardwired into the brain. As in so much of management according to the discoveries of neuroscience, all it requires is that we consciously direct our attention. Yet we do live in a world where Machiavelli is still read and venerated by some. On occasion, it's helpful to have some less intuitive tools at hand.

THE ART OF PERSUASION

From Plato's *Dialogues* to Dale Carnegie's *How to Win Friends and Influence People,* we have a long history of people offering advice on how best to get our way. Often people object that such tactics are manipulative and believe that there is something immoral about their use. But we've got to remember that the brain making these moral judgments evolved to enable us to get others to do what we want them to. Since the brain is wired to help us in that endeavor, the judgment of what is moral or immoral should probably be restricted to the ends and not the means.

The psychologist Robert Cialdini took a scientific approach to the subject in his book *Influence: Science and Practice*, and he has come up with six different tactics. Whether or not we can bring ourselves to use them on others, it's important to be aware of them because others will undoubtedly use them on us. Some of them are so fundamental to how humans interact, odds are we've used them without even being aware of it.

This is certainly the case when it comes to *reciprocation*, because it's the glue that holds social groups together. When people do something for us, we feel obligated to do something for them in return. When we're the first to do the favor, we accrue social capital that we can then call on later. Cialdini uses the example of one subject in an experiment giving a soft drink to another and then later asking the person to buy raffle tickets. On average those that had received the gift of the soft drink first bought twice as many raffle tickets. If we do favors for people without being asked, we predispose them to respond to our requests for help later on.

We've seen that we strive to keep our version of reality consistent and will either suppress or rationalize any information not in keeping with it. We can use this psychological dynamic to our advantage by getting people to first agree to a position and then asking them to take an action that is in line with that position. Cialdini calls it *commitment and consistency*. There's an old sales technique that poses a series of questions that will certainly be answered in the affirmative and then follows up with a request to buy a given product. It goes something like this: "You love your family, don't you? You wouldn't ever want them to be unprotected, would you? If something happened to you, wouldn't you want them to be taken care of? You'll want to buy this life insurance policy, won't you?"

The reason this technique works is because of the hierarchical organization of ideas in the brain. As we've seen, those high-level ideas evoke thoughts and actions in harmony with them. To make use of this technique, we don't have to be as smarmy as the life insurance salesman. We can just establish agreement on a set of principles that will lead naturally to the action we desire someone else to take.

Because the brain is first and foremost social and because membership in our prehistoric groups was beneficial to our survival, we can use *social proof* to motivate desired behavior. We can think of it as peer pressure because it plays off our need to be accepted by others. The knowledge that those we want approval or acceptance from are doing something is a strong reason for us to do it as well. We can make use of this need by calling attention to how many people are engaged in a given behavior, or we can systematically build peer pressure by convincing people one by one until we've created a grass roots movement. Targeting high-status people, or thought leaders, first will work best.

Liking is perhaps the most intuitively obvious tactic, but also the one that seems most ignored in practice. When we like certain people, we are more willing to do what they want us to do. Because of this, it's worthwhile for us to spend the time to build friendly relationships before we need to call on someone for a favor. While the easy way to figure out how to build such friendships is just to consider what we like in a friend, there are some general principles. We like people who are like ourselves, so it's important to establish a commonality of interests. And we like people we spend time with. Then there's the one you learned as a child: if you want a friend, be a friend. We like people who like us, so we just need to like people, and they'll like us in return.

In more than two decades of giving management seminars, I have used the phrase, "the research shows," thousands of times, yet nobody has ever asked me what research. We have an incredible respect for *authority*. In a classic experiment, Stanley Milgram showed that when instructed by a researcher in a white lab coat, subjects were willing to administer life-threatening shocks to total strangers who gave the wrong answer to a question, even when they claimed to have a potentially fatal heart condition. But we have more respect for the authority that comes with expertise than the authority that comes with a position in a corporate hierarchy.

Cialdini's last technique, *scarcity*, might have its roots in the Darwinian struggle for survival in an environment of limited resources. Something about hearing that it's the last one available or that the offer is good for one day only drives us to action. This is the tactic that I have the most difficulty with. I see its use as primarily limited to customer relationships, and decisions made under its influence produce more than their share of buyer's remorse. As a favorite of car salesmen, it has a well-earned bad reputation.

Although these tactics do test as being effective, perhaps their use should be restricted to those times when we're trapped in a Prisoners' Dilemma dynamic or when we encounter disciples of Machiavelli. If we're really out to do the right thing not just for ourselves but for others, then we need only to embed a neural network of principle at a high level, and the right behavior will follow. We just make life more difficult for ourselves if we don't make use of our brain's innate ability to proactively build good working relationships before we have to call upon them.

PEOPLE

Deny it as we might, business is all about managing relationships. The objective paradigm leads us to believe that we can just pursue our goals without giving much thought to anything else. The cognitive paradigm, though, highlights counterintuitive relationship effects that can become self-defeating. In most of our relationships, there's another prisoner whose interests are both aligned with ours and yet in conflict.

The only thing for us to do is empathize with those we interact with, anticipate how they will act, and then select an approach that creates the response we want. At the same time, we have to keep in mind the other key relationship between the past, present, and future. Fortunately, our brains come equipped with the wiring to do so. Our mirror neurons, and the theory of mind they enable, allow us to quickly and effectively adopt the perspective of another.

First, though, we must suppress our own perspective, and that can require actively shifting our attention from ourselves to others. But again, the brain is wired to facilitate this. All we have to do is hold the thoughts in our minds that relationships are important and that we need to be proactive about managing them. Neuroscience's explanation of how our minds work is just the kind of hard data that convinces our logical minds to attend to relationships and put aside our own view in favor of that of others.

Rather than see ourselves living and working in a Newtonian world of billiard balls, we need to recognize the constellation of relationships that determine our success or failure in business. Our relationships with customers, suppliers, peers, and even our bosses should be managed proactively. To assist us in empathizing, we can make use of questions to gather information and garner commitment. Our innate ability to appreciate and tell stories gives us a deeper understanding of what motivates people and a means to predispose their minds to take the action we desire.

Our brains have evolved to facilitate social interaction, and we can trust them to give us the information we need to build good working relationships, but at times we may wish to avail ourselves of Cialdini's influence techniques. If nothing else, we need to be aware of them in a world where Machiavelli's *The Prince* is still selling robustly four centuries after it was written. But because they merely leverage the way the mind naturally works, we probably make use of most of them without even knowing it.

There is, of course, one relationship we haven't talked about— the one between the manager and the employees. While all relationships can be difficult because of the tension between cooperation and competition, the managerial relationship is complicated by power, which skews everything. What we might expect to work doesn't, while what does work is often counterintuitive. Once again, though, we're aided by the insights of brain science.

FOUR

MANAGING UPSIDE DOWN

"I watched, amazed, as she opened the refrigerator and various cupboards, found bottles and a glass, then poured herself a gin and tonic. She took the drink to the TV, turned the set on, flipped from one channel to another, then, as though in disgust, turned it off again. She selected a glossy magazine from the table and, still carrying her drink, settled in a comfortable chair. Occasionally, as she leafed through the magazine she identified something she saw, using the signs of ASL, the American sign language used by the deaf."

Why is enjoying a drink while viewing television or leafing through a magazine so amazing? Because Jane Goodall isn't watching a human being, but a chimpanzee named Lucy. Even after spending a lifetime studying chimps in the wild, the primatologist is still taken with how much they resemble us. When we see animals behaving like humans, it throws even our simplest acts into relief. It's like a metaphor, causing us to see in a new light what we've taken for granted. Because chimps are closely related to us and share over

98 percent of our genes, it's as if we're watching an earlier version of ourselves. It's particularly illuminating when it comes to relationships involving power.

Just like early human tribes of hunter-gatherers, chimpanzees live in bands of twenty to forty with a clear hierarchy and an alpha male at the top enjoying privileged access to food and mates. He becomes the alpha by being the strongest and maintains his position by cleverly creating the appearance of even greater strength through behavioral displays that cause him to look more ferocious than he is. He jumps up and down, shakes branches, and hurls rocks into the bush. The display throws the community into a chaos of pants and screaming.

The better his display, the greater the chance the alpha's intimidation will be successful and he won't have to resort to the risk of actual fighting to maintain his status. One alpha male, Mike, learned to kick four-gallon tin cans in front of him to make such a racket that no one would challenge him. Figan, an adolescent who would rise to alpha status himself one day, was seen practicing kicking cans in imitation of Mike.

No chimp in the band is untouched by the alpha's display of who's in charge, and each must determine how best to manage the relationship with him. Most of the lower-ranking males pay court. They approach cautiously, and when given the signal that it's safe, they kiss his thigh or lips, and then both engage in mutual grooming. Some may decide to challenge the alpha, in either overt or subtle ways. Just before his bid for alpha status, Mike nonchalantly turned his back on the reigning alpha during a display. Others just stay far away. But all "need highly developed social skills—particularly those males who are ambitious to attain high positions in the dominance hierarchy. Low-ranking chimpanzees must learn deception—to conceal their intentions or to do things in secret—if they are to get their way in the presence of their superiors."

It has become fashionable today to use the term alpha to describe the man or woman at the top of an organization, and it is questionable how far to take the parallel between humans and chimpanzees. Michael Gazzaniga notes that most male chimpanzee behavior is aimed at the goal of becoming the alpha male, and he believes that the same is true of humans. Anyone who has ever worked in a large organization has experienced the human version of displays, deception, withdrawal, and thigh kissing. The relationship with the alpha determines the quality of chimps' lives, and so they mobilize all of their social intelligence to compete, cooperate, or avoid. The same is true of humans and their managers.

The role of the manager in a large organization is fraught with problems, and when we see it as just a slightly more civilized version of alpha status, we can understand why. Whether we're a chimpanzee or a corporate employee, we don't like being controlled by others. Not many of us care for the boss, either, and most of the stories our culture tells about bosses are far from complimentary. There's Dagwood Bumstead's Mr. Dithers, there's Dilbert's pointy-haired boss, and there's Michael, the branch manager of Dunder Mifflin in *The Office*.

Even beyond the discomfort of submitting to the alpha, our standard management practices don't create warm feelings. The approach they entail is more suited to forms of life lacking the ability to think. Since they offend employees and become self-defeating, the most effective managers, according to neuroscience, are the ones who do the least in the traditional sense of management. But because those who are promoted to management are usually the high achievers in an organization, it's particularly difficult for them to back off. The solution is to turn the relationship upside down and redefine what it means to be the boss.

EXTENDING THE METAPHOR TOO FAR

Peter Drucker ranked Frederick Winslow Taylor's effect on the modern world with that of Sigmund Freud and Charles Darwin, yet Taylor is hardly a household name. Nor are the time and motion studies he pioneered quite on the order of psychoanalysis or the theory of evolution. It is Taylor, though, who is responsible for the way we manage.

Although he was the product of a wealthy Quaker family, Taylor chose a career as a machinist. He joined Bethlehem Steel, where he demonstrated a talent for improving the productivity of machinery used in making steel. His first major success came when he pioneered a process to produce superheated steel cutting tools that quadrupled the speed of lathes. But it was the common shovel that led to his fame and the transformation of management.

He was given the job of designing a more efficient shovel for men to load coal into blast furnaces, and he approached it like a scientist. He observed the men shoveling coal, measured how many pounds were in each shovelful, and calculated the total amount shoveled over the course of the day. He then experimented with different amounts of coal per shovelful, and found that twenty-one and a half pounds was just the right amount to keep the men working efficiently all day and moving the most coal. When he redesigned the shovel to hold that amount, the company was able to reduce the number of men shoveling coal from 500 to 140.

But Taylor realized that the design of the shovel was only one part of the productivity equation. The other part was how the men used the shovel. Applying the same approach he had used to improve the efficiency of machines to the people working on the machines, he broke the task down into its component parts, made careful measurements, and concluded that there was "one right way" to do the job. Those employing a fluid motion and putting both shoulders behind their thrust were clearly more efficient, so he taught all of the men to shovel that way, and there was another significant increase in productivity.

Managers had long been accustomed to reengineering their machines, but the human side of production had remained stubbornly resistant to any improvement attempts. This all changed when Taylor looked at the men as if they were machines. He called his approach Scientific Management, and managers found the application of scientific method to human work enormously attractive. Taylor quickly acquired an international reputation, and soon legions of his disciples could be found roaming through factories around the world with clipboards and stopwatches.

Taylor's approach wasn't limited to just industrial work. Every task in life could be performed more efficiently, he believed, even the domestic ones. The layout of the modern kitchen is the result of Scientific Management, and according to his wife, he also designed a better method for cooking eggs and baking pies. He is responsible for the idea that we should attend to the most efficient way of using our time and doing our work. From daily planners to our fear that we might be wasting our time, Taylor's influence is still felt far and wide.

He wasn't interested just in making more money for the owners of Bethlehem Steel. He envisioned himself as the savior of the workingman, and hoped that his Scientific Management would usher in a new age of cooperation between managers and employees. Rather than leaving them to fight over how big a slice each got, his idea was to increase the size of the pie. Just like Aristotle, he believed that men were reasonable beings and motivated by economic self-interest. It was only logical that if they were paid for the amount they produced in a given time period, they would eagerly embrace a more efficient way of working to improve their earnings.

However, those he was intent on saving didn't share this view. They had always had the freedom to do their jobs as they saw fit, and they took pride in their skill and independence. With Taylor's method, though, young men with college educations and stopwatches determined how the men would do their work. All that was important was that they precisely follow the process laid out for them. In the words of Samuel Gompers of the American Federation of Labor, Taylor reduced the working man to no more than a "cog in a machine."

Taylor's work redefined the role of the manager. He (it was nearly always he) became the brains of the organization, the one who determined how everything was to be done. But the more the manager did, the less the workers needed to do. Because he separated thinking from doing and decision making from the work, the jobs became so unattractive that close supervision was needed to ensure that, in Taylor's view, the inherently lazy man did not get away with "soldiering." When the manager assumed virtually all responsibility, the workingman didn't need to take any, as the role of each in the relationship complemented the other.

Twenty years after Taylor's rise to fame, another productivity experiment undercut his fundamental premise that reasonable men want to maximize their earnings. Researchers studying men wiring switching banks at Western Electric's Hawthorne Plant in Cicero, Illinois, found that production and earnings were consistently held to about two thirds of what was possible. When asked why they held back on their production, the men answered that they thought if they produced more, management would just lower the rate per piece.

When he extended the machine metaphor to workingmen, Taylor assumed that their minds were of no consequence. In fact, at one point he said, "I care not a whit for the thinking of the working man." Ironically, it was the men's thinking that caused Taylorism to fail. But his influence still permeates the way we work today. It is behind the way we design organizations, define jobs, measure performance, and incentivize. It's also behind the rising number of hours that we think we have to work and the nagging feeling that it's never enough. Carrying a BlackBerry and checking e-mail on Sunday are evidence that Drucker wasn't exaggerating Taylor's impact on the way we live.

THE FEEDBACK FALLACY

With its echoes of domination by the alpha and the damaging legacy of Taylorism, the relationship between a manager and an employee is challenging for both. The key to making it work, the conventional wisdom holds, is objective feedback on performance backed up by rewards and punishment. In effect, it's the only tool a manager has to shape behavior. In most corporations, regularly scheduled performance appraisals are conducted to provide such feedback and to ensure that the compensation of the employee is aligned with the objectives of the business.

But a landmark study at General Electric found that the company's performance appraisal system not only didn't work, it produced results that were virtually the opposite of what was intended. We readily accept that receiving information on how we're doing is the best way to improve our performance. It's built in to the way we raise our children, it's the purpose of the grading systems in schools, and it's behind the design of performance management systems in companies. But GE found that a manager's praise had no effect on performance one way or the other, while the areas that a manager criticized showed the least improvement.

Given how central feedback is to the role of the manager, one would expect that the publication of this study in the *Harvard*

Business Review would have revolutionized management. Yet forty years have gone by, and most managers are still giving feedback to their employees in the same old, ineffective way. It's as if the study never happened. When a manager's feedback fails, either it isn't noticed or the cause of the failure conveniently becomes an employee who is defective. Such is the way the mind works, and it's why our conventional management practices, logical as they appear to be, are doomed to fail.

This study also challenged the basic premise of behavioral science by showing that reward and punishment don't work the way we thought they did, but this wasn't the first time the behavioral science model was shown to be flawed. A decade earlier, the social psychologist Leon Festinger found in a simple experiment that reward produced the opposite effect of what was intended. The reason he discovered for this counterintuitive result explains not only why performance feedback fails, but why we don't notice the failure and why the conclusions of the GE study could go unheeded. At the same time, it gives us an incredibly effective management tool for the mental world we inhabit.

In the experiment, men were instructed to perform boring tasks for an hour. When they were finished, they were told that there were actually two groups involved in this experiment. The one they were in wasn't told anything before the experiment, but the other group had been briefed that the tasks would be enjoyable. The experimenter then asked the men to substitute for the person who usually did the briefing. The men were divided into two more groups: Those in one group would be paid a dollar for their participation and those in the other would receive twenty dollars. After they were done giving the briefing, the men were asked to rate how enjoyable the tasks really were.

The behaviorist model predicted that those receiving the larger reward would rate the tasks as more enjoyable, but the opposite turned out to be true. Those paid only a dollar rated the tasks as more enjoyable than those paid twenty dollars. Both groups of men were being asked to lie, to tell others that tasks they found boring were interesting. While twenty dollars was enough of a reward to justify the lie, apparently one dollar wasn't. The men who received the smaller reward experienced dissonance between their belief in their honesty and their willingness to lie about the tasks. Because this kind of internal contradiction is uncomfortable, they reduced the dissonance by convincing themselves that the tasks actually were enjoyable and that they weren't lying. Festinger called the effect *cognitive dissonance reduction.*

Given that we now know the mind creates our experience, it isn't surprising that the men would so easily change their view of the tasks. But at the time, this evidence of the power of the mind to change our reality was earth-shattering. It just didn't fit with either common sense or science. As the pioneering social psychologist Elliot Aronson put it, psychologists were forced to conclude that because "human beings think, they do not always behave in a mechanistic manner." But just as is the case today with research in neuroscience, this revolution in our understanding was largely ignored by those outside of the scientific community. It's too bad, because the theory of cognitive dissonance would have predicted the failure of GE's performance-appraisal system.

One way to understand how cognitive dissonance reduction works is to imagine how you feel when someone offers to give you feedback on your performance. The typical response is not, "Oh great, I'm going to have an opportunity to improve," along with a nice warm feeling. More often than not, the prospect of feedback is experienced with a sense of dread, particularly when it's coming from an alpha with a huge influence on one's career. If the feedback we receive conflicts with the self-image that we have spent a life-time honing, creating cognitive dissonance, it will be experienced as uncomfortable, and we will do what we can to eliminate the discomfort.

The most productive response would be for us to take the feedback to heart, change our self-image from infallible to fallible, and work at learning a new way of behaving that incorporates the feedback. But this kind of change is the most difficult because of our deep-seated need to maintain our self-image. It's much easier for us to keep our self-image intact by rationalizing away the feedback, and either attributing the cause of the performance failure to external factors out of our control or discounting the source of the feedback. When the source is our bosses or people we don't especially care for, this is an attractive option. We question their ability to evaluate us, or their motivation.

The theory of cognitive dissonance also explains the failure of praise to improve performance, but it, too, requires that we incorporate mind into our view of why humans behave the way they do. In a study on reward, children were divided into two groups and given math puzzles to solve. In the first group, the children were rewarded for solving the puzzles. In the second group (the control), there were no rewards. The rewarded children initially did tend to spend more time on the puzzles. However, when the rewards were discontinued, they spent less time than they had before and less than the unrewarded group. This can be explained by drawing a distinction between intrinsic and extrinsic motivation. Intrinsic motivation comes from within—it is tied to our need for achievement and fueled by the neurotransmitter dopamine released by an area of the brain known as the nucleus accumbens. Extrinsic motivation, working for a reward, comes from outside of us—it is the motivation for the bonus at work, the compliments of people we care about, the

treat we give our children for good behavior. The extrinsic motivation created by the rewards in the experiment led to a decrease of
intrinsic motivation.

Because the reward was held out as the reason for the children
to work on the puzzles, they saw it as the only reason. When the
rewards were discontinued, they felt that there was no longer any
reason to continue trying to solve the puzzles. The net result was
that the reward had exactly the opposite effect of what was intended
and of what we believe about rewards. Rather than motivating them
to work on the puzzles over time, the use of the reward demotivated
them. (This effect can be mitigated a bit by rewarding the performance rather than just the act of trying to solve the puzzles.) Since
people are motivated intrinsically, the extrinsic reward of praise during the performance reviews at GE didn't motivate higher performance. People were already doing the best they could.

Punishment has also been shown to have an effect opposite of
what we intend. In one experiment, two groups of children were
placed in a room with some attractive toys. Each group was told not
to play with the toys, but the first group received a mild threat of
the consequences of disobedience while the second received a severe
threat. Several weeks later the children were again placed in the
room with the toys. Those who had received the mild threat were
much less willing to play with the toys than those who received the
severe threat. In the absence of a truly compelling reason, the children had convinced themselves that it was their decision not to play
with the toys. Again, the strong extrinsic motivator decreased the
intrinsic motivation.

These experiments demonstrate that in order to understand the
effects of reward and punishment, including feedback that is experienced as either, we have to incorporate mind. It's not that we don't
desire reward and dread punishment. It's just that how we view

them is a result of everything else going on in our minds. Since extrinsic reward can make us feel that we have no other reason to do something, we might be better off rewarding behavior we want extinguished and then withdrawing the reward. Because punishment can make us more eager to do something, it makes sense to avoid using it.

MINDING BEHAVIOR

The effects of reward and punishment aren't as straightforward as we might've thought, and our need to reduce cognitive dissonance will determine how we respond to them. As Aronson put it, "Unlike rats and pigeons, human beings have a need to justify their past behavior, and this need leads them to thoughts and feelings, and behaviors that don't always fit into the neat categories of the behaviorist." In the physical world, reward and punishment are just what they are. In the mental world, they are what we think they are, adding a level of complexity to their use.

But it isn't only our reason that determines our response to rewards and punishment. Because the limbic system, which is responsible for our emotions, is much older and more deeply rooted in the brain than our newer prefrontal cortex, our feelings have a tendency to trump our reason. The sociologist George Homans believed it was our feelings that were responsible for reward and punishment producing the opposite of what was intended. While Frederick Taylor believed that a person's reaction to the prospect of a reward would be the result of a rational calculation, Homans recognized that it wasn't that simple.

He found that a reward is only effective if it's valued, but all too often, the one dispensing the reward gauges its value differ-

ently than the one receiving it. The boss may see a 5 percent salary increase as valuable, while the employee finds it so negligible
that it's an insult and creates feelings of anger. Rather than being a
motivating reward, it becomes a demotivating punishment. He also
found that the value of a reward is a function of its frequency. With
the very best of intentions, the boss may liberally reward people with
praise, but rewards wear out with use as we become accustomed to
them. The five hundredth time the boss praises the employee for a
good job will not have the same effect as the first time. In fact, the
employee very well may come to expect the praise and experience
feelings of disappointment if it isn't forthcoming.

As Homans put it, "When a person's action does not receive
the reward he expected, or receives punishment he did not expect,
he will be angry; he becomes more likely to perform aggressive
behavior, and the results of such behavior become more valuable to
him." When unexpectedly we aren't rewarded or are punished, the
amygdala kicks into gear, and we become aggressive toward the person responsible. Hurting that person is then experienced as rewarding to us.

The 5 percent salary increase the boss gives you when you're
expecting 10 may be perceived as punishment and prompt aggression. The constructive criticism that you unexpectedly receive when
you believe you are doing an acceptable job will also prompt aggression. It doesn't make any difference how the boss intended either,
because in the mental world, what you believe something to be is
what it is. Nor do you rationally calculate that 5 percent is better than
nothing or that feedback is important for self-development. Instead,
when you are being punished, it feels rewarding to punish in return.
Ironically, it makes it rewarding to persist in the criticized behavior.
This is what may have been responsible for the failure of criticism in
the GE study.

Even beyond the aggression that punishment stimulates, its use is a problem for other reasons. If the behavior your manager would like extinguished has brought a reward, the punishment to prevent that behavior must be strong enough to overcome the lure of the reward. If the motivation is to avoid punishment, you won't necessarily refrain from the proscribed action. Instead, you'll just try to avoid being punished. If, as a child, you are punished for stealing candy, you are not necessarily going to stop stealing. Instead, you're going to work to avoid getting caught.

If getting less of a reward than we expect makes us angry, getting more makes us pleased. As Homans explains it, "When a person's action receives a reward he expected, especially a greater reward than he expected, or does not receive punishment he expected, he will be pleased; he becomes more likely to perform approving behavior, and the results of such behavior become more valuable to him." The first part of this is straightforward: Unexpected rewards have unique value. It is the second part that is counterintuitive: Punishment not delivered also has unique value. So when a person expects punishment, it is much more effective to withhold the punishment.

When I was a student at an inner-city high school in Detroit, I would on occasion sneak out of the building to smoke a cigarette. One day a teacher saw me and asked what I was doing. With the kind of logic only a teenager can come up with, I explained that I had come outside to smoke a cigarette since smoking was not allowed in school. The teacher informed me that I risked punishment. As I prepared to receive it, he told me that the next time I wanted to leave school, I should come to him and get a pass so that I wouldn't be punished. I was stunned. This incident didn't stop me from leaving school, but it did dramatically change my attitude toward that teacher. Hardly a motivated student up to that point, I started paying more attention in his class and worked hard to master the material.

It was a significant turning point in my life, and it eventually led me to become an educator myself.

In general, reward works to reinforce behavior when it is clearly paired with the desired behavior, when it is used sparingly, when it is valued, and when it is greater than expected. However, extrinsic reward, as we have seen, tends to diminish intrinsic motivation. While punishment may extinguish undesired behavior, it runs the risk of stimulating aggression, it must be quite strong to deter one from rewarding behavior, and it stimulates behavior to avoid the punishment. It appears to work best when it is expected, but withheld.

We like rewards and we don't like punishment. When we reward people or when we punish them, it appears to work. What we don't see is what goes on in the minds and hearts of the people we reward or punish. It is not immediately observable when our rewards diminish intrinsic motivation or when our punishment creates aggression. Nor can we tell how the person feels about us or what action they will take subsequently. This makes a manager's use of reward and punishment, and feedback that may be perceived as either, rather risky.

MANAGEMENT THAT WORKS
FOR THE EMPLOYEE

In light of the theory of cognitive dissonance, it's not surprising that the conclusions of the General Electric study have been ignored for forty years, because the study called into question the very role of a manager. Rather than accept that the premise behind management is wrong and have to sacrifice the alpha status that goes along with the role, it's much easier to just ignore the study's conclusions. After all, what we observe tends to confirm that reward and punishment work.

Reward and punishment are not intrinsically bad. It's their source that causes problems. As the cognitive paradigm predicts, it's the effects of the managerial relationship itself that produce counterintuitive results. When reward and punishment are dispensed by managers, employees are put in a subordinate role. In *Punished by Rewards,* Alfie Kohn makes a convincing case that all reward systems—whether at work, school, or in the family—are resisted because they are perceived as manipulative. As we've seen, the more responsibility a manager holds, the less an employee has to accept. When Taylor made managers the prime movers and gave them reward and punishment as their only tools, he pretty much ensured they would fail.

Given the overwhelming evidence that the managerial relationship as it's usually configured is self-defeating, managers should stop doing most of what they're doing today. Consider the following half dozen managerial practices:

1. Reward good performance as often as possible.
2. Punish poor performance.
3. Give timely feedback on performance problems.
4. Prescribe corrective action for performance problems.
5. Set measurable objectives.
6. Make an effort to closely supervise employees.

Each of these strike us as logically the right thing for managers to do, but they all fail in practice. We've already seen why reward, punishment, and feedback don't produce the results we intend or produce the opposite. But the same is the case for any action that puts the manager in a dominant role. When the manager prescribes corrective action, the employee does not have to take responsibility and has no motivation to make it work. The same is true of setting objectives. Plus, if employees don't meet the objectives the manager has set, they can claim they were too aggressive. People don't want to be closely supervised, and when they are, the managerial relationship quickly turns into a game of cat and mouse.

Since abstaining from these practices would seem like an abdication of responsibility, what should a manager do? Turn the tables and put as much responsibility on the employee as possible. Employees should set their own objectives, critique their own performance, and if there is a performance shortfall, determine what corrective action needs to be taken. When they are the ones responsible for their performance, the psychological dynamic of the relationship works for the manager, because the employee's self-esteem is positively correlated with their performance and the success of any corrective action.

The traditional role of a manager is Aristotelian, but it needs to become Socratic. Rather than tell employees what to do and create all of the negative relationship dynamics, the manager needs to ask. Rather than hand objectives to the employee, the manager should ask the employee to set them. Rather than give employees feedback on their performance, the manager should ask them how they think they're doing. Rather than tell the employees how to fix a problem, the manager should ask them what they think they should do to fix it. This is, of course, counterintuitive, for it turns the relationship upside down. As the prime mover of the organization, the employee now calls the shots and the manager is in a support role.

For the manager, this isn't an abdication of responsibility. In fact, it's a considerably more difficult way to manage. It's quick and easy to give an employee direct feedback, and there is a kind of pleasure to be derived from smacking a performance problem with some critical feedback. It takes more time and is more difficult to come up with a questioning strategy so that the employee self-critiques. For this kind of management to work, the manager must have patience and spend a good deal of time giving the employees the information required for them to self-manage.

Employees need to understand the dynamics of their industry and how their company is positioning itself. They need to be clear on the strategy and what kind of thinking and behaving is required to implement it. They should know specifically how what they do contributes to success or failure. But they also need real-time information about how the business is doing, and feedback on the success or failure of their efforts. It just can't come from the manager.

Instead, managers will need to install systems to provide employees with an objective source of feedback. This can be part of a goal-setting process in which performance against the metrics of the business is checked periodically, and it can include customer survey data and 360 degree feedback. Information on the overall performance of the business and any changes that might affect the employees can be provided by online systems that track the business, but some managers also make use of a periodic memo or newsletter.

Any reward or punishment employees earn should similarly be self-administered or dispensed by an objective system. As much as possible, the reward should approximate profit. There are many different ways to do this, but all link compensation to a set of objective measures tied to the performance of the business. Depending on the role, it may be production, sales, or customer satisfaction that is measured, or a combination to ensure the balance of activities needed for both short- and long-term success. Some businesses even use peer appraisals when there is no easy way to measure the quantity or quality of results. The measures can be individual, group, or both. So that there are no Prisoners' Dilemma dynamics, it shouldn't be the manager who evaluates the performance.

Regardless of how good the systems are, there will still be a need for human contact. Objective data is not a substitute either for the emotional connection that makes employees feel more committed to a business or for real-time, unplanned communication. Regularly scheduled one-on-one meetings will facilitate this kind of contact, but care should be taken that they don't appear as close supervision. An interesting alternative is scheduled office hours when employees are free to drop by if they want. Team meetings are a good way to build mutually supportive relationships and to ensure focus and alignment. Managers just need to be careful that they don't become an occasion for alpha displays.

This kind of participative management is not coddling or soft. It's just the opposite. When managers are setting objectives, giving feedback, prescribing corrective action, and dispensing punishment, it's harder for tough decisions to be made and acted upon. Few managers are eager to address performance problems head on. No one wants to cause distress to another person, and good managers will always question whether the objectives they set were achievable and the feedback they provided was fair. As a result, poor performance goes unchecked for far too long.

But when employees are setting the objectives and providing the feedback, the manager's self-doubt and emotion are removed from the equation. If the employees set the objectives and didn't achieve them, they should be held rigorously accountable. There is no reason why they should be sheltered from the competitive pressures the business is under. If corrective action doesn't work, their fate should be the same as that of a company which fails in the marketplace. Under this approach, tough performance management becomes much easier.

The new role of the manager, in the world according to neuroscience, is virtually the opposite of the old one. She doesn't order;

she asks. He doesn't set objectives; he provides the information to enable the employees to set their own objectives. She doesn't give feedback; she solicits self-feedback. He doesn't dispense rewards; he puts in place systems that self-administer. Employees don't work for her; she works for the employees.

It's like a tennis game: Whenever the employee tries to put the responsibility on the manager, the manager just sends it back over the net. But it takes self-awareness and discipline to pull this approach off. The manager has to guard against going for the expediency of telling rather than asking, and against the temptation of a periodic alpha display. The manager also has to understand the employee's version of reality to know how best to package communication and how to deal positively with any performance problems that can't be batted back. Finally, the manager must accept a relationship devoid of most of the perks that used to make the job so attractive.

REVERSING TAYLOR'S LEGACY

Taylorism is built into the design of most organizations that have been around for any length of time. It's in the structure, the control systems, and the job descriptions. But as we've seen, it's also in the managers thinking that they need to be in control: setting objectives, giving feedback, dispensing rewards and punishments. The first step for any manager who wants to improve performance is to recognize how the traditional role leads to suboptimization and self-defeat.

In newer organizations, particularly those in high technology, there is no legacy of structure, systems, and processes, so they have the luxury of "hardwiring" a different approach to management into their organizations. They can set up self-managed teams that use peer appraisals, install systems that help employees get feedback from the organization, and establish career managers to serve as advocates on compensation and promotional issues. Many believe such approaches are necessary to attract and retain younger, highly educated professionals. But the ultimate justification for them is that they lead to greater commitment, higher motivation, and better performance.

Perhaps what this new approach requires from management is clearest in traditional companies that have made the transition to a more employee-centric style, and there's no better example than Frederick Taylor's old employer, Bethlehem Steel. For the better part of the twentieth century, the company was one of the most successful in the United States. By the 1950s the company made so much money that eight of the ten highest paid executives in the world worked there, and it was said that if one blast furnace was needed, they would build two.

The line between the workers and the managers was clearly drawn by the company and reinforced by the union. Each mill had a country club built alongside it exclusively for management, and an office building well removed from the grit of the steel-making process. At the Sparrows Point Works in Maryland, there was a company town with streets designated by letters of the alphabet, and employees had to live on the street that corresponded to their rank in the hierarchy. In Bethlehem, Pennsylvania, workers lived on one side of the city and management on the other. There were different dining rooms in the headquarters building for different levels of the hierarchy, and they were furnished accordingly. It was even said that the high-level executives had shower priority at the country clubs.

But by the early eighties, foreign competition, substitute materials, and the mini-mills had transformed the industry, and the

integrated steel makers were no longer profitable. One by one, Bethlehem's country clubs were sold off and the mills shut down. Still,
Taylorism reigned supreme. The general manager of one of the divisions was pulled out of a training session on participative management by the president, who wanted to know why he was wasting
company time and money on such things. At another division, a
study team recommending cost-saving measures was told by the
general manager that they had to earn the right to implement their
ideas by first cutting costs.

The inefficiency of the company's approach to management was
highlighted by a comparison with one of the mini-mills. With about
the same revenues, Nucor employed seventeen people at its headquarters, while Bethlehem had over seven hundred. Nucor made
steel at a cost of little more than one man hour per ton compared
to Bethlehem's twelve. With the business dying and nothing left to
lose, many in the company were willing to turn the traditional managerial relationship upside down.

At the Structural Products Division, a team of supervisors was
given a free hand to redesign the business with my help. After a
good deal of work, which included extensive research, site visits to
cutting-edge companies, and in-depth planning sessions, their new
organization was unveiled. They went from over four hundred professionals and managers to eighty professionals arranged in self-managed
teams. Every phase of production was to be run by a dedicated team,
and all decisions were to be made with the participation of those who
would be affected, including the union. Even performance appraisals were to be done by the teams. Effectively, all supervision was done
away with, and people were trusted to do the right thing.

The general manager and his executive staff redefined their
roles to support the employees. They moved from the six-story headquarters building with closed offices, sitting outside the plant, to a

one story metal building with an open bullpen in the center of the mill. For the first time in the history of the company, an all-hands meeting was held for both the union and management to discuss the changes, and information that used to be held close to the vest was shared widely, including financial results.

In the first year of operation after the changes, $85 million had been cut from expenses on revenues of $800 million. The second year's results matched the first, and the case was made for the division's new approach to management. It wasn't just that it was good for the people or that it was in line with the latest discoveries of neuroscience. It saved money, over $170 million in two years. Unfortunately, though, it wasn't enough. The business was still losing over $30 million a year, and the company could no longer afford the luxury of keeping the mill open, even though it had been the flagship plant. The decision was made to shut it down.

When I heard the news, I drove to Bethlehem to meet with the team I had worked with on the redesign of the division. At lunch with a supervisor who had been one of the most skeptical members of the team at the beginning of our work, I wondered aloud if there was anything we could've done differently. He told me that we had done the best we could, and that we'd succeeded in convincing other divisions of the company to adopt our approach. It just wasn't enough to overcome the drastic changes roiling the markets for structural steel. Then he added, "I've been here thirty-five years, but the last two have been the best of my career."

FROM CONTROL TO SUPPORT

Hierarchies and battles for control mark all primate communities, from chimpanzee bands in the wilds of the Gombe National Park

Primate Reserve to corporate organizations in glass and steel high rises. In the modern age, such relationships became even more difficult when the machine metaphor was extended to managerial relations. Add in behavioral science, with its disregard of mind, and the role of the manager became challenging at best and self-defeating at worst.

The only solution is for managers to stop thinking they can control behavior, whether through feedback or reward and punishment. Instead, they need to recognize that the process of natural selection holds inside a corporation as much as it does outside in the marketplace. People will behave the way they want, regardless of how rational we judge them to be. The best we can do as managers is to create an environment that selects for the behavior we desire.

As long as we remain in control, the relationship dynamic will work against us, driving our people either to passivity or outright aggression. This means the managerial relationship needs to be turned upside down, and for the manager it is going to feel like an abdication of responsibility. But it's not important what the manager feels, only what works. Rather than tell, we need to ask, when it comes to setting objectives, providing feedback, or deciding on corrective action. When the employee is the one responsible, the relationship dynamic is leveraged.

The role of the manager is now to provide the support and information the employee needs to self-manage. This can be built into the organization through design, like Bethlehem's self-managed teams. As Taylor's old employer demonstrated, when managers are eliminated, people step up and accept responsibility. Ultimately, though, it comes down to the willingness of the individual manager to consciously resist being in control. This creates an organization that is a better place to work and makes a lot more money.

FIVE

ORGANIZING LEVERAGE

Slime mold can teach us a lot about how to work together, per-haps because without brains they're incapable of Aristotelian logic. The species Acrasiales lives among the rotting leaves on the forest floor as individual organisms, ingesting bacteria they sur-round with their flesh. They're very prolific and reproduce every two or three hours, so the geometric growth in their population quickly exhausts the food supply in a given area. Then something quite unique happens.

One of the organisms, known as a founder, begins emitting a gas that attracts the others. They migrate toward it and form clumps, and then the clumps begin to move toward other clumps. Soon, the slime mold appears as streams of living matter, all moving in the same direction. The different streams ooze toward a central point, and a mound forms that grows upward into a stalk. When all the streams are incorporated, the stalk falls onto its side and becomes a slug about two millimeters in length. In this form, the Acrasiales make their way across the forest floor in search of an area where food is more plentiful. As the slug moves along, other individual organisms join up and become part of it.

When the slug reaches an area with more food, its migration stops and it again rises up in the shape of a stalk. The stalk grows taller and taller until a roundish ball of spores forms at the top. Once the stalk reaches a sufficient height, the spores are dispersed. As each lands on the forest floor, it opens and releases a new organism. And then the whole process begins again. The slime mold exist as individual organisms feeding on bacteria until the food supply is exhausted and they join together to search for more.

There are actually people who study such things; they're called animal sociologists, and they see slime mold as a metaphor for the ideal human organization. Each individual creature enjoys its independence until communal effort is needed to ensure an adequate food supply. The creatures then coalesce around leaders, forming small groups that merge into larger ones. Whether at the head of the slug or the rear, whether forming the base of the stalk or the spore mass at the tip, each one fulfills its role as an integral part of the whole. Each acts selflessly to ensure the release of new organisms from the spore mass.

The individual organisms don't chafe at their role as part of the slug. They don't envy those that form the head of the spore mass. The followers don't resent their leaders, nor do the leaders flaunt their power. Clumps don't compete with one another, sabotage the efforts of other clumps, or try to go their own way. All of their organized behavior happens without job descriptions, performance objectives, or incentive plans. Yet each tiny little creature plays its part perfectly. Although unfortunately named and oozing a trail of slime, they have it all over us when it comes to organized effort.

We battle for alpha status and don't care to be subordinate to anyone. We rate our success relative to others and envy those who we believe have a more privileged position. If there's more than one group, odds are there will be competition between them rather than collaboration. Truly selfless behavior is the exception. The organizations we create to run our businesses aren't very effective at fostering teamwork, nor do they tend to be warm and friendly places to work.

The enviable teamwork of slime mold is hardwired into its genes. A good percentage of our behavior is hardwired as well, but by what Richard Dawkins has called the selfish gene. We are in a competition for survival, and the winners get to pass on their genes. Although our sophisticated mental apparatus may appreciate the virtues of collaboration, it is no match for the instinct of self-preservation. We look out for number one. As one middle manager at a telecomm company put it, "if it comes down to a question of making my team successful or being able to send my son to college, it's a no-brainer."

Even when we buy into goals that require cooperative effort, it's just not in us to selflessly play the role of the stalk and support the spore mass. Nor are we eager to join a clump, and if we do, we don't want our clump to join together with others. Having evolved from hunter-gatherer bands, our orientation is still to the smaller, more immediate group. In his classic "Robbers Cave" experiment, Muzafer Sherif demonstrated how averse human beings are to being part of a larger group. Twenty-two boys were divided into two homogeneous groups, and separately transported to a camp at a state park in Oklahoma. Initially, the two groups were kept apart, but as soon as they learned of one another, each group wanted to run the other off. "These kids were not just playing at war. In a very short time, they had gone from name-calling to sticks and stones."

Our business organizations allow us to achieve goals not possible through individual effort, but attempts to get us to work together always butt up against the imperative of our genes. The challenge for all managers is to overcome first our selfishness and then our inclination to identify with the smaller, more immediate group. The conventional wisdom on how to accomplish this, just as in the case of management, is a product of our Aristotelian logic. As a result, virtually everything we do creates more problems than it solves.

Neuroscience offers us a better way to organize, but once again its insights will strike us as counterintuitive. Given our unconscious reduction of cognitive dissonance, our resistance to being controlled, and the hierarchical organization of neural networks, we'll get better results organizing to leverage people's natural inclination rather than attempting to thwart it. The hierarchy and functional specialization believed to be necessary in large organizations are eliminated, and in their place, a more natural process, not unlike how slime mold function, drives the focus and alignment required for organized effort. There's also a way to organize for group effort that dispenses with formal structure altogether. It leverages what we have that slime mold doesn't—a brain.

THE LOGIC OF ORGANIZATION

Most likely, the first attempt to achieve the benefits of large-scale collective action was in the military. A larger army confers an advantage, but only if it's an organized force and not a chaotic mob. As a practical matter, it isn't possible for a general to direct the activities of thousands of troops. There are just too many people following the conflicting imperatives of their selfish genes. At best, maybe he can effectively provide direction to ten people, and they in turn each can provide direction to ten more people for a total of a hundred. Each of these could then provide direction to ten more for a total of a thousand, and so on and so on. By creating a *hierarchy* of levels with a manageable *span of control,* a general could establish a *chain of command* to direct the activities of an army with as many soldiers as there are individual organisms in the Acrasiales slug.

This approach comes with its own set of problems. Whenever something is communicated through more than one person, it is subject to distortion, as we've all seen in the party game in which a message is whispered from person to person until it bears no resemblance to what it was originally. The further down the hierarchy the message travels, the greater the distortion. So to be effective, military organizations issue very precise orders with the stringent requirement that they be implemented exactly as directed. This requirement is backed up with the threat of Newtonian force, and not much independent thought or freedom of action is allowed. Well aware that their lives are at stake, most soldiers willingly accept the terms of their employment.

For most of history, armies were the only large organizations facing competition and requiring focused activity and tight management. By comparison, business enterprises remained quite small, at most made up of a handful of skilled craftsmen. But the industrial revolution changed all that when it brought about the *specialization of labor.* As Adam Smith described it in *The Wealth of Nations,* there are advantages to dividing the job of making pins into a series of discrete tasks assigned to different people. When someone performs the same job over and over, Smith explained, he learns from his experience to do it more efficiently, and productivity goes up exponentially. But when a job is broken down into its component parts, there is an even greater need for coordination, and the *functional organization* we're familiar with today evolved to provide it.

Even so, business organizations remained small enough to be easily managed until the middle of the nineteenth century. The average one employed no more than five hundred people and was usually located in a single mill building, or even on just one floor. In an organization of this size, it's possible for the manager to be close enough to the business to have relationships with all of his employees and to personally direct their work. When a business grew larger, though, the manager encountered the same problems as the general of an army.

This was precisely what happened with the railroads. There had never been anything like them before, and they put enormous demands on management. Given the need for a huge investment in rails and running stock, railroads had to be large to be economically viable, and by their very nature, their operations were geographically dispersed. Hands-on management wasn't possible, but tight control was even more of a necessity to ensure that a train running in one direction did not crash into a train traveling in the opposite direction. Passengers also expected a standard fee schedule and reasonably uniform treatment at any of the stations they might stop at.

The railroads quickly grew into huge business enterprises. By 1890, the Pennsylvania Railroad employed over one hundred thousand people, and all of its various activities had to be carefully synchronized. The only organizational models of sufficient scale to meet this challenge were from the military, and it was a young man named Harrington Emerson who brought them to the railroads. As a seventeen-year-old, he was present at the decisive defeat of the French by the famous Prussian general, Helmuth von Moltke. The general knew that while a large group of soldiers was an advantage in battle, it could be a disadvantage when it came to moving them into place or housing and feeding them. His solution was to organize them into smaller corps that could be combined into larger ones, and to make extensive use of staff to plan, refine, and standardize the operations of the army.

When Emerson later earned a degree in mechanical engineering and went to work for the railroads, he applied what he had learned from von Moltke. As a result of his work, all three features of the modern business organization were in place: hierarchy, a functional organization, and the use of staff to refine and standardize operations. In later years, Emerson became a colleague of Frederick Taylor's.

The railroads transformed local and regional markets into national ones, fueling the growth of the large companies we're familiar with today to serve them, such as Swift, Ford, AT&T, and U.S. Steel. They also became the organizational model for all others to copy, and their structure, systems, and practices were imported wholesale. But just like a metaphor extended too far, the military model, with its tight control backed up with Newtonian force, didn't necessarily fit businesses outside of the railroad industry. Relationship effects were inevitable when staff work replaced the thinking of the workers, and close supervision was required for employees who were seen as becoming increasingly lazy and passive.

The focus of this kind of organizational structure, with its carefully defined areas of responsibility and lines of authority, is on control, not on how work is done. As a result, legions of staff people and middle managers are required to ensure that organizational handoffs take place efficiently and nothing gets lost in translation. Still, given the tendency for different functions to take on an identity of their own and become fiefdoms, cooperation breaks down, and work moves haltingly through the organization.

The marketing function creates specifications for a product and passes them off to engineering. Engineering finds it can't design a product that meets all of the specifications, so it compromises on what it hands off to manufacturing. Manufacturing receives a design for a product too difficult to build, so it also makes changes. When the product is finally produced, marketing finds that it no longer meets the needs of the customer. Conflicts between the different functions must be shuttled up to the top of the hierarchy to be resolved, slowing down the process of getting a product to market and moving decision-making away from those who understand the issues best.

Making matters worse is that staff organizations find themselves in conflict with the line. Finance sees spending out of control while the line functions find themselves hamstrung by unrealistic budgets and controls. Human Resources is appalled at how people are treated, but the line sees HR programs as a needless intrusion. Precious time and resources are invested in creating strategic plans that the functional managers put on a shelf and ignore. Potentially even more serious is that the line abdicates responsibility for the issues that are handled by staff.

While hierarchy, a functional structure, and the use of staff were all intended to solve problems resulting from the organization of large groups of people, they ended up creating even more. Neuroscience would argue that the cure is worse than the disease, but that neither is really necessary. The more structure we put in place, the more we go against the grain of human nature. Rather than attempt to counter our natural inclination, we should accept and leverage it. While the theory of evolution establishes our inherent selfishness, it also highlights our tendency to cooperate under certain circumstances, and this tendency can be used to our advantage.

IT'S OUR NATURE

We're selfish, but not all the time. Under the right conditions, we want to be part of a group, as Solomon Asch demonstrated in his experiment on the human need to be accepted by others. He brought a subject into a group that was discussing whether line A or line B was longer. After listening for a few minutes, the subject was asked to give an opinion. In the initial trials, the group chose the line that was clearly and objectively longer, and the subject agreed with them. But then the group members, who were actually confederates of the experimenters, chose line B when line A was clearly longer. The great majority of the time, the subject agreed with the group on their choice. Moreover, the subject came to really believe that B was longer, as the conscious mind's need for group acceptance overcame the judgment of his or her senses.

Apparently, the desire to be part of a group has an evolutionary basis, just like our selfishness. Since our genes are only replicated through our offspring, the advantage of caring for them is clear. Those of us with children know viscerally how this works. We willingly put aside our interests for theirs. A good night's sleep, time for our own activities, and dinners at our favorite restaurants are displaced by nighttime feedings, interminable trips to the playspace, and happy meals. We don't need to learn how to be parents; we're hardwired to respond to our child's every little whim.

The evolutionary biologist William D. Hamilton argued that our *kin selection,* with its selfless behavior toward our children, gave rise to other altruistic behavior. When we lived in bands of hunter-gatherers, we would most likely have had some degree of relatedness to the other members of the band. Because we shared genes with them, we would be driven by our instincts to take actions for the good of the group. Once the value of cooperation with our close relatives was demonstrated, it would be extended to unrelated members of the band.

Cooperative hunting in bands would have produced a better result for our prehistoric ancestors than hunting individually. Sharing food among the members of the band would lead to the survival of a greater number than if one person hoarded a surplus while others starved. If all individuals called out a warning to the group

whenever a predator was near, rather than simply fleeing and looking out for themselves, fewer would become prey. When we recognized the survival value of this *reciprocal altruism,* other social
feelings and behaviors would also have been selected.

If we recreate the kind of group environment that gave rise to
it, we can leverage our reciprocal altruism to encourage the cooperation we need in organizations. According to George Homans, the
scientist who factored emotion into the use of reward and punishment, it doesn't take very much to do that. Homans studied all kinds
of groups, from the workers who wired the switching banks at Western Electric to street gangs, and he found that the group dynamics in each were very similar. When he tracked the interaction of
couples living in married student housing at MIT after the Second
World War, he found that the main criterion for developing supportive relationships was proximity. Those who lived closest to one
another and had the most interaction became friends.

This explains why functional specialists tend to coalesce into
tight groups. With similar backgrounds and professional interests,
they have enough in common to form friendships. Their day-to-day
interaction, facilitated by their proximity, then causes them to identify with one another and form into a group. The Robbers Cave
experiment showed us how quickly this can happen and to what
lengths members can take their group identity. It also highlighted
how to make smaller groups coalesce into larger ones. The coun-
selors were able to get the campers to overcome their antipathy for
one another by inventing an imaginary threat from a third group. In
business, competitors are a ready-made common enemy.

The work of Asch, Sherif, and Hamilton shows us how to build
focused, cooperative groups. Given the natural inclination to identify
with a group and the need to be accepted, all managers have to do
is create the environmental conditions where frequent interaction

will lead to group identity. This will require physical proximity, a common threat such as competition, and a work group that doesn't exceed the size of a prehistoric band. When these conditions are met, cooperative behavior will naturally occur.

THE FREE-MARKET ORGANIZATION

Because our view of how to get people to cooperate is based on what's worked in the past, and because most of the time we're dealing with organizations that are already in existence, we keep thinking about how to solve problems that earlier solutions have created. Instead of worrying about how to get beyond hierarchy, a lack of cross-functional cooperation, and conflicts between line and staff, a better approach is to think about the best way of running a business with human beings who don't like being controlled and identify best with small groups.

That's exactly what the redesign team at Bethlehem Steel did. After a century of running their business with an organization modeled after the railroads they used to make track for, they decided to redesign it from the ground up. They wanted an organization that would support the implementation of their new strategy while facilitating the self-managed teams they were instituting.

Integrated steel mills like Bethlehem's were rendered obsolete by a simpler and cheaper technology. Rather than spend a billion dollars in capital for a facility to make steel from coke and iron ore, a mini-mill could melt scrap in an electric furnace that cost only about $150 million. This put Bethlehem at a huge cost disadvantage if steel was just a commodity to be purchased at the cheapest price. But the group of supervisors knew that their product wasn't just a commodity for all of their customers.

While some customers were only interested in the lowest price, others wanted the technical expertise Bethlehem had amassed during their century in business, and still others wanted custom payment terms, special shipping, and warehousing. The company's monolithic functional organization couldn't discriminate between these different customers nor deliver what they wanted. So three teams were put together to address the needs of these different customer groups. Each team was staffed with the people from all of the functions needed to make and deliver steel. It wasn't important who was in charge, for they were going to take their direction from the customer anyway. But in order for the groups to be manageable, they had to stay small.

Perhaps because they started with the needs of the business rather than the organization as it already existed, they created what organizational theorists would see today as a cutting-edge structure. Since it was focused on the customer, it was *market-oriented*. Because it facilitated the flow of work, it was *process-based*. With no one hung up on who was in charge and all decisions reached through consensus, it was a *self-managed team*. The steelworkers didn't know about organizational design, only about how to make and sell steel, so they didn't use any of these terms. They simply thought of their organization as the best and cheapest way to serve their customers.

There was just one problem. There was only one mill, and because it represented a huge capital investment, there was no way this asset could be duplicated for each market group. To produce an adequate return on investment, it needed to operate at full capacity, and long runs of commodity products were the best way to do that. This put its objectives in conflict with the two market groups that needed shorter runs of customized products.

For a time, the problem of the mill threatened to become a huge bottleneck that would sink the new organization, but then the group arrived at a solution that just seemed obvious. The mill should be looked at the same way customers viewed the company. It should operate as a separate business and structure its relationships with the market groups like those between a supplier and its customers. Each group would buy the services they needed from the mill and pay what was required. Short runs of customized products would cost more than long runs of commodity products, but that was acceptable because they would sell for more.

This structure did require a few more functional specialists so that one could be assigned to each group. But it eliminated all of the people needed to manage the hierarchy and the relationships between the functions. The net savings, as we've seen, were huge. By focusing on the market environment, by ensuring that key relationships were intragroup rather than intergroup, and by using market dynamics to manage those who couldn't be brought inside the groups, Bethlehem was able to eliminate hundreds of millions of dollars of inefficiencies and better serve its customers.

THE ENTREPRENEURIAL ORGANIZATION

Despite its innovations, Bethlehem's organization was relatively traditional. While it did leverage the natural inclination to be part of a group and minimized issues of control through self-managed teams, it still relied on salary tied to the achievement of objectives to motivate the right behavior, and we've seen the problems that can create. The supervisors were limited in what they could do because the Structural Products Division was part of a larger company. But their solution to the problem of the mill suggested that free-market dynamics could be used to manage all of the relationships in the business, not just those with the mill.

Such an organization, rather than having the invariable structure of a machine, would be a dynamic process more like natural selection. Focused on meeting the demands of the market environment better than the competition, it would be as purposeful as any organism in nature, with the selfish goal of maximum profit. Roles and relationships would evolve over time to meet any changes in the competitive environment. It would be made up of independent, entrepreneurial businesses, with customer-supplier relationships managed by market dynamics. The inside of the company would operate the same way as the external market.

Why shouldn't the relationships between "customers" and "suppliers" within a company be managed by a free market? The inherent conflicts between different functions, departments, and even individuals would then be resolved on the basis of money, just as in the example of the mill at Bethlehem Steel. We have a much kinder view of the gearheads in engineering, the slick willies in marketing, and the bean counters in finance, when they're our customers and paying us. We're also much more willing to put ourselves out when, rather than being compensated with a fixed salary, there's the prospect of being rewarded with profit.

In such an organization, all of us would run our own business, offering services at rates competitive in the market. If we did a good job and satisfied our customers, we'd flourish. If we didn't, our enterprise would go out of business. In areas where this wouldn't work because of the nature of the work or because the measurement systems would be too complicated, like production teams with highly interdependent jobs, we could create partnerships or small businesses. It wouldn't be necessary to implement the approach fully. Approximating the ideal would still bring benefits.

Free markets are highly efficient. Attempts to control them by imposing top-down structure create inefficiencies, as the decline of the Soviet Union and its planned economy illustrated. In the United States, the overregulation of airlines and telecommunications led to bloated costs and a lack of innovation. In both industries, deregulation brought both lower prices to the consumer and a host of new offerings. The Sarbanes-Oxley legislation passed in the wake of the Enron and Worldcom debacles has produced the unintended consequences of burdening companies with excessive costs for compliance, discouraging qualified people from joining boards of directors, and prompting an exodus of talent from public companies to private ones.

While the meltdown of the global financial system has its roots in a lack of regulation, no one is recommending doing away with the free markets that are the core of our economic system. If anything, the excesses in the subprime mortgage market are further evidence of how people will naturally pursue their self-interest and will be constantly on the lookout for loopholes in existing regulations. But while some degree of control will be necessary, we'll want to keep it to a minimum to avoid producing unintended consequences. The more we're able to align the pursuit of self-interest with the goals of the business, the less we'll need formal strictures to prevent inappropriate behavior.

Before the appearance of the large corporation, industries were made up of small businesses linked by customer-supplier relationships. When our country was founded, in the late eighteenth century, most American citizens were self-employed entrepreneurs. Small farmers raised sheep, and when it came time to harvest the wool, they hired independent shearers to remove the fleece. Spinners operating out of their homes turned the wool into thread, and weavers turned the thread into cloth. The cloth was cut and stitched into clothing by seamstresses, and the clothing was sold by retail merchants.

All of the people in the process were independent business-people. If their work was efficient and of high quality, they earned the reward of profit and were selected out by the competitive environment for future work and survival. There were no performance appraisals, strategic plans, or interminable management meetings. Thankfully, there were also no motivational seminars or management consultants. While spinning wool by candlelight or sewing for twelve hours a day to earn a living probably didn't lead to a great quality of life, at least there weren't any bosses to complain about.

There are still remnants of this approach today. The residential construction industry, with the exception of a handful of large companies, is comprised mainly of small entrepreneurial firms. A general contractor retails the project, oversees the process and schedule, and hires subcontractors to perform the bulk of the work. If they perform well, they get more work. If they don't, they have to find employment elsewhere.

Outsourcing today is in many ways a return to this model. The current trend is for a company to focus on its strategic advantage, where it can gain the maximum profit, and outsource everything else that would be a distraction. Even the monolithic domestic automobile industry has moved from Henry Ford's model of raw materials entering one side of the River Rouge factory and assembled cars leaving from the other. Component manufacturers now produce everything from brake systems to seats. There's even a firm that outsources innovation to Russian PhDs who lost their jobs when the Cold War ended.

In the 1920s, Alfred Sloan took what was then seen as the radical step of decentralizing General Motors and breaking it up into five companies with their own automobile brands, marketing, engineering, and manufacturing. The benefits Sloan gained, such as the market orientation that enabled GM to overtake Ford, would help make any organization more effective. Rather than limit decentralization to the top of the hierarchy, why not drive it down into the organization as far as possible? Modern information technology makes such "radical decentralization" much easier now than it was in Sloan's day.

Such an approach enables people to control their own destinies. From a Darwinian perspective, it's aligned with the urgings of our selfish genes. From a market perspective, it's more efficient and effective. From a cultural perspective, virtually every organizational innovation since the Western Electric Hawthorne studies has been aimed at fostering democracy and initiative in the workplace because it's good for both people and the business. Moving to an entrepreneurial organization is just the next step. While it may not be possible in all businesses and some control may still be necessary, it's worth shooting for.

CULTURE

Market-facing and process-based organizations can overcome the problems created by hierarchy and the functional groupings of specialists, especially when they're made up of small, self-managed teams. The entrepreneurial organization goes even farther toward eliminating cumbersome and inefficient structures by using market dynamics to manage key relationships. All of these innovations leverage natural selection as a better way to manage human activity.

But we have yet to incorporate the real insight of neuroscience—the dominant role of mind. Regardless of what structure, systems, and processes are used or how effective they are, it is impossible to prescribe how people should behave in every instance now and in the future. There are just too many variables, unpredictable changes, and ways to work around control systems. In fact, the more we attempt to prescribe what people do, the more we lose the advantage of the mind's ability to change how it works through learning. But given the primacy of mind in the mental world we inhabit, it's possible to control the behavior of a group without resorting to any structure whatsoever. All we need to do is shape the culture that shapes the thinking.

Culture is a convenient way of thinking about patterns of behavior in an organization that aren't hardwired by policies, procedures, or structure. Popularly, it has become a black box used to explain, in the absence of anything else, the failure of an organization to implement its strategy. The conventional wisdom, based on Aristotelian thinking, sees culture either as a thing or a set of observable behaviors. When Porter Goss took over the CIA, he attributed its intelligence failures to a "broken culture."

But in light of the mind's primary role in creating the world we inhabit, a better way of thinking about culture would be to see it as the mind-set of the organization. Because our mind-set is structured as a story, culture can be thought of as the collective story the members of an organization tell themselves, driving the way they perceive the world and act as a result. In the case of the CIA, the story wasn't aligned with the mission and goals of the organization.

If there has not been a conscious effort to shape the cultural story, the odds are that it will not be aligned with the organization's strategy. Since culture is collective and transmitted from person to person, it has continuity over time. When the strategy changes, the culture doesn't necessarily change with it. Even in a stable environment, without attention and careful orchestration, the culture evolves informally and can be at odds with the business. The men wiring switching banks for Western Electric created a culture that held back productivity. No matter how much structure is in place, it makes sense to consciously shape culture by managing how the organization's story is being told.

Research on the use of stories to further social movements suggests how this should be done. Sociologist Ronald Jacobs has studied such narratives and he believes that "Individuals depend on the existence of shared stories—or collective narratives—in order to express their sense of self. . . ." Successful movements, Jacobs has found, convince "people that the movement narrative coincides with their own personal narratives," and that their participation in the movement will further their individual goals. But they must "emphasize agency and ultimate success, rather than fate or ultimate failure," and they will need to do this more effectively "than other 'major' collective narratives."

As we've seen, the most effective stories are romantic, where the "heroes represent ideals and villains represent threats," and people are united "in the pursuit of a utopian future." In a corporation, people want the business to meet its goals for both rational and irrational reasons, but they also want to be part of something important and feel that their work is significant in a broader sense. When it's done well, the company's vision statement, the "happily ever after" of the cultural story, is the collective expression of this desire. It encourages people to move beyond a fair day's wage for a fair day's work.

When I started out in the corporate world, I worked for the computer manufacturer Digital Equipment Corporation. Because of the kind of work required to build large, expensive computer systems, the company had adopted the matrix organization of the aerospace industry, with most people reporting to both the manager of a business unit and the manager of a function. This hybrid structure aims for both customer focus and the advantages of a traditional functional organization.

Paradoxically, having two bosses gave employees more freedom to make decisions than having one boss, because it was up to them to resolve any conflicts between the two. This decision-making authority was reinforced by the company's founder, Ken Olsen, who was fond of saying, in contrast to the views of Taylor and Emerson, that no one knew as much about a job as the person doing it. It was up to each employee to determine what to do and how to do it.

This could certainly be a recipe for chaos, and there was a fair amount. It was also relatively easy to take advantage of the situation, and at one point I had a boss who lived on the coast and rarely showed up for work on nice beach days. But the company believed that whatever productivity was lost from these causes was more than made up for by the increase in commitment the culture encouraged. The company's incredible success, even when it employed well over one hundred thousand people, was evidence that this was the case.

The story the company told was on the order of the Arthurian quest for the Holy Grail. There were posters throughout the building that showed a photograph of the earth taken from outer space. At the top was the company name, and at the bottom was the line, "We change the way the world thinks." For me, this vision for the company was incredibly inspirational. Along with it came a set of stories, almost myths, about the Herculean efforts of people working to make the vision a reality, and the stories were true. In fact, people became so consumed by their jobs that the company produced a video cautioning employees to be careful about how much work they took on.

The corporate story was reinforced in every way possible. Ken Olsen sent out a memo once a month to all employees with his observations on the state of the company. Managers encouraged employees to "push back" and not just blindly follow the direction they gave. Work units were kept small and were distributed in two hundred facilities around the world, each designed to be like a college campus. There were no closed offices, even for executives. It's been twenty-five years since I left the company, but I still look back on my experience fondly. Although the company is today part of Hewlett-Packard, there's an active Digital alumni association, complete with newsletter.

The starting point for creating the cultural story is to determine precisely what kind of thinking and behavior is necessary for the company to implement its strategy. The story is then constructed with a plotline that pivots on how people change to overcome any obstacles in the way of achieving their vision of the future. It will describe precisely how people need to think and act, but at a high level. In line with Jacobs's research, the vision of the future should be aspirational and meet the needs of both the business and the individual.

The next step is to tell the story. Because the employees will create their version of it based on their total experience of the company, all of the details of the experience should be managed tightly. It should be conveyed in new-hire orientation, at training programs, and through all company communications. There should be a concise vision statement and regular updates on progress toward its accomplishment. Everything that can be orchestrated should be, from the behavior of managers to the physical environment.

Although our genes might be selfish, human beings know the value of cooperation, even when it requires a degree of self-sacrifice. We will work for the good of the group, especially if it enables us to achieve something we aspire to and can't accomplish on our own. The cultural story is how we can shape and leverage our natural inclination to be part of something bigger than ourselves. If we do it right, formal structure and control systems aren't even necessary.

GROUPS, MARKETS, AND MINDS

One can envy slime mold. It perfectly balances independence and collective effort. When the depletion of the food supply requires collective effort, the organisms coalesce to form first a slug and then a stalk with a spore mass on top. Each one willingly sacrifices itself for the good of the community and the next generation. No cumbersome organizational structures are necessary to control their behavior.

Human beings aren't so willing to sacrifice. We have evolved to be selfish and to look out for ourselves. Life is a zero-sum game and we're locked in competition for survival. Most organizational structures, systems, and processes try to thwart this natural inclination. Paradoxically, the hierarchy, functional specialization, and division into line and staff, created to ensure collective effort, end up producing just the opposite.

But by creating small groups physically co-located and by leveraging reciprocal altruism, our need to be accepted by the group, and the threat of competition, we can eliminate the barriers to collective action. In larger organizations, we can install market-oriented and process-based structures to create focus on the market and enhance workflow. We can go even further and make use of the process of natural selection that governs human activities by using free-market dynamics to manage customer and supplier relationships.

With structure or without structure, our greatest success will come from orchestrating how people think about their groups, by consciously shaping culture through a narrative. The most effective stories target our highest aspirations, are easy to identify with, and make it clear what people need to do to implement the business strategy. In fact, strategy should be the starting point for the design of any organization, and the kind of strategies the cognitive paradigm gives us, as we'll see, require the cooperation and commitment only a carefully managed culture can foster.

SIX

THINKING STRATEGICALLY

The war has gone on for nine years, and the advantage has swung back and forth. Then, just as victory seems to be within their grasp, a mysterious plague descends on the troops. A prophet proclaims the cause to be the abduction of a Trojan priestess by the Greek commander, Agamemnon. If the plague is to end, the seer explains, she must be returned to her father and a sacrifice made to the gods.

Agamemnon does not take this news well. Reluctantly, he agrees to send her back, but he then demands the priestess Achilles has taken in return. The great warrior takes the demand as an insult and goes for his sword. But just as he is about to make short work of his boss, the goddess Athena drops down from heaven and stops him. He obeys the goddess, but he then retires to his tent and refuses to continue fighting in the war.

This argument is the subject of the first story we have in the Western world, Homer's *Iliad*. Although these are two of the greatest heroes who have ever lived, the behavior of both can't help but strike us as childlike and self-defeating. Agamemnon alienates his best warrior and loses the advantage he brought the Greeks, while Achilles should have known that killing one's boss is never going to lead to good things, and his subsequent refusal to fight put both his comrades and his cause in jeopardy. Their behavior drives us to ask just what these men could've been thinking. The answer is nothing. They're not thinking at all. There's no thinking anywhere in the epic. There is no reflection, no deliberation, and no introspection.

Instead, our heroes act just like objects in the physical world governed by Newton's laws of motion. They go right at each other, letting force determine the outcome, and not just in this argument, but in the way they fight the war as well. There's no attack on the flank, no maneuvering, and no clever feints to mislead the Trojans. In fact, there's no strategy at all. Day after day for almost ten years, the Greeks just hammer on the Trojans and the Trojans hammer back. It's finally Odysseus who wins the war for the Greeks, not with superior force, but with strategy. The Trojan horse was his idea.

According to his plan, the Greeks left it on the beach as a sacrifice to the gods, and then sailed away. The Trojans debated whether or not to bring it into the city, but when sea serpents conveniently devoured those against the move, the horse was dragged inside the city walls. That night, Odysseus and an elite band of warriors hidden inside climbed out of the horse and opened the city gates to the returning Greek army. The rest is the history of the Western world, which may not have existed if it hadn't been for Odysseus.

He didn't go right at the Trojans and use force to breach the gates of the city, as Achilles had tried to do. Instead, he tricked the Trojans into opening the gates for him by presenting the wooden horse as something other than it was. This is the same way a metaphor works, and just as the old Yankee's pickle changed the thinking of the town's people, the sacrificial horse changed how the Trojans thought and acted. It wasn't Achilles' physical strength that won the Trojan War, but Odysseus' cleverness.

Whenever he found himself in a tight spot, Odysseus would work his way out of it by presenting himself as something other than he was, and the form this deception always took was a story. When he returned to Ithaca after his travels, he found a hundred suitors vying for his wife's hand. To trick the suitors into letting down their guard, he fabricated a story about himself as a blind beggar. Although he quickly became the butt of the suitors' jokes, enduring far worse insults than Achilles did, he never lost sight of his goal of revenge. When all of his preparations were completed and the time was right, he sprang his trap and made short work of the suitors.

In the person of Odysseus, the wisest of all men according to Zeus, Homer teaches the Western world how to think strategically. It is the same whether one is confronted with a hundred greedy suitors, an army of the finest warriors, or a one-eyed Cyclops. We focus on the long-term goal, formulate plans to achieve it, and calmly exercise self-control to ensure the plans are executed. Rather than directly challenge force with force, we leverage our resources by changing the thinking of our opponents so that they behave the way we need.

Our objective paradigm causes us to view conflict in terms of Newtonian force. Whether it's a one-on-one relationship, a military battle, or business competition, we see it as a contest where the strongest party wins. But because the world we inhabit is not physical but mental, the actions we take all too often have self-defeating relationship effects, and we don't avail ourselves of actions that would prove more effective because they strike us as illogical. When we view the conflict through the cognitive paradigm, though, we recognize how the nature of a relationship can be used to our advantage, how the environment can be a source of opportunity, and how the mind is the ultimate source of competitive advantage.

STRATEGY ISN'T LOGICAL

Imagine that I am a large manufacturer of automobiles, with huge fixed costs, excess capacity, and relatively low margins. My purpose is to maximize my revenues and profits for the quarter, because they determine how Wall Street values my company, affecting both the cost of capital for the business and my own compensation. From the law of supply and demand, I know that if I reduce my price, I will create a greater demand for my cars. I have data that allows me to calculate how much of a cut is needed to increase demand enough to raise total revenues and profitability. Based on my best logic, backed up by financial analysis, I cut my price a thousand dollars.

There is just one problem with this analysis—the market for automobiles is a web of relationships that includes customers and competitors. My behavior affects theirs, and theirs affects mine. My competitors, with access to the same data that I have and not wanting to see their products become less competitive, match my price cuts, and the supply and demand curves for the industry are shifted downward. With all of the companies now selling their cars at a lower price, I haven't gained any competitive advantage. My revenues are down and so are my profits.

But logic will object that this assumes constant demand, and total demand should increase with lower prices. While this is true at any given moment, it is not necessarily the case over time. The price cuts prompt a flurry of buying, until those who needed a car and those now able to afford one at the lower price have made their purchases. Having accomplished its purpose and helped to make the quarter, the price cut comes to an end and demand falls.

Logic obscures the interdependent relationships with competitors and customers, and it also prevents us from appreciating the role of the mind. Because the customers have minds, they are capable of using their past experiences to determine how best to act in the present. Observing the frequent bouts of price cutting in the automobile market over time, they learn not to buy until prices drop.

The ultimate effect of my logical price cut ends up being the opposite of what was intended. I have lower revenues and profits, and what's worse, a customer acclimated to waiting for price cuts. The quarter may have been made, but the unintended consequences stretch into the future. The next quarter will be even harder to make. Customers now waiting for the inevitable price cut will force the manufacturers to lower prices just to achieve the original level of demand.

Even with proprietary products and an absence of strong competitors, companies can still fall victim to relationship effects with their customers. Bausch & Lomb drove its managers with an annual goal of a 15 percent increase in both revenues and profits. As it posted quarter after quarter of these enviable results, its CEO was heralded in the business press as a visionary. After a while, however, when no more sales could be squeezed out of the market, it became clear that coercing managers with impossible goals wasn't quite as visionary as it might have appeared.

The company sold its products to distributors who then in turn sold to retailers. When the company was pressuring its managers to increase sales to the distributors by fifteen percent a year, it exceeded the capability of the market to absorb all of the product. With the aggressive goals hanging over their heads, the company's managers continually pushed the distributors to take more and more at the end of every quarter. Eventually, however, the distributors were so flooded with product that the only way to get them to buy more was to give generous discounts. Like automobile customers, the distributors had minds, so they quickly learned to delay their purchases for the quarter until the discounts were offered.

Soon, however, they held more product than they could do anything with and stopped buying all together. The unintended consequences were predictable—plummeting revenues and profits, and stressed-out managers. Creative accounting and fraud were next employed, but eventually the whole thing blew up with criminal indictments and a bankruptcy filing. Well before the cover stories in *Business Week* and *Fortune,* the CFO of one of the business units made an impassioned plea to simply accept missing a quarter. He was dismissed as naive.

Aristotelian logic distorted the view of both the automobile market and the distribution chain of Bausch & Lomb. As a result, actions intended to produce a certain result were actually producing the opposite. Because the cognitive paradigm focuses our attention on relationships, it enables us to anticipate such effects. When we factor in how the mind works, we're not only able to avoid falling victim to them, we're able to use them to our advantage.

THE SCIENCE AND ART OF STRATEGY

Clearly Odysseus was capable of a thought process that neither Achilles nor Agamemnon, nor for that matter the former CEO of Bausch & Lomb, were able to call upon. It seemed that he always knew just what to do to get the response he wanted from his opponents, and not only was he not surprised by relationship effects, he was able to use them to his advantage. Unfortunately, brain scans weren't available in ancient Greece, so we can't know for certain what was going on in his head, but we do have Homer's thoughts and the musings of a Princeton psychologist with an interest in both the classics and brain anatomy.

Julian Jaynes was an obscure researcher in the 1970s when he read about Roger Sperry's work with people suffering from epilepsy. Sperry had observed that seizures started as a burst of electrical activity in one region of the brain and then spread to others. Both hemispheres became involved when the electrical spikes traveled through the corpus callosum, the large bundle of nerves that connects the two hemispheres. Sperry's idea was to sever the corpus callosum and minimize the severity of the seizure by keeping it localized in one hemisphere.

To test his hypothesis, he performed his operation on fifteen patients. The results were stunning—the seizures stopped altogether. The only problem was that the patient literally became of two minds, and one didn't know what the other was doing. If a patient had his left eye covered and was presented with an apple, he could draw it but not name it. The reverse was true as well—an object viewed with the right eye covered could be named but not drawn. One patient was even observed pulling his pants up with one hand as he pushed them down with the other.

This anomaly led to the conclusion that the two hemispheres of the brain were specialized for different mental processes. Although it's not quite as simple as it first appeared, the left hemisphere of the brain, which controls the right side of the body, was seen to be the seat of our conscious reasoning. The right hemisphere, which controls the left side of the body, was believed to be where our emotions were located.

When Jaynes came across Sperry's research, he immediately thought of Achilles. The warrior was all emotion, and when reason made an appearance, it was in the form of Athena. The two cognitive processes were disconnected, just as they were in Sperry's patients, so Achilles experienced his reasoning as coming from the outside in the form of the goddess. Given that there are no references to conscious thinking in the *Iliad,* but an abundance of them in the *Odyssey,* Jaynes concluded that consciousness evolved in the period between the creation of the two epics.

The nature of this conscious thinking comes across in the way Athena convinces Achilles not to kill Agamemnon. She promises him a reward in the future worth three times what he was being asked to give up in the present. Freud called this *delayed gratification* and thought it was fundamentally how the conscious mind worked. He believed that it made possible the rise of agriculture, with its tilling of the soil and planting of seeds in the present for the promise of a crop in the future. Among her other duties, Athena was the protector of both agriculture and the civilization it gave rise to.

Today we do have brain scans, and they show that the nucleus accumbens, which we have seen is responsible for feelings of pleasure, matures before the orbital frontal cortex, which is the location of our faculty for long-term planning. The different rates of maturation of these two areas, in the view of Gary Marcus, explains why teenagers are "pathologically driven by short-term rewards." Odysseus, on the other hand, appeared to have a rather well-developed orbital frontal cortex.

So why do automobile executives and the former CEO of Bausch & Lomb fail to adequately anticipate the long-term consequences of their actions? Damasio's experiment with the decks of cards offers a hint. In the world of Aristotelian logic, we discount emotion in favor of objective reasoning. The right hemisphere of the brain, which is responsible for emotion, is also responsible for seeing wholes. This big-picture perspective recognizes that making the quarterly numbers is just a small part of running a successful business and can't be pursued at the expense of the longer term. When we discount emotion, we lose access to the big picture. It isn't as much a question of emotion *or* reason as it is using the two in tandem.

The night before Odysseus is to execute his plan to slaughter his wife's suitors, he is awakened by the laughter of his wife's maids cavorting with the suitors. He's tempted to make short work of them, "torn in thought, debating, head and heart." But in contrast to Achilles' need for the goddess of wisdom to control his emotions, he is the one who recognizes that it would jeopardize his longer-term goal. So he controls his desire for immediate gratification with the words, "Bear up old heart! You've borne worse, far worse. . . ." Signals were flowing freely through Odysseus' corpus callosum.

The execution of strategy requires delaying the gratification of our short-term emotional wants, but not at the expense of the insight emotion brings us. Perhaps the pendulum has swung too far, and we now favor our left hemisphere over our right more than we should. But we can bring that hemisphere back into play by consciously attending to the two aspects of our experience highlighted by our awareness of the big picture, relationships and the environment, and the cognitive paradigm enables us to do that. To keep our focus, we can coach ourselves as Odysseus did, or we can just tell ourselves a story.

LEVERAGING THE ENVIRONMENT AND THE MIND

Before there were corporations that needed to mobilize large numbers of people in pursuit of a common goal, there were armies facing the same challenge. The military established the pattern for how large business organizations are built and managed, and in fact the word strategy comes from the Greek *strategia,* meaning generalship. So if we want to understand how best to formulate a competitive strategy, the battle plan is not a bad place to start. One of the best examples is Henry V's classic battle against the French in 1415. It teaches us how to leverage both the environment and the minds of our competitors.

Henry had sailed to France to assert his claim to lands his grandfather had won. His first battle ended in victory, but it took longer, consumed more resources, and cost more men than he had anticipated. In his weakened condition, he decided to avoid any more battles, and just march symbolically up the coast to Calais and sail back to England. The night before he was to arrive there, he found himself on the edge of a newly plowed field near the small town of Agincourt. There, across the field, he saw the entire French army, outnumbering the English by twenty to one. They were fresh, well armed, and eager to claim the glory they felt they were due. The English were worn-out, homesick, and convinced they'd be defeated in the coming battle.

That night as he wandered among his dispirited troops, the king could hear the French feasting across the field, raising toasts to the victory they were sure to win the next day. In almost all traditional warfare, and business competition as well, victory favors the stronger force. Henry's only hope for survival was to come up with a plan that would turn the French advantage in numbers into a weakness. At some point during the night, looking out across the field and listening to the detested French, he figured out just how to do it.

The newly plowed field was muddy, and narrower on the English side than on the French. Henry had his men drive stakes into the ground on his side of the field at a height that would impale a charging horse, and he placed his infantry in front of them so that the stakes would be hidden from view. On the sides of the field, he deployed his archers with their longbows. Although the conventional wisdom held that Henry should've been in a defensive posture, his troops were deceptively arrayed as if for an attack.

When morning came, Henry spoke some final words to his troops and then launched the attack by signaling his archers to fire their arrows. Given their distance from the French, the arrows did no physical damage, but they infuriated the French leadership. Quickly, they mounted their horses and started galloping full speed down the field toward the English. But when they reached the narrower end of the field, there was no room for all of them. At just that moment, the English infantry stepped out of the way and exposed the stakes. The French were trapped with nowhere to go, and they were easy targets for the archers, who began raining arrows down on them. Nor was a retreat possible, for wave after wave of cavalry followed the leadership in quick succession down the field.

The French who didn't fall victim to the arrows were either driven into the stakes or trampled by their own cavalry. By the end of the battle, there were over six thousand French casualties, while the English lost only about a hundred men. Recognizing that he might need the French as allies in the future, Henry made a point of treating his captives graciously and later cemented an alliance with them by marrying the French king's daughter.

Conveniently for our purposes, Henry attended to all of the elements one must consider for a successful strategy and made the most of them. He analyzed the environment that he would be fighting in and recognized that it could be used to his advantage. The horses would find it difficult to get their footing on the muddy field, and the French cavalry would be too crowded together to fight when they reached the narrower English side of the field. He factored in the French mind-set of superiority and arrogance, anticipating that they would race down the field to his trap when his archers fired arrows at them.

In the spirit of Odysseus, Henry tricked the French by hiding the stakes blocking the end of the field and having his archers act as if they actually were attacking. This strategy intensified the competitive dynamic of the relationship, which worked to Henry's advantage and enabled him to change the greater numbers of the French into a weakness. Finally, he thought beyond his immediate goal of survival to strike an alliance with the French that might prove useful in the future. The best strategists anticipate the reactions to their moves and constantly ask, "What's going to happen next?"

BUSINESS STRATEGY

Because its roots are in the military, it's easy to think of business strategy as some sort of competitive shoot-out. After all, the competition is the enemy and the goal is to defeat the enemy. But this is extending the military metaphor too far. The difference between military strategy and business is the presence of a third party, the customer. The goal of the strategy is not to defeat the competition in a head-to-head battle, but to *meet the needs and wants of the customer better than the competition.* When it becomes just competitor against competitor, we get caught up in the relationship effects and lose sight of the customer, as we see when competition is focused on the single dimension of price cuts in the automobile industry.

As would be expected, given that free markets are Darwinian, the cognitive paradigm captures the nature of business competition better than the objective one. While species compete to meet the demands of the natural environment, companies compete to meet the demands of the market environment, and that is made up of customers. The big difference is that while the natural environment is dumb, customers have minds that shape their demands.

Just as in autos, the airlines are addicted to price wars, with the same disappointing results. One company that figured out how to move beyond the destructive head-to-head competition was People Express. Don Burr, the founder and CEO, came up with a strategy that although based on price, leveraged the changes in the environment and addressed the mind-set of the customers in a way that couldn't be matched by the competition.

In late 1979, when People Express was founded, the country was still suffering from the fuel shocks of the seventies. The skyrocketing cost of oil had caused the economy to stagnate, and it hit the airlines even harder than most industries because jet fuel was their largest expense. Since the price had gone up dramatically in a very short period of time, there had been no opportunity to drive efficiencies, and most carriers were flying planes that were highly fuel inefficient.

Besides, the airlines had been regulated and were used to the peaceful coexistence that kept both costs and prices high. That era had just come to an end with President Carter's signing of critical legislation deregulating the industry. Socially, the country had not yet entered the "Me" decade of the 1980s, and there was a strong populist ethic. With the hostage crisis dragging on in Iran, it felt as if the American ideal of democracy was under fire.

Most airline customers were either businesspeople flying on their company's dollar or relatively well-off private passengers, and both groups were largely price insensitive. However, there was a large group of potential customers who would consider flying as an alternative to driving or taking the bus, if they could do so for a reasonable price. These were the customers People Express decided to go after.

People Express's competitors were established carriers, and their strengths and weaknesses were just what you would expect from companies in a regulated environment. They knew their business and had the necessary plant, processes, and people in place to run them. They had established relationships with their suppliers, shareholders, and banks, and they had name recognition with customers. This gave them forward momentum.

However, because the industry had been regulated, they were complacent and invested in maintaining the status quo. The conduct of their business had become routinized. Standard operating procedures were in place, and corresponding neural networks had been embedded. They had high costs and were slow to innovate. Having become accustomed to a market in which selling just seats was sufficient, they didn't necessarily understand the wants of their customers or how to address them. If they thought about them at all, they would have most likely defined them with Aristotelian logic as more comfortable seats and fancier meals.

In contrast, as the new kids on the block, People had nothing in place to run an airline and everything had to be created from scratch. While this put them at a cost disadvantage on the experience curve, they also benefitted from the absence of legacy costs and practices. They didn't have a high-priced workforce with expensive pension obligations, entrenched processes that weren't efficient, or costly facilities. While most organizations and cultures evolve willy-nilly and aren't necessarily configured to implement the current strategy, People Express had the luxury to design their organization specifically for the implementation of their strategy.

Plus, they had Don Burr as their CEO. He was an experienced airline executive, having run Texas Air in the seventies under the legendary Frank Lorenzo, who went on to turn the old Eastern Airlines into the world's largest carrier. Burr knew both the strategic and the operational side of the business, and had the contacts to assemble a high-quality management team. Because he had worked on Wall Street, he was able to raise the kind of money needed to start and grow the airline. He understood what deregulation would do to the industry and how to take advantage of it. He was also charismatic enough to pump up a room full of investment bankers or maintenance workers, as the need might be.

There's no logical algorithm to follow to come up with a competitive strategy, no syllogisms or laws of logic that can be applied. But having considered the nature of the competitive environment, the needs and wants of the customers, the competitors' strengths and weaknesses, and our own, a neural network is embedded in our brains that will select out a strategy in harmony with it.

Such a strategy, just as in the case of the battle at Agincourt, must leverage our strengths relative to the competitors' to create an offering that will better satisfy the demands of the market environment. We can get a bit more direction if we make use of our theory of mind and think about our offering from the customer's perspective. There are only two reasons people buy a product or a service. Either the offering is cheaper or it's better. Cheaper is straightforward, and clearly that was People's dominant strategy.

The company gave up the established market of traditional flyers and took advantage of deregulation to go after the untapped price-sensitive market with a low-cost offering. Because they were not burdened with fuel-inefficient airplanes or legacy costs and practices, they could price their offering so that it was competitive with driving or taking a bus. Given their lower cost structure, they had an immediate competitive advantage over the established carriers. As a start-up, they were small enough not to be much of a threat anyway.

A purely low-cost strategy will only work for a while; eventually either existing companies or new entrants to the market will duplicate it. But if the company can differentiate its offering at a minimal incremental cost and not undercut its low-cost strategy, it can more effectively attract and hold on to its customers. It can then fend off any competitive attacks based solely on price.

Another way of thinking about it is that meeting the customers' basic needs is just the ante that gets you in the game. The real advantage comes from going beyond what customers need to what they want. In the world according to neuroscience, the key differentiator is going to be mental, not physical. While it isn't always obvious what customers want, the more we understand the story they're telling themselves, the better we'll be at discovering and addressing what motivates their buying decisions. There may be individual variations, but the overriding story will be a masterplot of our culture.

Don Burr realized that the masterplot foremost in the minds of his target market was the story of American democracy, "We the people" coming together to build a "more perfect Union." This is deeply rooted, and taps into those high-level ideas that we've seen drive much of our behavior and thinking at lower levels. People Express leveraged this story both inside and outside the company with its people-centered organization, employee ownership, and name. Customers weren't just buying a seat, they were voting for democracy and the American way.

This not only created a buzz for the airline, it made customers more willing to accept the long lines and waits in the Newark North Terminal that occurred all too frequently. It also made it easier to attract the kind of employees who were willing to work for a lower wage plus stock, enabling the company to keep operating costs down. In the mental world, a seat is not just a seat and a job is not just a job. They are what we believe them to be, and that is a function of the story we tell. People Express told a great story, and it changed the competitive dynamic of the marketplace.

Brilliant as any strategy may be in concept, it isn't enough to ensure success. More companies fail because their strategy isn't implemented than because it isn't robust enough. The relationship between the formulation and implementation of the strategy doesn't receive the attention it should, both because of our Aristotelian logic and because those formulating the strategy usually aren't the ones who will implement it. But every aspect of People's organization was designed to operate just like natural selection, both to keep costs down and capitalize on the populist theme.

In place of the hierarchical management and standard operating procedures of the established carriers, People Express used self-managed teams that determined their own work processes. In place of rigid job descriptions, enforced by the established carriers' unions, the airline had the flexibility to rotate people through different jobs. Rather than fixed salaries, stock ownership aligned with profitability made up the bulk of compensation. The aspirational mission of showing the world how to run a business democratically took people beyond a fair day's work for a fair day's wage. As a result, operating costs were low, morale high, and customers satisfied with a "unique" flying experience. By 1984, People Express had become not just the fastest growing airline, but the fastest growing business ever.

THE MIND OF THE STRATEGIST

Within six months, though, People Express was bankrupt. Given the high profile of the company and its success in implementing so many of the management practices that would later become fixtures of companies like Apple and Google, there's been a lot of speculation about what caused its demise. Some were quick to fault its wide-open organization and employee-centric policies. Others believed the airline just grew too big for the established carriers to ignore, and their deeper pockets enabled them to win the ensuing price-cutting battle. Don Burr attributed the cause to the rise of yield management software, which enabled the airlines to adjust prices on individual seats in response to demand.

But an experiment called the Stanford Marshmallow Test suggests that the reason for People Express's failure can be found in the orbital frontal cortex of Burr's brain, the same area Gary Marcus believes is responsible for the high-risk decisions of teenagers when it's underdeveloped. Four-year-olds were placed in a room with a one-way mirror and a marshmallow on the table in front of them, and they were given a choice. They could eat the marshmallow right away, or if they waited twenty minutes for the researcher to leave and come back, they could have two marshmallows.

Given the impetuousness of four-year-olds, the results are not surprising. About a third ate the marshmallow right away, a third tried to wait but couldn't make it, and a third waited the full twenty minutes for the researcher to return. But what the researchers learned when they revisited these kids fourteen years later is surprising. Those who were willing to wait the twenty minutes for the other marshmallow tested on average over two hundred points higher on the Scholastic Aptitude Tests. The four-year-olds are now in their forties, and follow-up research has found that they are also more popular, have had greater career success, and score significantly higher on intelligence tests. They have proven to be great strategists. The ability to make the decision to delay immediate gratification for the promise of greater gratification in the future pays huge dividends.

There was one critical decision Burr made that led directly to People Express's bankruptcy filing, and it seems to have been made without any input from the orbital frontal cortex. By the end of 1984, the company was growing quickly, but not quickly enough for Burr. He became convinced they should move beyond a regional focus and go national. Given the hub-and-spoke model of the industry, this meant a western hub was needed in addition to the eastern one in Newark. But rather than sticking to the strategy that had brought them success and build it from scratch, Burr went searching for an acquisition.

When a carrier named Frontier Airlines in Denver became available, he decided to buy it. In itself, this was a questionable move. Anyone who's worked on Wall Street, as Burr had, knows that fewer than one third of acquisitions are successful. Even more of a concern was that the key to the company's competitive advantage was innovative human-resource practices and procedures that were not going to work at an established carrier, let alone a unionized one like Frontier.

But perhaps most curious was how the acquisition took place. Burr was experienced enough in the financial world to understand the need to calculate the highest price he could pay for Frontier and not go over it, but he ended up going way over it. The acquisition sank People Express, which became loaded with debt and unable to implement the kind of cost-saving measures that had proven so successful. Why did Burr pay more than he should have? Because there was another bidder for the company and his name was Frank Lorenzo.

It's open to debate whether Burr's former boss actually wanted the airline, or just wanted to drive the price up so high that it would bankrupt Burr. Apparently, there was a bit of bad blood between the two because when Burr left Texas Air to found People, he took the whole executive team with him, including Lorenzo's personal secretary. One can't help feeling that Burr's desire to beat out his former boss got in the way of his business sense. In any case, Lorenzo played the competitive game to the hilt and let Burr bankrupt himself. When People Express ran into financial trouble, Lorenzo picked up its assets at a fire-sale price.

In retrospect, one can't help wondering why Burr went after an airline that didn't fit his strategy and paid far more for it than he should have. But anyone who has ever been involved in an acquisition has felt the thrill of the hunt, and the bidding war with Lorenzo can't help but recall a similar competitive escalation that occurred three thousand years earlier between Achilles and Agamemnon. Just like a teenager, Burr became involved in the emotions of the moment and lost the long-term perspective the orbital frontal cortex offers.

According to the *Iliad,* the battle against the tug of immediate gratification is a story as old as our culture, but we're not doomed to lose it. Researchers have found that performance on the Stanford Marshmallow Test improves when children stop thinking about the marshmallow as "yummy and chewy," and start thinking about it as being like a "cloud." This is just like the cognitive reappraisal we saw change the emotional response to the picture of the woman crying. It does appear that people can train themselves to be better at delaying gratification.

Psychologist Jeremy Gray thinks the best way to avoid falling for the lure of immediate gratification is to clearly envision the future, and this approach is tailor-made for ensuring that strategies are implemented. Even if we were capable of remaining reasonable in the face of emotional temptations, there are just too many decisions to be made for our logic to handle. Instead of being driven by our conscious reasoning, implementation should be driven by the story with the vision of the future we tell ourselves. It's the only way to ensure that all of our decisions and actions are in sync and that we're not being distracted by the activity of the nucleus accumbens.

The more we tell the story, the more it's embedded in a neural network, and the more comprehensively it drives our thoughts and actions. But the story will only work if we really believe it. As a discipline, every one of our decisions should be checked against it, just as Odysseus checked his desire to murder his wife's maids. Perhaps People Express would still be in business today if Burr had had the benefit of the latest research in neuroscience and exercised a little bit of Odysseus' knack for telling a story and sticking to it. Then maybe he would have opted for slower and more reliable organic growth. That's been Southwest Airlines' strategy and they have now become the most successful airline ever.

THE COUNTERINTUITIVE STRATEGIST

Odysseus' strategy changed the wooden horse from a siege engine into a sacrifice to the gods. Henry's strategy changed the French strength of greater numbers into a weakness. Don Burr's strategy changed an airline seat into a vote for the American way. In each case, the strategy changed how people thought in counterintuitive ways, so that the nature of the competition wasn't just force against force. In the mid-1990s, a small high-technology start-up named Cambridge Technology Partners revolutionized the information technology services industry by taking a counterintuitive approach to the formulation of strategy itself.

When I first interviewed the CEO, I learned that he'd never attended college or business school, with the exception of an exec-utive education program. Instead, Jim Sims left high school to join the Navy, where he was trained as a computer technician. After the service, he went right to work for a computer manufacturer. He was so charismatic and such a natural salesman that he quickly rose to the top and became a sought-after CEO. When venture capitalists were looking for a leader for an interesting high-tech start-up, Jim seemed like the ideal candidate. By the time I became his consul-tant, he had already taken the company from just under ten to over a hundred million dollars in revenue.

I was puzzled by how this guy became such a consummate

businessman without the requisite formal training, so I asked him one day. He explained it by describing his years selling newspapers on a street corner in Detroit. "A bunch of us used to stand on a street corner at a stoplight. When the light changed red, everybody would run to the cars at the front of the line, but I would run to the cars further back where there was no competiton.

"You know, the papers used to cost seven cents. Now, most people would ask for a paper, give me a dime, and tell me to keep the change. The margin wasn't bad, but the real opportunity was the people that gave you a quarter. As if looking for their change, I would take off my gloves one finger at a time and then start searching all of my pockets. I would just keep them waiting until the light changed and people started honking. Then they'd tell me to keep the change and would drive off." Early on, Jim had learned to go where the competiton wasn't and to anticipate and leverage the responses of his customers.

CTP was in the business of developing applications using client-server technology. This industry was virtually locked up by the technology consulting divisions of the then Big Six accounting firms. These firms already had relationships with the finance departments of most large corporations, so it was easy for them to cross-sell information technology services. Newcomers to the market had little chance of getting a hearing, let alone a contract.

All of this changed because of a brilliant MIT professor with a flair for the theatrical. He held seminars for chief information officers to introduce them to the latest client-server technology and graphic user interfaces. At night, he would have his graduate students dummy-up screens so that the CIOs could experience what a custom-designed application using the technology could do for their businesses. They were so impressed that they immediately wanted to hire the professor to build the applications. He had started CTP to meet the demand for these services. When the company ran into problems, the venture capitalists took it over, and brought Jim in to run it.

With offices located in Cambridge, midway between Harvard and MIT, Jim was quickly able to build a talented staff. With his sales expertise and the staff's knowledge of the technology, they set about reinventing the business. Rather than formulate strategy by starting with customer needs the way People Express did, they went at it counterintuitively. They started with the customer's frustrations and dislikes, and then designed an offering that would eliminate them. This one change then led to a completely different approach to all aspects of the business.

The biggest dislike in application development has always been projects that run over time and budget. It makes it impossible for CIOs to plan and effectively manage their business. Worse yet, such projects destroy their credibility with the line. To eliminate this source of frustration, CTP decided to offer guaranteed fixed-time, fixed-price contracts. The company knew that this strategy couldn't be easily matched by the competition because all of their systems, including compensation, were based on billing for time and materials. To match CTP's offering, they would have to completely redesign their businesses, and the cost and time involved would be prohibitive.

To make this one change work, others were needed. For the company to guarantee a fixed time and a fixed price, they had to eliminate change orders and midcourse corrections. Standard practice in the industry was for the client to give the vendor the specifications for the application, and inevitably this handoff would lead to misinterpretations, which then would require adjustments. The way around this was for the client and vendor to create the specifications together. CTP's approach was to form a team made up of representatives from both who would spend a week working together to create the specifications.

But this was an expensive proposition, so it led to other changes. CTP turned what had been a service into a product by putting a fixed price on the process of creating the specifications. To make sure the team used their time effectively, they staffed each project with a trained facilitator, and this allowed them to address another key frustration. Most development projects focused only on the technology, and inevitably there would be behavioral issues when it came time for implementation. With the participation of the facilitators, these issues were identified and addressed up front.

There is always friction in the relationship between the consultants and the clients, particularly when it comes to sales, but the team approach prevented it from occurring. In other firms, the vendor would sit across from the client and pitch their services, but at CTP there was no pitch to sell services. Instead, at the end of the week-long workshop to develop the specifications, the CIO would come in for a presentation given by his people on what the application should look like. Effectively, the CIO's own people were the ones selling him on the application. Not only had Jim changed a service sell into a product sell with a fixed price, he had the client selling himself.

One simple shift, from meeting needs to eliminating frustrations, led to a counterintuitive habit of mind, an idea lodged at a high level, which was then brought to bear on all aspects of the business, even turning problems into opportunities. Since the company was growing so quickly, it was forced to hire a number of young developers right out of school. Given the business model, these people were in front of the client from day one, in contrast to the established industry practice of having only senior people meet with the client. The necessity quickly was recast as a virtue. As the president described it to me, "Initially we were concerned how clients would respond, but we just stressed how much fun it was to work with young, bright, energetic people. After a while, they saw them that way too."

ENVIRONMENT, RELATIONSHIPS, AND MIND

Strategic thinking is fundamentally how the conscious mind works, and most likely it was an adaptation that evolved to address human conflict. We stand back, decide what we want for the future, and arrange our activities in the present to achieve it. It's basically the same thought process whether we're up against a monster with a taste for human flesh, suitors who are after our spouse, or an army we'd like to defeat. Given the mental Darwinian world we compete in, we attend to the environment, relationships, and mind.

The big difference between strategy in human conflict and in business is the presence of the customer. Our goal is not to focus on defeating the competition, because the relationship effects will only pull us into a destructive downward spiral, but to meet the needs and wants of the customers better than they do. When we consider the environment, the customer, and the competition's strengths and weaknesses relative to our own, we prime the mind to come up with a sustainable competitive strategy that ensures we'll be either better or cheaper.

Ultimately, though, in a mental world, the real competitive battle is going to be fought in the mind. By addressing the way people think, we can move beyond the battle of force against force that typifies competition in the Newtonian world. The place to start is with the stories people tell themselves. The more we understand what they are, the better we'll be at formulating strategies to take advantage of them or change them. As Henry did, we can use the arrogance of our competitors against them, and as Don Burr did, we can address hidden motivations that customers might have.

But the most important mind to consider is that of the strategist. We need to recognize the pull of our desire for immediate gratification and accept that it isn't our conscious reasoning that directs our actions. Instead, it's our high-level beliefs and values that determine what we do. To ensure that we act in line with our long-term goals, we've got to keep in mind the vision of the future we're striving for and frequently check ourselves against it. But we also need to be willing to challenge the conventional wisdom so that we can completely reinvent the business the way CTP did. For in the world according to neuroscience, the mind of the strategist is a powerful competitive advantage, but only when it's disciplined and focused on the future.

SEVEN

CHANGING MINDS

The idea that someone would purposely try to drive a dolphin crazy is enough to stop us in our tracks. It seems so incomprehensible that we have a hard time making any sense out of it. We think of dolphins as those playful little mammals that always seem to have a smile on their faces and would never harm anybody. Why would anyone want to drive one crazy? How would anyone drive one crazy? What does it mean for a dolphin to go crazy? There don't seem to be any reasonable answers to these questions, and that's just the point. The same kind of frustration we experience pondering them is exactly what Gregory Bateson was trying to create in his experiment with driving a dolphin crazy.

Bateson was a man with incredibly wide-ranging interests. With his first wife, Margaret Mead, he had studied the indigenous culture of the Balinese and concluded that it was free of many of the conflicts that troubled ours. He went on to work with schizophrenics and formulated the double-bind theory, which proposed irresolvable dissonance as the cause of the disease. Later he participated in the design of the twelve-step process that Alcoholics Anonymous uses to help people overcome their battle against addiction. The theme that tied together all of his work was how people made sense of the world. He considered our Aristotelian logic to be plagued with problems, with schizophrenia and addiction as just two of the more extreme examples, and he saw a more natural use of the mind as preferable.

Since porpoises were believed by many to be more intelligent than human beings, they attracted Bateson's attention, and he spent the sixties and early seventies studying how their minds worked. Bateson felt that, like the Balinese, the way dolphins made sense of the world freed them from many of the problems that afflicted human beings in the developed world. But while identifying a better way of thinking is one thing, being able to adopt it is quite another. Ultimately he came to believe that the greatest challenge we face is change. His experiment with the dolphin was an attempt to understand under what conditions we would change from one way of thinking to another.

By this time, the theory of cognitive dissonance had established that our response to reward and punishment was not as straightforward as the behaviorists thought it was. The mind intervened: discounting, rationalizing, and ignoring dissonant information, driving behavior that didn't fit their model. Bateson wondered what would happen if the dissonance was of a kind that couldn't be so easily reduced by our Aristotelian logic. Would it cause us to change the way we think? His experiment was designed so that there was no way to make sense out of how a reward was dispensed, and so as a result, there was no way to respond logically.

He taught the porpoise a series of tricks and rewarded the performance of each trick with a fish, as expected. Next he stopped rewarding every trick and only gave a reward after three tricks were performed. The porpoise quickly became accustomed to this change. But then Bateson withheld the expected reward no matter how many tricks the porpoise did, and determined to only reward it when a completely new trick was performed. The porpoise responded by performing every trick it knew, either singly or three at a time. When it received no reward, it acted just the way George Homans had predicted: it got angrier and angrier.

But when there was still no reward after even more tricks, it started "to go crazy, exhibit signs of extreme frustration or pain. What happened next in this particular experiment was completely unexpected. . . . The animal not only invented a new trick (for which it was immediately rewarded); it proceeded to perform four absolutely new capers that had never before been observed in this particular species of animal." Caught in the dissonance between the expectation of reward and its absence, the porpoise, after much struggle, learned that new tricks were required for a reward.

We can think of it like this. The porpoise had learned to play the game of reward and punishment, and one of the rules was that "if you repeat the tricks, you get a reward." There was no rule in the game allowing for the invention of completely new tricks, nor was there a rule that allowed for changing the rules. In effect, the dolphin was imprisoned within the game. When Bateson didn't reward the tricks the dolphin already knew, he invalidated the rules and ended the game. No longer knowing what rules to abide by, the dolphin was initially frustrated, but then started generating random behaviors until it hit on the performance of a completely new trick. When it then received a reward, the dolphin realized it was playing a new game with the rule, "if you perform a new trick, you get a reward." It experienced a paradigm shift.

Bateson's experiment didn't just demonstrate how smart dolphins are. It captured a fundamental truth about what it takes for intelligent beings to change. We live according to an implicit set of rules that govern the way the world operates and specifies how we need to behave in response. We've called these rules Aristotelian logic. Given that we make our experience conform to the way we think the world is by reducing any cognitive dissonance, everything we encounter operates according to this set of rules.

The only way for us to change our thinking, and the behavior it gives rise to, is to realize, like the dolphin, that the rules no longer hold and the game has ended. For that to happen, we must experience "reversals of logic" that demonstrate the rules are no longer valid. The resulting cognitive dissonance can't be reduced by any other means than a new paradigm, which comes with a different set of rules.

Neuroscience teaches us that we can formulate more robust competitive strategies, design organizations that will perform at a higher level, and manage people so that they realize their fullest potential. All of these powerful insights come to naught, though, if we don't implement them, and that requires not just a change in behavior, but a change in the thinking that drives the behavior. Because the paradigm responsible for our thinking is self-reinforcing, the only way we can move beyond it is to experience the kind of dissonance that invalidates it.

Thankfully, neuroscience also teaches us how to create that kind of dissonance. It's through the skillful use of the counterintuitive. Our attempts to change the behavior of either individuals or organizations within the objective paradigm will fail because they will fall victim to relationship effects. But if we first use reversals of logic to invalidate the paradigm and change the way people think, we'll be able to get the kind of behavior we need to transform our businesses. Stories are the best way to create and manage this kind of dissonance.

WHY CHANGE FAILS

When the venture capital money arrived, one of the first things the founder did was plunk down $2 million to buy a ski chalet. As we stood on the porch, he explained that it would be a good place for the software developers to write their code. "They can sit out here and look at the mountains," he told me, pointing out the view. "It will stimulate their creativity." Although he had a well-earned reputation for being a bit over the top, I couldn't help but be impressed with this former professor's concern for the well-being of his people. The new ski chalet was the site of the strategic planning session we were holding with the executive team that afternoon.

We started the meeting after lunch. About an hour later, when the team was considering different strategic options, the founder jumped to his feet and proclaimed that the ideas being generated were worthless. "The only people in this room that aren't idiots," he announced, "are the engineers that graduated from Carnegie Mellon and Caltech." This excluded over half of the executives, most of whom were just business school graduates from Harvard and Wharton. The room grew silent, and there were looks of agony on the faces of the executives, regardless of the school they had attended. I decided it was an appropriate time for a break.

I took the founder aside and explained to him that his observation might very well be valid, and I could understand his disappointment, but the way he expressed it was detrimental to the team. It drove a wedge between the business and technical people, and the company's success depended on a strong cooperative relationship between them. I told him there were other ways to deal with his frustration, and I recommended that he briefly apologize when the meeting resumed. In my experience, it would head off any bad feelings that might derail our process, and, if anything, increase the team's respect for him.

When the meeting resumed and he rose to his feet, I expected him to make a brief statement that would get us back on track. "Let me be clear about what I said," he stated professorially. "The only people in this room that aren't idiots are the engineers from Carnegie Mellon and Caltech." With that, he promptly sat down. For all intents and purposes, the meeting was over. For the next six months, the company spun its wheels as most of the executives were either preoccupied with managing the founder or trying to avoid him. Finally, the venture capitalists bought him out and removed him from the company. By then it was too late. The window of opportunity for the company's offering had been missed, and $30 million in funding was gone with virtually nothing to show for it, except a ski chalet.

I don't believe that the founder was just blowing off steam or indulging a taste for making people feel miserable. I think he was genuinely trying to raise the quality of the ideas being generated. His attempt to improve how people were thinking was driven by the paradigm he used to organize his experience of the world. In the Newtonian universe, the application of a little force, in the form of punitive criticism, is what's needed to move people to change. Colloquially, it's known as a kick in the butt.

Of course, we know this would never work. Even leaving aside the fact that people generally don't have that kind of control over the quality of their intelligence, his approach came across as domineering, and like Achilles, human beings resent being controlled. His statement also created the same dynamic that hampered G.E.'s performance appraisal process, reinforcing the behavior it was intended to extinguish. It became in the best interests of those who weren't engineers to become even more idiotic, if possible. At the very least, he ensured that they would withhold their participation to avoid punishment, and there weren't many comments from the business executives, intelligent or otherwise, for the rest of the meeting.

Because I'm well aware of this dynamic, my attempt to change the founder's behavior was carefully managed so that it would not be construed as punitive. Instead of criticism, I acknowledged that the founder's comment very well may have been valid. Focusing on the goal we were all trying to achieve, I simply offered straightforward advice, although what might have been objectively reasonable to me wasn't necessarily so to him. Regardless, my reasoning didn't prove to be any more effective at creating change than his criticism.

Although Aristotle believed that people were rational and that superior reasoning would motivate them to change, we know it's not that simple. Emotion always plays a role in our decision making and we've all experienced it trumping our reason. Even though the founder saw his comments as perfectly rational, clearly there was emotion behind them and behind the way he responded to my advice. Even if he'd been coldly rational, he still would have reduced the dissonance created by my comments in favor of his position. That's what most of us do when our logic is being challenged.

The problem with both the criticism leveled by the founder and the neutral advice I offered is that both were attempts to drive change from the outside. While the application of force might work in the physical world—regardless of whether it's benign, punitive, or rewarding—it doesn't in the mental world. As Socrates demonstrated, people are more likely to change when the motivation comes from within, and when we ask rather than tell.

THE MORE THINGS CHANGE

The difficulty of changing an organization really came home to me when I worked for a telecommunications company trying to transition to a deregulated world. One of the managers hired me to teach his people how to participate in joint performance appraisals. His employees had nicknamed him "Thumper," because the data center he managed had a raised floor that sounded like a bass drum when he stomped across it. The training courses started at 8:30 in the morning, and if they weren't full, he would thump into people's offices and order them to attend, without the slightest concern for what they might be doing. The scuttlebutt around his group was that his management style had been honed when he worked as a POW interrogator during his time in the military.

A new performance appraisal system was just one component of a corporate initiative to change the culture of the company. There was also a new set of prescribed behaviors, along with a PR campaign and management seminars to promote them. These were targeted at creating a more participative work environment to foster the commitment and innovation needed to compete in the company's recently deregulated market.

One day, the committee that had been appointed to drive the initiative was to meet with its sponsor, a senior executive appointed by the CEO. On the wall of the conference room the meeting was held in, a poster trumpeted the initiative and listed the new behaviors. Within fifteen minutes, the executive had violated every one of them. None of the other people attending the meeting, all long-term employees, noticed anything out of the ordinary.

The CEO had undertaken this initiative because he was convinced that his new strategy would only be successful if the people responsible for its implementation radically changed their behavior. In fact, he was so committed to it that he saw the $25 million it cost as an absolutely essential investment. In this, he was far ahead of most of his peers. It's not unusual for a company to formulate a new strategy and then fail to execute it because the old organization remains intact. The CEO not only recognized the need to make the necessary structural changes, he was determined to address the critical issue of culture as well. The new behaviors listed on the poster were indeed the ones needed for the company to succeed. The problem was that no one other than the CEO really embraced them. The only thing the $25 million did was enrich a group of consultants.

In many ways, changing an organization is the sum total of changing all of the individuals in the organization. When a change initiative is based on the objective paradigm and designed with Aristotelian logic, reasons, threats, and/or incentives are the motivators for change. Because they don't work for individuals, we can hardly expect any different outcome with groups of individuals. But changing an organization is even more difficult than changing individuals, because direct contact, for the most part, is not an option. The change must be worked through the organization. Should there be a breakdown at any level, whether executive or managerial, the initiative will fail.

We're quite adept at reducing cognitive dissonance and maintaining a consistent view of the world, even when a conscious effort is made to change it. Thumper's employees didn't think for a moment that the training heralded a change in how they were going to be managed. They just assumed, in keeping with their view of his character, that the training was a corporate initiative he was being forced to go along with. Even the committee tasked with driving the initiative never believed that it was going to lead to real change. They'd been through so many other initiatives before that they referred to the current one as the "initiative du jour."

At a minimum, for a change initiative to take hold, all aspects of it must be aligned. The vision, the strategy, the organization, the culture, and the management practices need to be integrated. Even then, though, success is not guaranteed. The problem with Thumper and the executive was that while they might have bought the need for the initiative and knew they had to support it, they never really believed in it. It's just not possible for all behavior to be hard-wired, and because behavior is ultimately driven by what goes on in our minds, the nuances of our behavior will communicate what we really think. A change initiative is only going to work when the way we think changes.

Even if all aspects of the organization were aligned to support the initiative and it addressed the way people think, its chance of success would still be questionable. Because our minds are automatically reducing cognitive dissonance, we don't necessarily become aware of information that is at variance with our view of the world. The only way we'll be prepared to accept the possibility of change is when there's a marker we're forced to attend to that proclaims the world is going to be different going forward. Otherwise, odds are nobody will even notice that there is an initiative in place.

And there's still one other issue that makes change so difficult. While our Aristotelian logic leads us to believe that we're separate from the world, we are enmeshed in a network of interdependent relationships. Because what we do affects others and what they do affects us, actions don't always produce the results we expect them to, as we saw with price-cutting strategies in the automobile industry. The cognitive paradigm captures these relationships, and the effects we get when we attempt any kind of change are not unlike what happened when we first used the insecticide DDT. Not only did the insects die, but so did the birds that ate the insects, the predators that ate the birds, and so on through the food chain until the DDT started to poison us. There were unintended consequences.

Systems scientist Jamshid Gharajedaghi believes that "the actions intended to produce a desired outcome may, in fact, generate opposite results." As an example, he points to the war on drugs. The U.S. government has spent billions of dollars to fight drug use, but the result has been the unintended consequence of creating a huge criminal enterprise to supply drugs. The harder it is to bring the drugs into the country, the higher their cost, the greater the profitability, and the more attractive is the business to criminal elements. This powerful industry now thrives on the fact that the drugs are illegal, and of course, does everything it can to create and supply demand.

Relationship effects are, as we've seen, at work in the use of reward and punishment. Increasing the motivator of extrinsic reward can decrease intrinsic motivation, and punishment can end up reinforcing the behavior we're trying to extinguish. Because the relationship effects are obscured by our Aristotelian logic, we may not even recognize that our actions have a result that is the opposite of what we intend. Instead, like Porter Goss at the CIA, perhaps we'll simply blame the culture.

THE ILLOGIC OF CHANGE

A farmer is particularly proud of his mule and boasts about its wonderful qualities frequently. One day he's talking to his neighbor and going on and on about how terrific this mule is. It's smart as a whip, he claims, works tirelessly, and will do whatever you ask it to. This last claim is finally too much for the neighbor.

"How can you brag that your mule will do whatever you ask?" he demands. "Mules are stubborn, and I've never met one even half as obedient as you claim yours is."

The farmer is unfazed by this challenge, and responds that his claim is indeed the truth. But the neighbor is unwilling to accept what he's sure is an exaggeration, and demands, "Show me!"

So they go out to the barn, and there in the back is the mule in a stall. They walk toward the stall, and just as they get there, the farmer bends down, picks up a two-by-four, and smacks the mule over the head with it. Caught by surprise, the neighbor asks, "What are you doing? You said your mule was obedient and would do whatever you asked."

The farmer replied, "Yes, he will, but you've got to get his attention first."

Getting his attention first is exactly what Bateson had to do in order to get the dolphin to change from repeating old tricks to creating new ones. We are very much prisoners of our paradigms, attending to information that confirms them and cleverly reducing any that is dissonant. The only way to escape from the paradigm is to stop its automatic processing. Two-by-fours may work with mules, but a little more subtlety is necessary for human beings.

At a biological level, our paradigms are neural circuits that have become acclimated to a set of inputs, perceptions, or ideas. When the expected input occurs, there is a minimal level of neural firing in response. But if the input is different than expected, a host of new neurons fire. The two cerebral hemispheres appear to be quite specialized in this regard. Neuropsychologist Elkhonon Goldberg believes that "the right hemisphere is particularly adept at processing novel information and the left hemisphere is particularly adept at processing routinized, familiar information." What captures our attention and stops our automatic processing, according to neuroscience, is the new.

This startling revelation is, of course, not so startling. As journalists say, "Dog bites man is not news; man bites dog is news." If the conscious mind were an evolutionary adaptation to enable us to respond flexibly to the unexpected, as many cognitive scientists believe, it makes perfect sense that the new would grab our attention. In the absence of the new, our mental processes proceed automatically and unconsciously. One way of thinking about the new is that it is anything contrary to our expectations. It stops us and forces us to stand back and reflect.

Studies have shown that it does take longer for us to process novelty than the expected. We know from fMRIs that the unfamiliar creates heightened activity in the prefrontal cortex. Biologically, the unexpected is responsible for more firing in the area of the cortex thought to be the site of reflective consciousness, and in the right hemisphere of the brain that processes wholes. Psychologically, it pulls us back and directs our attention to the big picture. We become aware that something is amiss with the game we're playing—the paradigm we're using can't make sense out of what we've experienced. We're ready to entertain new ones.

But it's not just anything unexpected that will have the effect we want when we set out to change the way people think. It's got to be the kind of dissonance that can't be reduced by any of the other strategies we like to employ, such as ignoring, discounting, or rationalizing. Because the rules of the game we're playing are Aristotelian logic, we need reversals of logic, the counterintuitive, to get the result we want.

Social psychologists have found that dissonance of this kind stops our brain's automatic processing and forces us to question the validity of the paradigm we use to structure our experience. Rather than keeping our view intact by reducing the dissonance, we change the way we think, revising or scrapping our model of how the world works and the appropriate way to behave. Rather than change the input to the model, we change the model.

We undergo a "cognitive restructuring" to create a "new integration." Our existing worldview is swapped for one that incorporates the dissonance and resolves what had appeared as a conflict. This happens when the dissonance is at such a high level that it is "embedded in a large network of knowledge, beliefs, and feelings," when it's valued and embraced rather than feared and avoided, and when there is no other viable way to reduce it.

Perhaps the most common experience of this kind of dissonance is failure. When we are successful, there is no reason to reflect on what we're doing or change it. Success positively reinforces our current way of operating. But when we fail, our automatic processing is stopped. We are then driven to ask questions, to dig deeper, and perhaps to change how we think and behave. It is thought that the big step forward in how the early Greek scientists made sense of the world was their active search for information that would disconfirm their theories, in contrast to the ancient Egyptian tradition of blindly accepting received knowledge.

This is why we euphemistically refer to failures as "learning experiences." Rather than shunning them, they should be embraced and mined for any insights into how we can operate better. While our tendency may be to protect our fragile self-image, it is far more productive for us to challenge it. Instead of looking for instances of confirmation of our views, we should actively seek out disconfirmation. When someone offers to give us feedback, we really should think, "Oh great, I'm going to have an opportunity to improve."

USING THE COUNTERINTUITIVE
TO DRIVE CHANGE

Not only does the counterintuitive grab our attention and serve as a marker of change, the actions that make change happen will also frequently strike us as counterintuitive. For example, rather than continue to fight against drug use, a growing number of law enforcement professionals believe we should legalize it. Such a step would eliminate both the expense of fighting drugs (including housing abusers at great expense in prisons) and profits for the criminals. Without those profits, criminals would leave the industry, and the supply would decline. The money spent on enforcement could be reallocated to treatment and programs encouraging people to abstain. The fear, of course, is that the level of abuse would rise when drugs became legally available. The opposite, however, has been the case in European countries where use of safe, nonaddictive drugs, like marijuana, is not aggressively suppressed. The experience of Prohibition also supports legalization.

Similarly, a counterintuitive action is the best way to change the dynamic of an escalating conflict. In a disagreement in which both parties raise their voices louder and louder until they're shouting at one another, lowering one's voice not only has a calming effect, it eliminates any reason for the other party to yell. Its illogic subverts the logic of the other person, breaking the vicious cycle of feeling compelled to respond to the action of another with more of the same.

Psychotherapist Paul Watzlawick explained why the counterintuitive works so well by drawing a distinction between ". . . two different types of change: one that occurs within a given system which itself remains unchanged, and one whose occurrence changes the system itself." Actions within a system he called first-order changes, and they will appear eminently reasonable in a world that operates according to Newton's laws of motion. Force needs to be matched with force, violence with violence. These are the kind of changes that create the relationship effects we've seen at work in price-cutting strategies and the use of reward and punishment. It was first-order change that I used in my attempt to persuade the founder to apologize.

Watzlawick calls actions to change a system second-order changes, and they will appear to those within the system as exactly the opposite of what should be done. These are the counterintuitive actions like competing in Prisoners' Dilemma to get cooperation, legalizing drugs to cut down on their use, and attacking the French when logic says you should be in a defensive position. As Mahatma Gandhi showed, responding to violence with nonviolence ends the vicious cycle by invalidating the logic of escalation. The rules no longer hold, and the game is changed.

Watzlawick illustrates the difference between first- and second-order change with the example of a couple on a sailboat. To balance the boat, the man sits on one side and the woman sits on the other. The man moves a little further out, unbalancing the boat, and the woman is forced to move out to rebalance it. As she moves out, the man moves out to counter her movement and regain the balance. This competitive dance continues until both are hanging way off their respective sides of the boat. In other words, they are in a relationship in which their behavior is interdependent. Each move out forces a counterbalancing move out on the part of the other. This is first-order change.

Their sailing trip could be a lot more comfortable if they were sitting further in, more securely inside the boat. The solution is for one of them to do exactly the opposite of what they have been doing to maintain the balance, and paradoxically it will initially destroy the balance rather than improve it. One of them just has to move in, forcing the other to move in as well. Inside the boat, this would be counterintuitive. From outside the boat, where one can see the big picture, it is clearly the only solution. This is second-order change.

Watzlawick demonstrates the power of second-order change in his treatment of a young couple burdened with overly attentive parents. When the parents come to visit, the mother cleans, and the father does all the household repairs, regardless of the couple's protestations. The parents also insist on paying for groceries, restaurant bills, and any other expenses that come up during their visit. The couple is frustrated by this overdose of parenting and would like it to end. They have already tried the logical solution. They vigorously cleaned the house and made any needed repairs before the parents' visit. During the visit, they fought to pick up restaurant checks and to cover the cost of groceries.

Demonstrating that they did not need their parents' help was to no avail. Apparently, the parents envisioned the game as one of positive escalation. They must have thought that the more they did for the couple, the more the couple did for themselves. There was no reason to change their behavior because it obviously was working. The house was clean and in good repair, and the couple was working to keep it that way. So Watzlawick's advice to the couple was to do exactly the opposite. Rather than demonstrate their independence, they needed to demonstrate their dependence.

Following his advice, they made sure that the house was particularly dirty and in need of repairs the next time the parents came to visit, and they eagerly let the parents pay for any and all expenses. As a result, the parents decided to cut their visit short, explaining to the couple that they were becoming too dependent on the parents for help. When the couple was striving for independence and the house was well taken care of, the parents had, in their view, been good parents by helping the children, and so their behavior was reinforced. But when they saw the couple becoming more dependent on them, they recognized that their behavior was not producing the results they wanted, and good parenting had to be redefined as letting the "overly dependent" children fend for themselves.

The way to come up with the appropriate counterintuitive action, according to Watzlawick, is to change the "conceptual and/or emotional setting or viewpoint." Changing the paradigm we use to make sense of a situation will highlight the action we need to take. In the physical world of Newton's laws, force needs to be matched with force. In the mental world of interdependent relationships, we should take the action we believe will cause the other person to behave the way we want them to. An easy way to change the conceptual setting is to set aside our point of view, and use our theory of mind to adopt the other person's point of view. When we do, we'll realize that the action required for change is usually the opposite of what we think it should be.

We've already seen how powerful the counterintuitive can be in strategy. At the battle of Agincourt, their unexpected attack transformed the weakness of the English into a strength. We've also seen how the less control we exert as managers, the more we get the behavior we need, and the less structure in our organizations, the better the performance. We've even seen that sometimes the best way to sell consulting services is to tell the prospective client that they don't want them. All of these actions fly in the face of our Aristotelian logic but make perfect sense in a mental world that operates through natural selection.

Unfortunately, we can't accept as a rule of thumb that we just do the opposite of what our reason would suggest. It's risky to tell someone aiming a gun at us to shoot, and responding to a competitor's price cut by raising ours isn't necessarily a viable strategy. But if we swap out the objective paradigm for the cognitive one, we'll get a view of the situation that will account for relationship effects. We can then determine what action to take to get the kind of response we want.

In the mental world, we don't find the direct connection between cause and effect that we do in the physical world, as the use of reward and punishment illustrates. So the best approach is to determine under what conditions the target of our change effort would behave the way we want, then take the counterintuitive action needed to create those conditions. In other words, determine what the rules of the game need to be and then do what it takes to invalidate the current game and establish a new one with the rules we want.

If we want people to start focusing on the work and not the reward, we can take a salary of only a dollar to dramatize our commitment to the company, as Lee Iacocca did when he took over as the head of a bankrupt Chrysler. If we want to break down the hierarchy and create more participative management, we can move our office from the fiftieth floor of our headquarters to the second, as John Reed did when named CEO of Citicorp. If we want to create a more informal, team-based approach to getting work done, we can show up at the office on our first casual Friday without our toupee, as one authoritarian manager at Bethlehem Steel did.

Because such actions are counterintuitive, they stop the automatic processing and signal that change has occurred, and because they're aimed at changing the way people think rather than eliciting a direct response, they avoid those self-defeating relationship effects. However, there is still a need for all actions to be consistent and send a unified message. The best way to ensure that is through a vehicle perfectly suited to change the way people think, the story.

CHANGING STORIES

As we've seen, using stories to change behavior is more effective than logical declarations. Because they don't proclaim truth, they don't create relationship effects or elicit attempts to refute them. They're the way our minds naturally work, so they're very accessible. Addressing both our intellect and our emotion, and the two hemispheres of the brain they reside in, they have a more profound effect than an argument. By calling our attention to relationships and environment, they prevent us from falling victim to the effects of first-order change. But the most powerful aspect of stories is their ability to fundamentally change how people think by pivoting on dissonance, a core attribute first noted by none other than Aristotle.

If we think back to stories we've experienced, our tendency is to view them as explanations. Starting with the state of affairs at the end, we recognize the series of events that caused it. The fall of Troy was caused by the abduction of Helen. The death of Hamlet was caused by his rash response to the murder of his father. The failure of People Express was caused by Don Burr's immature orbital frontal cortex. But that's not the way we experience stories in real time. We don't start at the end and look back. We start at the beginning and move forward.

When we experience stories in real time, they're about planning: having a goal with a sequence of actions to accomplish it. But a story about a plan would not hold much interest for us. It's when the plan doesn't work, when the implementation fails because something contrary to expectations occurs, that a story has its greatest value for us. Psychologist Jerome Bruner believes that "the impetus to narrative is expectation gone awry. . . ." Stories are, first and foremost, a way to deal with dissonance.

The overall plan of our strategist, Odysseus, is to sail home to Ithaca, but the action of the epic revolves around the series of obstacles he encounters. Aristotle called an obstacle of this kind a *peripeteia* and defined it as a change "from one state of things . . . to its opposite." Just as when the porpoise didn't receive the reward it expected for a trick it performed, the peripeteia alerts us to the fact that the world is not as we thought. So just like the porpoise, when we are immersed in the story, we search for a way to deal with it. As Bruner puts it, "The story concerns efforts to cope or come to terms with the breach and its consequences. And finally there is an outcome, some sort of resolution."

But unlike the porpoise, we experience the dissonance within the context of the story. We don't have to suffer a series of trials and errors. The resolution is given to us. Rather than it occurring randomly, the process of change can be managed. Like a counterintuitive action being selected so that it causes the game we want to be installed, the peripeteia can be selected to ensure the kind of resolution that is desired.

When we think of change this way, it becomes much easier to come up with those counterintuitive actions that Watzlawick believes are critical to second-order change. The beginning of the story is a given, for it's the current state. The end of the story is the future we desire. We have a clearly defined strategy for our organization and everything is in place for its implementation. The dissonant event, the peripeteia, is what it takes to stop the way people are thinking now and create the new way of thinking that will drive the behavior we need to achieve the future state.

It would be difficult to imagine a more boring story than one about a company that increases its return to shareholders or one about a firm on the verge of bankruptcy that cuts its expenses and returns to profitability. But all too often, this is the story that management tells. A story that's going to engage people needs to be a romance in which people accomplish great, meaningful feats. For Bethlehem Steel, the story was about people working together as a team, overcoming a history of arrogance and mistakes to save a great American icon. For Cambridge Technology Partners, the story was about David slaying the Goliath of the IT business with a slingshot of superior intelligence.

The test of the peripeteia is whether it gets us from the present to the future in a believable way. When we watch the movie in our mind's eye, we have to be convinced that it works and we can buy it. It's believable that a steel company under threat of bankruptcy would abandon the perks of management, particularly when it installs self-managed teams and moves to a new building, complete with a new sign and an opening ceremony. But it's less believable that an automobile company with a history of ineffective change initiatives, a lineup of uninspired cars, and an intact hierarchy is really going to change this time around.

That's the other great benefit of a story. It forces us to attend to every detail if it's to be believable. The setting, the characters, and the action all must be aligned. Nothing can be out of place, and there can be no mixed messages. An effective initiative that's going to change how people think is like theatre. Every scene must be perfectly crafted, every role precisely performed, and all of the action flawlessly executed.

DISSONANCE THAT CAN'T BE REDUCED

The discoveries of neuroscience make it clear that there is a much better way to think about business, a way that leads to more powerful strategies smoothly implemented through smart organizational designs and effective management. But these new ways of doing business only have value if they're put into practice, and that requires change. Unfortunately, the approaches to change our Aristotelian logic drives are doomed to fail. In the mental world we inhabit, cause and effect are not as directly linked as they are in the physical world. Reward and punishment all too often produce the opposite of what we intend, and reason is notoriously unconvincing to those that don't already agree with its conclusions.

The problem is that our minds have evolved to maintain the

status quo. As a species, we are quite good at reducing any dissonance that threatens our view of the world, including the kind that might motivate us to change. But paradoxically, it's this same ability to reduce dissonance that makes it possible for us to change. When the dissonance is at a high level, when it's counterintuitive, and when it's of the kind that can't be easily reduced any other way, it can drive a paradigm shift that will change both how we think and how we behave.

This kind of dissonance renders the logical rules of the game invalid. We are then prompted to recognize that there is a different game with different rules. When change is well managed, the new game drives precisely the kind of thinking and behaving that our change initiative targets. While, in certain cases, just doing the opposite of what's expected will create the dissonance we need, more often than not, it's better if we start with the kind of thinking we want and create the dissonance that will lead to it.

Working through a story is the easiest way to do this. Stories pivot on the peripeteia that changes how we think, and as we've seen, stories affect us in very profound ways. To create a story to manage organizational change, we specify where we are and where we need to be, and we look for the kind of event or marker that is both believable and will lead us from the one to the other. But to really be effective, the story should address our higher aspirations and be presented with the same passion and attention to detail as great theatre. It is the role of the leader to make sure that happens.

EIGHT

LEADING IDEAS

One of the more curious findings of neuroscience is that I don't exist. I do have a social security number, a place of work, and a home address, so in the eyes of the government, my professional colleagues, and my family, there is indeed a Charles Jacobs. But my sense of who "I" am, the identity I've honed for a lifetime and that occupies me from morning to night, is only an illusion. This isn't just my issue—your "I" is an illusion as well.

But as sure as I'm sitting here, I know that I exist. I can look down and see myself as I type on my laptop, my arms reaching out and my hands over the keyboard. I can distinctly remember getting up this morning, going for a run, and eating my breakfast. When I turn to look at the table next to my chair, I can see a picture of myself with my family when we were on vacation last year. If I needed any more evidence, I'm quite aware that I'm thinking about all of this, and according to René Descartes's dictum *Cogito ergo sum,* that's proof enough that I exist.

The problem is that all of this evidence runs smack up against the results of a simple experiment that would seem to prove that I don't exist. When two images are flashed on a screen in succession a short distance apart, it appears that a single image is moving from the location of the first to the location of the second. This psychological effect is known as the phi phenomenon, and we're quite familiar with it because it's how movies work. Although a film is just a succession of still images, we infer movement from seeing one after another and experience the action as seamless.

If we introduce color into a demonstration of the phi phenomenon, though, something very odd happens. When a red dot is lit for a fraction of a second and then, after a brief interval, a green dot just a short distance away is also lit for a fraction of a second, the red dot appears to move toward the location of the green dot, just as in the black and white version. But then about midway, its color miraculously changes from red to green.

We know that the dot isn't really changing color, that it's just an illusion created by the subsequent lighting of the green dot. But we see the dot change color *before* the green dot is lit. This is impossible unless we can foretell the future and know that the green dot will be lit. Even if this were the case, how would we explain what happened to the original red dot when we saw it turning green?

The results of this experiment fly in the face of common sense. We know we can't foretell the future, so how do we explain the dot changing color? The answer offered by neuroscience is to accept that there is no "I" that exists over time. There's no connection between our perception of the red dot and our perception of the green dot, because the "I" that thinks there is and perceives the change in color is just a figment of our imagination.

Our common sense holds that there is an "I" that perceives the world around us and controls our thoughts and actions. It is often envisioned as a little man or woman who resides in our head, a homunculus who sits back observing and controlling our life. When our attention is directed elsewhere, it is the homunculus who does the directing. Most of us also feel as if there is a homunculus existing in the heads of those we interact with.

But, of course, there's no homunculus in our heads or anyone else's. Our skulls are chock-full of brain cells, and there's no room for a little person. Setting aside this folk image, there's also no part of the brain that corresponds to a screening room or control center. Even if we accepted the idea of an "I" that directs our attention and controls our actions, despite the phi phenomenon, we'd still be faced with the question of who or what directs it.

According to neuroscience, our perceptions of the world exist as the firing of nerve cells in local networks distributed throughout various areas of the brain. We become conscious of any given one when our attention is drawn to it and it becomes part of a larger network linking more areas of the brain. There can be a number of such perceptions existing simultaneously, and Daniel Dennett suggests that we think of these as "multiple drafts," different ways of making sense of our experience.

Depending on whatever else is going on in our minds at the time, one draft or another will be favored because it's a better fit. Although each is as discrete as the individual frame of a movie, our experience of them over time yields "something rather like a narrative stream or sequence." In the case of the phi phenomenon, the draft of the moving red dot is replaced by the draft of the moving green dot, and we see the dot appear to change color. In the case of "I," the succession of drafts creates the illusion of an identity existing through time in the same way that the succession of still images creates a movie.

The implications of the multiple-drafts theory cause many people to violently object to it. If there is no "I" existing over time, there need be no reason to assume personal responsibility for one's actions. A clever lawyer could mount a defense claiming that the defendant standing in front of the court is a person different from the one who committed the crime. We'd have to accept that the spouse sitting across from us at dinner is not the same person as the one we married. In fact, the one who ate the entrée is different from the one eating dessert. Even more disconcerting is the fact that the "you" who read the previous page is a different "you" than is read-ing this one. While common sense tells us that this is ridiculous, we must remember that common sense is, according to neuroscience, also just one of the multiple drafts created by the firing of a distrib-uted neural network.

It doesn't cost us much to hold on to the illusion that there is an "I" and to continue to believe that the spouse we greet at night is the same one we said good-bye to in the morning. But we can no longer trust that either our view or theirs is an objective record of what hap-pens or that we have the ability to control our thoughts or events in the world the way we thought we did. A world that is created anew every moment requires very different ways of thinking and behav-ing than the stable and enduring one we thought we inhabited.

The phi phenomenon raises a fundamental question about lead-ership: if there is no "I," just who or what does the leading? The answer neuroscience gives us challenges our conventional view of a leader as one that is in charge. Rather than view leaders as dominant alphas, it makes more sense to see them operating like Socrates. In place of forcefulness, they need an understanding of the minds of those they set out to lead and the aspirations those minds create. As in the case of management, organization, and strategy, histori-cal models help us create a profile of what it takes to be an effective leader in business. But we also have the benefit of good hard data about which leadership practices produce the best results.

LEADING BILLIARD BALLS

At the beginning of the movie *Patton*, the biopic of the famous World War II general, George C. Scott walks out on a stage with a gigantic American flag as a backdrop to address his troops. He's dressed impeccably in a uniform of his own design, with jodhpurs tucked into riding boots, a waistcoat covered with medals and accented with a blue sash, a steel combat helmet, and an ivory-handled pistol. Planting himself firmly, he begins his speech with that raspy trademark voice at a volume that makes it clear he's in command.

He starts out by telling his men "no bastard ever won a war by dying for his country," but by making "the other poor dumb bastard die for his." Patton was a student of history with a belief in his own reincarnation, and he had learned the lessons of Odysseus well. With these inspirational words setting the tone, he goes on to clarify his expectations. "I don't want to receive any messages from the front that we are holding our position," he orders. "We're not going to hold on to anything. . . . We're going to advance constantly and go through the enemy like crap through a goose." Patton had also learned the value of a well-turned metaphor.

He follows up this image with another one of cutting out "the enemy's guts and using them to grease the treads of our tanks." To address any concerns the men might have about their courage, he tells them that they'll know what to do when they stick their hand in "a pile of goo" that used to be their best friend's face. Such frightening and graphic images suggest that in Patton's leadership model, fear is a powerful motivator.

When we think of leaders, we often get an image like the one Scott conveys of Patton. The courage and raw power he projects are similar to what made Achilles such an attractive hero to the Greeks. We view him as strong, dominating, and courageous, without any second thoughts or hesitation. We can see him charging headlong into battle at the front of his troops, but we certainly can't imagine him disguised as a beggar and allowing insults to be heaped on him by his wife's suitors, like Odysseus.

There is research substantiating that this kind of authoritarian leadership does work when there is a crisis and people are accustomed to being given direct orders. Besides, Patton had demonstrated success in battle, and all soldiers would prefer a glorious victory over defeat and death. But everything we've learned about the mind and relationship effects would lead us to predict that Patton's approach would ultimately backfire, and it did. All of Patton's great accomplishments in battle were quickly forgotten when he attempted to motivate a shell-shocked soldier to return to battle by slapping him repeatedly in the face. Shortly after, the general died in disgrace.

Patton's model of leadership has had an enormous effect on the business world. For most of the last half of the twentieth century, the men, and they were mostly men, running our large corporations had learned about leadership in the military during the Second World War. Orders, the use of force, and intimidation became their preferred tools, and their necessity was justified by the aggression and passivity created by their use. When times change, the organizations and cultures that shape our behavior don't necessarily change at the same rate. The objective paradigm and the leadership it gives rise to are still firmly entrenched.

We've seen Patton's style of leadership in the founder of the software company haranguing his managers, in the president of the steel company seeing participative management as a waste of time and money, and in Thumper barging into people's offices. It's become legend in Donald Trump's "you're fired" and in the antics of the "Queen of Mean," Leona Helmsley.

I've run into it repeatedly throughout my career in ways that border on the comic. I've witnessed the CEO of a health-care company demand at an executive meeting that the COO fix the leak in his private toilet because he was in charge of operations. I watched the president of a household goods manufacturer throw his glasses at his vice president of manufacturing and, when asked why he did it, answer that he had nothing heavier to throw. When my first consulting firm was acquired, my new boss told me I acted like I had a burr under my saddle, as if I were a pack animal, and asked the CEO in my presence what he could "force" me to do.

Although there is something that we can't help but find attractive about Patton and wish to emulate, when it comes right down to it, his leadership is simply not effective. While fear and veiled threats will get compliance in the short term, we know that they stimulate aggression. We do find strong leaders comforting, particularly in times of crisis, but the relationship effect produces lower self-confidence and difficulty deciding what to do when there's no one shouting orders. Besides, slaps in the face have never motivated anyone to do anything other than slap back.

The deeper problem is that Patton's leadership model doesn't fit the world of thinking beings. In the physical world, there is an agent for every action. Somebody has to use the cue to impart force to the billiard ball. But as the phi phenomenon demonstrates, that's not the way the mind works. Our thoughts and behavior aren't controlled by us or by anybody else. They are driven by the narrative draft that fits best with the mental environment. Leadership isn't about forcing people to do our bidding, but about telling a story so that they want to do what we need.

WHAT LEADERS NEED TO KNOW

Weighing in at close to five pounds, with twelve hundred pages of double-columned small print, and subtitled, *Theory, Research &*

Managerial Applications, Bernard Bass and Ralph Stogdill's *Handbook of Leadership* is not the kind of book one reads just to pass the time. In fact, it's not the kind of book that many would read at all. It's a compilation of thousands of studies on leadership, presented one after another after another. Few in the business world bother with it, and that's a shame, for this book is a treasure.

There aren't any hot new models, five-step processes guaranteed to produce dramatic improvements, or anecdotes extolling companies that were successful because they did A, B, and C. But there are well-documented descriptions of carefully controlled studies of every conceivable approach to leadership, along with the results each produces. It's full of just the kind of hard data managers love, and all of it is directed at making them more successful.

While the experience of reading it is just what you would expect from its appearance, every so often you come across a finding that just stops you dead in your tracks. There's the study that reviewed pay-for-performance programs, which are a fixture of most corporations, and found no linkage between pay and performance. There's another one that found reward and punishment are actually effective, as long as the work is "repetitive, boring, and tedious." Then there's the one showing that the effect of a reward depends not on what it is, but on the employee's perception of the manager's reasons for giving it.

There are also a wealth of studies on authoritarian and democratic leadership, directive and participative decision making, and the results of focusing attention on people versus production. We learn which kind of leadership works best with intellectually challenging jobs and with mindless ones, with skilled employees and unskilled ones, and with managers who have knowledge of the work and ones who don't. We find that some forms of leadership improve employee satisfaction, others increase performance, and still others improve teamwork. There are even studies on what kind of leadership works better for the long term or for the short term.

The problem with the handbook is that there is so much information in such detail that readers don't walk away with any better understanding of what kind of leadership they should embrace. There are just too many interdependent variables to consider and too many different kinds of leadership to choose from. Stogdill himself claimed that there were as many different definitions of leadership as there were people defining it.

Determining what works best in a given situation is even more difficult because leaders aren't very good at recognizing what kind of approach they're using. According to a study of 360-degree feedback programs referenced in the handbook, what leaders think they're doing is not the same as what their employees think. Managers are consistently rated lower on key dimensions of leadership by their employees than they rate themselves, especially when it comes to being participative.

But there's one message that comes through loud and clear in the book, and it's that transactional leaders are less effective than those who hold out the promise of transformation. *Transactional* leadership, as the name suggests, is a simple exchange. Most commonly, it's work from the employee for money from the leader, but it can include other kinds of exchanges, such as loyalty for job security, friendship for consideration, and commitment for opportunities to develop. This kind of leadership is what defines most managerial relationships.

Transformational leadership is very different. It is not about an equitable exchange, but about the opportunity for employees to become fundamentally changed if they sign on to follow the leader. What changes, of course, is the way the follower views the world and thinks and acts as a result. This kind of leadership is often seen as charismatic or inspirational, and it offers the prospect of employees realizing a more profound purpose in their work. The relationship with a transformational leader is more exciting, and followers are more engaged.

It was the political scientist James McGregor Burns who first used the terms "transactional" and "transformational." In his 1978 classic, *Leadership,* he offered the likes of Winston Churchill and Franklin Roosevelt as examples of transformational leaders. Both men came to power during a time of crisis and enabled their followers to triumph over adversity so severe that they'd never seen the like before. While both called on people to make great sacrifices, they held out an attractive vision of the future that would be realized as a result. People were asked to change, and when they did, they achieved more than they thought possible.

While we might like to think of ourselves as a Churchill, most of us in the business world are transactional leaders, and the odds are that we're managing an exchange with our people based implicitly on the use of reward and punishment. Because most managers are uncomfortable with punishment, they shy away from it, leaving them with only rewards at their disposal. Other than the limitations we've already noted, the problem with rewards is that they can only reinforce current behavior. There is no way for a transactional leader to drive the kind of fundamental change we refer to as transformation.

Given the limitations of reward and punishment and the way big ideas work on the mind, it should come as no surprise that transformational leaders consistently outperform transactional ones. This is true whether we're looking for a quantum leap or just incremental improvement, for transformational leadership has been demonstrated to increase performance even when just used to supplement transactional leadership. We may not be facing anything comparable to the Battle of Britain, but we should still aspire to be transformational leaders simply because it's more profitable. Besides, it's a much greater challenge for the leader and a lot more fun for the followers.

A PORTRAIT OF A
TRANSFORMATIONAL LEADER

It's the beginning of what is shaping up to be the greatest challenge you and your people are likely to ever face. You've bet your career, and right now the odds aren't looking all that great. Even though everybody knows that you're way overmatched, you've tried to put the best face on it you possibly can. Then just at the moment when you need all the support you can get, your top guy starts to grumble about needing more resources. It's the last thing you need to hear, and certainly you can be excused for giving free rein to your anger.

But that is not how Henry V chose to respond at the battle of Agincourt, at least according to Shakespeare. When Westmoreland, his cousin and one of the captains of the English troops, wished for more troops from England, Henry's response was to give what has come to be seen as perhaps the greatest transformational leadership speech ever, inspiring the likes of Winston Churchill and John F. Kennedy. Even though Shakespeare's version is "just a story," it is perfectly in line with what the research tells us a leader needs to do to be effective. It's just a bit more accessible than wading through Bass and Stogdill's abstracts, and as stories do, it addresses the feelings as well as the intellect.

While most of us would probably be tempted to answer Westmoreland with a sharp rebuke, the young king didn't see his captain's remark as a problem, but as an opportunity to assuage the doubts probably all of his men shared. Henry sees the small number of troops as an opportunity and not a problem. He tells his captain and his troops that they don't want any more men. If they have more and lose, there will just be more men who die. If they have more men and win, they'll just have to share the glory.

Four centuries before scientific research had established the key dimensions of transformational leadership, Shakespeare gives us a perfect example in the character of Henry V. Methodically, the king goes on to address every issue needed to inspire his troops. Though he is the supreme commander, he refuses to order his men into battle against their will, and offers them money and transport if they decide not to fight. Of course, there's nothing wrong with stacking the deck in favor of the decision he wants with a statement like, "We would not die in that man's company / That fears his fellowship to die with us."

Now that Henry has their attention, he gives them not one, but two visions of the future they're fighting for. "From this day to the ending of the world / But we in it shall be remembered," he tells his men, holding out the promise of immortality. This is certainly inspirational and raises the stakes to a grand level, but most of us would prefer a payoff that we don't have to die to get. So he paints a picture, with just enough detail, of a holiday they'll celebrate in the future, sharing a mug of ale with their friends and showing off the scars from the wounds they received at Agincourt. Without antiseptics, the greatest fear next to death would be a wound, for it would almost certainly prove fatal. But just as he did with the number of troops, Henry shifts how his men think about the prospect of being wounded.

But Henry's not done yet. Given the potential for relationship effects, Henry cannot be on a pedestal. In the most frequently quoted lines of the speech, he demolishes the hierarchy: "We few, we happy few, we band of brothers. / For he today that sheds his blood with me / Shall be my brother." But enticing as the promise of brotherhood is, Henry must bring his men back to focus on the present moment if he is to get the best performance from them possible.

So he returns to those men home in England whom Westmoreland had wished for. They are not the fortunate ones, Henry proclaims, for they "Shall think themselves accursed they were not here." We're back where we started, but with a critical difference. We have experienced Aristotle's peripeteia, and the battle and the men's place in it are now seen as the opposite of what they were before. The world is transformed and the men are transformed.

What a contrast with Patton's speech before his men went into battle! There's no demand to constantly advance, emphasized with a graphic image. Instead, it's up to Henry's men whether they'll fight or not. In place of "a pile of goo," a wound is likened to a badge of honor. Nor are there any "dumb bastards." The men are brothers to one another and to their king. While Henry holds out the promise of transformation, all Patton offers to inspire his men is the statement that "all real Americans like the sting of battle."

Henry's greater effectiveness comes from his ability to empathize with his men, create a romantic counternarrative, and present it in a way compelling enough to transform their view of the world. At the same time, he is as humble as Socrates, preferring the place of a brother to his spot on the pedestal, and like Socrates, Shakespeare's Henry knew the world he inhabited was mental. His final words to his troops as they go off to battle are, "All things are ready, if our minds be so."

Of course, it's neither fair nor scientific to use fictional portrayals to argue for the superiority of one leadership approach over another. But Henry's speech does illustrate everything we've noted effective managers do, and what Bass and Stogdill tell us transformational leaders do. Leaders who inspire outperform any other kind, not just on the battlefield, but in business as well. Besides, stories are just paradigms, and Henry's gives us an apt model for business leadership.

TRANSFORMATIONAL LEADERSHIP IN BUSINESS

It's doubtful that any of us in business will find ourselves facing death and the defeat of our country like Henry. Most of us would also look ridiculous in a doublet and tights, spouting Shakespearean verse, and promising immortality to our followers. But given the limitations of transactional leadership and the proven capacity of transformational leaders to improve both the performance of the business and the satisfaction of the employees, it makes sense for us to figure out how to carry over to the business world what Henry does in this speech. We can boil it down to five key actions.

SHIFT THE PARADIGM. Given the mind's ability to reduce cognitive dissonance and configure our experience of the world so that it agrees with our beliefs, expressing anger won't work to change people, nor will reason. What will work is to transform how people think about the world, particularly when times are tough and a turnaround is needed. A failing business can be seen as an opportunity to break with the past and redesign the business the way you want it to be. Or you may want to present turning around the business as the challenge of a lifetime, one that if your people can pull off, will give them the confidence to do just about anything. If there just doesn't seem to be any way to put a better face on things, you can simply acknowledge the situation and stress the fact that there is no option but to deal with it the best way they can.

MAKE IT PARTICIPATIVE. Bass and Stogdill present numerous studies demonstrating that participation improves both performance and employee satisfaction. There are caveats on the use of participation, as when employees are new to their jobs and lack the skills and knowledge to make informed decisions. But studies of 360-degree feedback show that our employees rate us as less participative than we rate ourselves, so odds are we won't be participative enough. We can probably err in the direction of too much participation without much risk.

CONVEY AN ASPIRATIONAL VISION OF THE FUTURE. As we saw in Henry's speech, the vision of the future should take people beyond themselves, but it should also have a more immediate experiential appeal. In business, all too often, the vision is neither aspirational nor experiential enough. When the CEO of a telecom company announced to his four hundred top managers that his vision of the future was "an increase in shareholder value," his audience, not owning nearly as many shares as he did, responded with a collective yawn. One manager later facetiously remarked to me that if the CEO had been alive, he never would have given such a speech.

The vision also needs to be credible, not too much of a stretch. No one is going to buy that a fast-food restaurant is going to make the world a better place, but employees will buy into a vision of having the most satisfied customers of any outlet in the industry. The prospect of creating a new product, service, or new way of doing business can be very inspirational. "Changing the way the world thinks" worked for the employees of Digital, while the potential to save jobs and pensions was more than enough for people at Bethlehem. For most of us, it's just doing what we do as well as we can and striving to be the best, whether we're designing a chip, making steel, or serving fast food to hungry customers.

Just as we saw with stories, the more experiential the vision is, the more powerful it will be, so the achievement of the vision should be made as tangible as possible. This can be done by creating a picture of what it will be like when the vision is realized. Maybe it's the scene in the office the day your customer satisfaction ratings are the top in the industry, or maybe it's the setting of the celebratory dinner when you sign that new customer.

TELL THE STORY. As we've seen, people are going to embrace a story to make sense of their experience. As the phi phenomenon suggests, there is no "I" that creates this story. Instead, our attention is drawn to any one of the stories that exist in our neural network, based on its fit and how appealing it is. A transformational leader offers a counternarrative that is a more attractive version of events than the story people are currently telling themselves. Perhaps Westmoreland's story was about the defeat of the English army while the desperately needed troops lounged at home in bed. Henry's counternarrative was about a band of brothers performing heroic feats.

All too often, the story employees tell is about just getting by, about incompetent and venal management, or about destructive corporate politics that make it not even worth trying. The counternarrative is easy to come up with. People join together, change the way they work, and accomplish great deeds. As Henry's speech demonstrates, this story can be told with a few key details that evoke scenes, like the scars and the mug of ale. Its power is in the fact that it addresses more than just the intellect and is not a logical argument that has to withstand scrutiny. It would be easy to demolish Henry's case for having fewer men.

We shouldn't underestimate the power of the story. Given that we create the world, rather than record it, and that ideas in high-level neural networks create thoughts and behavior in line with them, even one idea can cause far-reaching changes in the way the mind works and transform both us and the world. During the last half century, social psychologists have repeatedly proven the power of ideas to change minds and behavior.

One experiment demonstrated an effect similar to that of Henry's explanation of why more men weren't desirable. A college class was informed that they would have a guest lecturer. Half of the students were given a description of the lecturer that included adjectives like "cold," "industrious," and "critical." The other half's description was exactly the same, except the adjective "cold" was replaced with "warm." After the lecture, the students rated the professor. Those who were told he was warm gave him significantly higher ratings than those who were told he was cold. During the class itself, the "warm" group participated more and asked more questions. The differing evaluations were based on the same observable behavior.

The students were primed with an idea, just as a leader's story primes the minds of the followers, but the effect isn't limited to how people perceive a situation. In a psychological effect known as the self-fulfilling prophecy, an idea really does objectively alter the world. A change in perception affects behavior in a way that causes the new perception to become true.

Researchers administered an IQ test to students at an elementary school. Afterward, their teachers were told that some of the students were "bloomers," and would show significant IQ growth in the coming year. In reality, the students were average, but when tested again at the end of the year, they showed a marked increase in IQ scores. The teachers behaved differently toward the "bloomers," and that caused them to develop in line with the teachers' expectations.

These experiments teach us how to control the creation of another's reality. If we prime our family with the belief that dinner is going to be wonderful, on average they will tend to experience it that way. If we tell the cook that he or she is wonderful, he or she just might perform at a higher level. If we really believe that someone is wonderful, we might unconsciously do things that will make the person wonderful. In one landmark study in the business world, priming was used to dramatically increase the performance of salespeople. With just one idea, we can not only change how people think and act, we can improve the quality of their thoughts and actions. The most powerful way to convey that idea is through a story.

CREATE FOCUS AND URGENCY. Henry had no need to create any more urgency or to focus his troops. The presence of the vastly larger French army did it for him. In a corporation, though, it's easy for people to become complacent, so it's important for the leader to let the followers feel the competitive pressure, but not to the extent that it makes them insecure. The leader also must make sure that people stay focused on what's critical for success. If the key to winning is customer satisfaction, selling, or expense control, it should be a critical part of the leader's story, and it should be repeated often enough to cause structural changes in the neural networks that drive the necessary thinking and behaving.

THE CHARACTER OF THE LEADER

The distinction between transactional and transformational leaders was translated into terms more familiar to the business world by Abraham Zaleznik in a seminal article in the *Harvard Business Review* entitled "Managers and Leaders: Are They Different?"

He saw managers as the direct heirs of Frederick Taylor, primarily interested in incremental improvements. In contrast, he saw leaders as creative, concerned with ideas, and viewing themselves as agents of change. From his perspective, much of their power comes from having been through a traumatic experience and emerging from it stronger than they were before. Since they are effectively "twice born," they are highly empathetic and able to help others work through the discomfort of change.

There might just be something to this notion of a twice-born leader. None of us would question the strength, courage, or effectiveness of John F. Kennedy, Winston Churchill, or Franklin Roosevelt. We look back at these three as strong, charismatic men, but there were questions about the character of all three earlier in their lives. Churchill had a penchant for self-promotion even when it required a bit of fabrication, Roosevelt was a wealthy playboy, and Kennedy's main asset seemed to be a father willing to buy elections when necessary. But each encountered failure or trauma, and as Zaleznik suggested, drew strength from it.

The character and heroics that Churchill displayed during the Second World War were preceded by the eight years he spent on the sidelines after his leadership was rejected by the British people. Roosevelt's transformation of the American economy and psyche during the Great Depression followed his devastating bout with polio. Kennedy's brilliant leadership during the Cuban missile crisis came after the dismal failure of the invasion of the Bay of Pigs that ended with the United States abandoning the invading Cuban troops. All three of these men were first humbled by personal failure, and only then demonstrated the empathy that made them so successful as leaders.

Henry, too, had encountered hard times in his life, and he was well aware of his own fallibility. This enabled him to accept people for who they were and not think he could force them to be something else. The kind of character needed to be a transformational leader seems to start with an acceptance of one's own fallibility. By the same token, the software company founder's punishing criticism of others is right in line with his inability to acknowledge his own mistakes. If we're Don Burr, we don't even think for a minute that our pursuit of an expensive, unionized airline could be a mistake, nor do we admit it even after it bankrupts our company.

Which brings us back to the phi phenomenon. We can see how easy it is to get people to embrace a counternarrative as their own when instead of an "I" creating stories, the mental environment selects out one of the many available. All the leader needs to do is to offer a story that is more attractive. But if there's no "I," what or who is it who creates the story and offers it? The clue to the solution of this puzzle is in how we experience failure, and it's the reason twice-born leaders are so effective.

When we experience dissonance, as the dolphin did, it stops our automatic processing and creates activity both in the prefrontal cortex and in the area of the right hemisphere of the brain responsible for the perception of wholes. Failure on a grand scale, which our leaders experienced, is just the kind of dissonance to cause this to happen. Effectively, our attention is drawn to the existence of more than one paradigm, or draft, as Dennett would call it. The self-monitoring of the prefrontal cortex would then learn that one paradigm could be a better fit than another.

The new mental environment, shaped by the failure, would select out the paradigm that was a better fit, and this paradigm in the form of a story would guide the thinking and behavior of the leader. The story communicated to the followers would be the same one the leader was telling himself. Without a story firmly in place, we'd be just like Don Burr, at the mercy of our nucleus accumbens.

In order for leaders to consistently think and act in line with the story they tell, they've got to really embed those neural networks by believing the story and telling it over and over. Perhaps the best way to think about character is that it's an unswerving belief in the story we tell.

Transformational leadership is about rewiring our minds and those of others by telling a more fitting story, so the only tool the leader has to effect change is communication. But we can't just hurl graphic metaphors in a loud voice and trust the Newtonian laws of motion to get the result we want. We need to focus on the *relationship* with the receiver, and we need to recognize that the relationship is a function of the *environment*. Patton's "crap through a goose," experientially moving as it is, probably wouldn't play very well in today's business world.

While our three twice-born leaders had styles very different from Patton's, they were all equally effective at communicating their story. Churchill's power was in his bulldog expression, bow tie, and steady voice intoning phrases like "the world may move forward into broad, sunlit uplands." For Roosevelt, it was the pince-nez glasses, the cigarette holder, and the calming voice telling us "there is nothing to fear but fear itself." Kennedy's youth, good looks, and tousled hair were all part of the package that convinced America to "ask not what your country can do for you, but what you can do for your country."

Each of these men had a unique style of leadership that was very much a function of his character and the situation he found himself in. What works during war won't necessarily work when there's peace, what is effective in one country might fail in another, and what succeeds in the political environment probably won't play well in a corporation. I've seen a painfully shy, soft-spoken PhD effectively energize his R & D group with a halting, almost inarticulate speech. It wasn't nearly as entertaining as Patton's but it fit the followers and the environment. I've also witnessed a high school dropout with a vocabulary limited to four-letter words and a mouth full of chewing tobacco fire up steelworkers. What both had in common is that their style of communication fit who they were and the needs of their followers. They believed the story they were telling, and so they were authentic.

While what one has to do to be a transformational leader is pretty straightforward, the need to communicate expressively can be a bit intimidating. However, there is consolation in what we've learned about how the mind works. Through both priming and the self-fulfilling prophecy, people become what we think they are, as we saw in the case of the guest lecturer and the children who were identified as bloomers. While we're not big fans of bosses, we do like leaders. In fact, we hold the expectation that our leaders will be charismatic. If they can just avoid doing anything offensive, that expectation will become a reality.

STORYTELLING

The findings of neuroscience have eliminated many of the tasks associated with the traditional approach to management. Given the failure of reward and punishment and other extrinsic ways of motivating behavior, managers have no choice but to consistently put the responsibility for performance back on their people. At the same time, there is an even greater need for the kind of leadership that changes how people think. In a mental world, it is ideas that shape behavior, and it is the transformational leader's job to package the right kind of ideas into a story and to effectively communicate it to the organization.

Essentially, the only thing leaders have at their disposal is communication, but the example of Henry V shows that it's really all they need. He doesn't shoot the messenger who voices doubts all of the others share but instead takes his concerns as an opportunity to understand the mind-set of the followers and change the way they think. He makes sure that it is the men's decision to fight, and he articulates a vision of the future to motivate them. Teamwork is stressed, and to guard against creating dependency, he steps down from his pedestal. When we apply this model to the business world, it becomes a template for what a transformational leader needs to do in a corporate environment.

While a George Patton comes across with the strength and courage we usually associate with leadership, we know from neuroscience that it won't have the effect we want. The kind of leadership that works is more humble and therefore more empathetic. We see it in the likes of Churchill, Roosevelt, and Kennedy. Perhaps because they knew what it meant to be human and fallible, these leaders, with very different styles, communicated ideas that took people beyond themselves to accomplish more than they ever thought possible. That's the kind of transformation organizations need and people long for.

NINE

ALL THINGS ARE READY

Tracing the flow of information through the brain with an *f*MRI leads to the rather surprising conclusion that we can't possibly have the direct knowledge of the physical world we think we do. All we can know is its representation in the brain as ideas, so the world we experience is mental, not physical. The chair you're sitting in, the book you're holding in your hands, and even your own body, are just creations of your mind. This is not an easy notion to get our heads around, but it is a scientific fact with far-reaching ramifications for how we think and act.

Rather than sharing the same world, we all inhabit a world that is uniquely our own. Our backgrounds, experience, genetic make up, culture, thoughts, and feelings all affect how we put together our versions of reality, and it's a good bet there will be wide variations among them. Men and women, adults and children, managers and employees, customers and suppliers, liberals and conservatives, Christians and Muslims, all will see the world differently. So will identical twins.

At some level, we accept this difference. We acknowledge that people see certain clothing styles as more attractive than others, believe some foods taste better than others, and evaluate some potential mates more favorably. We recognize a wide range of views about everything from the nature of God to whose sports team performs the best. But we tend to believe that these differences are relatively minor shadings and that we all have the same core experience. So we are surprised when our different versions of reality collide. We're amazed that other people thought O. J. Simpson was innocent (or guilty if we believed him to be innocent), that our spouses really thought our behavior was self-centered, and that our managers believed 5 percent was a suitable salary increase, given all that we'd achieved during the year.

Even though the world of ideas we inhabit operates differently than the world of physical objects, our minds trick us into thinking and acting as if it doesn't. So we tend to see other people as if they're physical objects like stones or trees, and we don't pay enough attention to how they make sense of the world. Believing they, too, are governed by Newton's laws of motion, it seems we can move them around like pieces of furniture. But because people don't like to be forced to do anything, our actions don't produce the results we expect. In fact, they often produce the opposite of what we expect.

Although our view of the world entails a unique way of thinking as well, our minds take the way we think as the only way there is. We assume the laws of logic govern how we think, and there's no provision for how our thinking might distort what we think about. But our minds don't work through syllogisms. Our ideas are arranged in hierarchical networks, and any idea can affect other ideas by changing the chemistry of the brain. Rather than obeying the laws of logic, our reasoning is a competition of ideas, with the best one selected out by the mental environment. Our decisions, no matter what we think to the contrary, are made as much by our emotions as our logic.

If this isn't enough to get our heads spinning, there's the person who supposedly directs all of this. On that matter too, we appear to be operating under an illusion. There is no part of the brain that corresponds to an "I," and the mind doesn't function as if there is one. Much of our reasoning takes place without our conscious knowledge of it, there is no central clearinghouse for our perceptions, and we lack a consistent identity. We can't even trust the fidelity of our perceptions, for the memories that enable us to recognize them change each time they're accessed.

It's as if we live in a world that is a figment of the imagination, but we can't even claim that it's *our* imagination. This world has no physical basis that we can know and no continuity from one moment to the next. It doesn't operate according to the laws we think it does, nor do we think the way we believe we do. Alice's Wonderland seems sane by comparison, but at least she knew something was a little wacky. We refuse to believe that the world is anything other than what we've always believed it to be. It's just the way the mind works.

AND THE GOOD NEWS IS . . .

Even if the "I" is just an illusion, it's a serviceable one. We live our lives, keep body and soul together, strive for deep meaning and purpose, and have moments of great joy. In fact, most of us have lived our entire lives under the illusion of an "I" and an objective, orderly world, and have never noticed anything amiss. That's one of the charms of our minds. They're quite good at reducing any uncomfortable dissonance between the way we believe things to be and the way they "really" are.

Besides, neuroscience doesn't just leave us adrift in this strange world. It offers us a way of thinking and a way of acting that are a better fit with the real nature of the world and so are more effective. It teaches us that our view of the world is biased and that we need to account for how it differs from everyone else's. It enables us to avoid those self-defeating practices that haunt us with their unintended consequences, and to make use of the relationship effects that create them. Like a self-help book, it promises the keys to greater success and more happiness, but with the added benefit of actually being based on scientific research.

Although our views of the world are subjective, our minds also come with a remarkable ability to empathize, which enables us to appreciate the versions of reality that others live. We are able to step into the shoes of people, and see the world as they do. Paired with our instinct for storytelling, empathy lets us identify with their story and anticipate how they will behave. We can then figure out how we need to act to get the response we want. It may not be as direct and immediate as the use of the carrot, stick, or logical argument, but it has the advantage of producing the results we intend.

The world we can know doesn't operate predictably according to Newton's three laws of motion, but Darwin's concept of natural selection does a pretty good job of capturing how it does work. Although it doesn't give me the certainty of predicting where a billiard ball will come to rest, I can anticipate what will be the results of the way I act in a relationship, and I can use that information to my benefit. I can't move ideas around the same way I thought I could, but I can shape the environment to select out the ideas I want. It may not be as simple as what I'm used to, but it works.

My Aristotelian logic may not be how the mind works or a suitable way to think about the world of human activities, but a Platonic dialectic is. I can play one idea off another to come up with a better, more comprehensive idea, and that idea will then select out other ideas and behaviors in harmony with it. Rather than force my argument on people who will simply turn it to their advantage, I can shape their thinking with ideas and use questions to guide them to reach the right conclusions on their own. It may take longer, but they'll be more committed to the result.

At first, the new tools neuroscience gives us may seem a little daunting to use. It does take more forethought and more time to formulate and implement a strategy to encourage someone to willingly do what we want. A billiard ball world is easier to understand and manipulate than one that is a network of interdependent relationships. But these tools work better because they fit the nature of the world we live in. Our ability to reduce cognitive dissonance may obscure the failure of actions driven by our common sense, but they still fail.

MANAGEMENT ACCORDING TO NEUROSCIENCE

Because we're not managing in a physical world but in a mental world, much of what is taken for granted as the right way to manage is actually the opposite of what we want to do. But to be more effective requires only a simple shift in perspective. Instead of seeing the world through the lens of Newtonian mechanics, we start seeing it as a process of natural selection. Rather than viewing people as inanimate objects, we recognize that they're thinking beings acting of their own volition. Because of the way the brain is organized, if we can just keep this perspective in mind, we'll know the right things to do.

In the Newtonian world, all action is through the application of

force. In the world governed by natural selection, any action elicits
a countervailing action, just as one person leaning out on a sailboat
requires the other person to lean out as well. Because of these relationship effects, direct actions don't create the results we want, so
we're better off making use of the forces that are already at play. The
management revolution is about no longer *forcing* people to do things
but *encouraging* them. Because behavior is driven by thinking, management according to neuroscience is about changing minds.

Competition is force against force in the Newtonian world, with
the strongest coming out on top. In the mental world, the key to competitive strategy is to leverage how the other side is already behaving
or influence them to behave the way we want them to. We use our
power of empathy to understand how they will respond to different
actions, then select the one that gets the response we want. We may
need to prime people to see things differently or make use of relationship effects.

When it comes to business strategy, competitive advantage is
established by creating an offering the customer wants and the competition can't duplicate. This requires understanding how the customers think, so you can make your offering appealing to them, and
understanding how the competition thinks, so you can configure
your offering in a way they aren't disposed to match. Sometimes the
best place to start is with how you think. Taking a counterintuitive
view can highlight ways of differentiating a product or service others would never think of.

The same basic principle is at work when implementing the strategy. Rather than forcing employees to do something, we want them
to do it willingly. For managers, this turns the world upside down.
They don't tell, they ask. They don't dispense rewards, punishment,
or feedback that can be construed as either. Instead, they work for
the employees, acknowledging the selfish gene, and making use of

their energy, desire for accomplishment, and need for compensation. They put the responsibility for performance on the employees and supply the information and support that enable employees to self-manage.

When it comes to organizing large numbers of people, we'll get better results if, rather than trying to thwart their natural inclinations, we just accept how people behave and make the most of it. People do want to become part of a group when it's kept small, when the advantages of collective effort are stressed, and when the competitive threat is clear. We can structure organizations as federations of small entrepreneurial businesses, the relationships between them managed through free-market dynamics. Profit is substituted for salary, and selfishness is aligned with the goal of collective effort.

But the ultimate solution may be to leverage minds. Human beings will always come together in support of causes they believe in, and such collective effort doesn't require cumbersome structures and control systems. Besides, no matter how much structure is in place, it is never enough to prescribe all behavior. The rest is covered by what we have come to call culture. As the collective story the group tells itself, culture drives the thinking that drives behavior.

Strategies that leverage the mind and don't use force, management that works for the employee and doesn't try to control the uncontrollable, and organizations that operate just the way natural selection does—all will lead to better performance with less stress. But all require change, and that has always been the sticking point for efforts aimed at improving business performance. While the mind is quite adept at reducing the dissonance that argues for change, even convincing us that we've changed when we haven't, it is through creating dissonance that we are able to transform people and organizations.

But it's got to be the right kind of dissonance. Bateson's dolphin changed the way it thought when it didn't receive the expected reward and realized the game had changed. Because the game humans play is structured by logic, the illogical is the kind of dissonance needed to change the way we think. Taking a salary of a dollar a year or refusing to wear the toupee you've worn every day for twenty years is the kind of counterintuitive marker needed to alert people that the world is no longer the same.

Stories can effect change without the frustration the dolphin was forced to suffer, because they offer a ready-made way to resolve the dissonance. It's the role of the transformational leader to create the story that identifies the kind of change needed and to present it in a way that is meaningful and moving. It should align the needs of the individual with those of the organization, so that people see the necessary changes as a way to meet their desire to be part of something bigger than themselves and realize their fullest potential. At the same time, it must be immediately appealing. Immortality might be attractive, but most of us would prefer a payoff that doesn't require our demise.

The story needs to be communicated powerfully in both words and deeds, and it needs to be as experiential as possible for people to relate to it. This requires some skill, and the best leaders are emotionally expressive. Even so, their style should fit who they are. The strongest are often the ones who come across as the most humble, for, given the potential for relationship effects, leaders must step down from their pedestals so that followers don't become overly dependent.

There is plenty of data that links this management approach to superior performance, and there's no lack of anecdotal evidence showing that today's cutting-edge companies are managed this way as well. As we've seen, it's all supported by the latest scientific research on how the mind works. But even beyond this validation and the simple fact that it creates a better environment for people to work in, this kind of management is aligned with our deepest values. It brings democracy to the workplace.

From its invention in ancient Greece to its American incarnation two millennia later, democracy has consistently created superior performance in all domains of human activity. The Golden Age of Greece followed right on the heels of the establishment of democracy and witnessed accomplishments in the sciences and arts never since equaled. Although under a bit of stress lately, the American democracy is the world's leading economic and cultural power. Is it democracy that's responsible? In a survey of civilization's greatest economic powers, economist David Landes answers affirmatively. The open-mindedness fostered by democracy creates the entrepreneurship that drives superior economic performance.

But there's always been another case made for democracy, a moral one. It is simply the right thing to do if you believe that all people are created equal. Because of this, an approach to management aligned with the latest discoveries of neuroscience speaks to something profound in all of us. It addresses both our need for individual freedom and our desire to join together with other people to accomplish more than we ever could by ourselves.

THERE'S MORE TO LIFE

It's not just business that benefits from the insights of neuroscience. We use the same mind to make sense of all of our experience and to determine the best way of acting. When we shift paradigms and factor in how the mind works, our reading of the different situations we find ourselves in becomes more accurate, and the actions we take as a result are more effective. We get better at dealing with the most intellectually demanding dimension of our lives—our relationships with other people.

In all aspects of our lives, we should take advantage of the evolutionary adaptation that gave us the ability to think strategically about our relationships. Although it may be a rather jaded way of looking at the world, it's best if we take the notion of the selfish gene to heart and assume that all people are out for themselves. We can then figure out what they want by calling upon the ability to empathize that our mirror neurons and theory of mind enable. The more information we take in about them, the better we'll be at imagining the story they're telling themselves.

Once we know what they're after, we can then formulate a strategy that presents doing what we want as a way for them to accomplish what they want. In most cases, the strategy we need to employ will be straightforward. As Socrates taught us, it's better to ask than tell, but as Henry showed us, we can phrase the question in a way that will get the response we want. We may also want to prime the mind up front. If we're trying to encourage an airline gate agent to get us a seat on a crowded flight, expressing our dissatisfaction with our treatment by the airline and demanding what we believe we deserve is probably not going to get us very far. But commiserating with the harried agents and asking for their help, while expressing admiration for the job they do under such pressure, just might.

But there are times when a bit more is called for, usually when you're trapped in a competitive dynamic and are the victim of relationship effects. When a police officer pulls you over for a traffic violation and comes across as a bit belligerent, arguing that you weren't speeding isn't going to get you very far because it just feeds the competition. Instead, showing the officer the deference he or she would like may turn the dynamic to your advantage, just as it did when I agreed with the bankers that I wasn't the one to do the job.

We should also accept that no one ever wins an argument.

Inevitably, reason is countered with reason, and emotion with emotion. The facts are irrelevant, because each side will just use them to construct their argument. Counterintuitively, though, if one side stops arguing and acknowledges that the other side's point of view is valid, it defuses the situation and reduces the level of emotion. Just like one person moving in on a sailboat, it encourages the other side to do the same. It then becomes more possible for each to hear what the other one is saying and perhaps find common ground.

Strategizing relationships makes perfect sense, but it's easier said than done. The demand for his priestess kicked Achilles' amygdala into high gear, and it made no difference to him that his behavior then became self-destructive. The only hope we have of avoiding a similar fate is to self-prime our minds. When Odysseus is tempted to kill his wife's maids, he steadies his mind by talking to himself, so that it selects out patience rather than violence. The key to success, as we learned from the sea snail, is repetition. If I entertain an idea enough, it will reinforce the neural network by causing more synapses to grow and lowering the threshold needed for firing.

In the same way, the more I think about the importance of strategizing relationships and the more I practice it, the more it will become a habit of mind. Just the act of reading this book has rewired your brain and established new neural networks. Continuing to think about the ideas that are in it will develop habits of mind that will make you more effective in both work and life. But as neuroscientists put it, you must "use it or lose it."

NOW

So what do you do now that you've finished this book? Even though the ideas have been seeded in your brain and are shaping the mental environment at this very moment, the business world is action-oriented. Somehow, just contemplating big ideas doesn't seem like enough. Ever since Frederick Taylor, there's much to be done and not enough time to do it in. So it's going to require a lot of fortitude and discipline, because you need to take time out to stop and think.

Our emotions may make better gambling decisions in card games, but they can also lead us to kill our bosses and jeopardize the causes we've been fighting for. We do inhabit a mental world, but our reasoning is a product of our experience in the physical world, and it doesn't take into account those counterintuitive relationship effects that come back and bite us. So it's best if we slow down a bit, think strategically about the situation we find ourselves in, and then decide what action to take.

Think about opting for indirect rather than direct action. It's so quick and so easy to tell people what to do or to tell them how badly they're doing it. It takes longer to come up with questions to help *them* decide what to do or realize that their performance isn't cutting it, but the questions produce a better result. Questions build commitment and overcome the resistance to being controlled. They enable us to gather information that we may have assumed we already knew. And because people would rather talk than listen, questions build goodwill.

Questions are also a great way to change a disadvantageous competitive dynamic. The next time someone is arguing strenuously for his or her point of view, rather than arguing back, try asking a question, and see how the emotional level drops. Then listen to the answer and repeat it back in your own words. All of a sudden, the other person no longer has to fight so hard for airtime, or stubbornly hang on to one position. The relationship effect may have your opponent asking *you* questions in return and actually hearing what you have to say.

Another thing to stop and think about is consciously using natural selection as a lens through which to view your experience. All of a sudden, you'll see things differently. You'll start to realize how much of what you do is a function of your relationships with others and how much of what they do is a function of their relationships with you. You'll see how much control you actually do have over other people, even though it may be indirect, and why an unreasonable action may be just what the situation requires.

Using natural selection as a lens will also alert you to how much we're a product of the environment and direct your attention to ways of shaping it to your advantage. It will then become easier to abandon force in favor of creating the conditions that will encourage people to do what you want them to do. Next time you're in a difficult relationship with someone at work, try taking that person out for lunch or a drink, and see how it changes the interaction.

Rather than vainly fighting against the way things are, sometimes it's best to just let it play out. If you interrupt people when they're talking, instead of listening to what you have to say, they'll just be waiting for an opportunity to interrupt you. But if you let them talk, eventually they'll run out of steam and be more willing to hear what you have to say. As I learned at the bank, the best sales calls are usually the ones in which the prospect does most of the talking.

You might also want to think about consciously making more use of stories, both to understand and to shape how people think and act. When we tap into the stories others are telling themselves, we gain a clearer understanding of who they are and why they do what they do. We become better able to predict how they will respond, so that we can generate the kind of actions that will get the response we want. Understanding our own story gives us a better sense of who we are and why we act the way we do, perhaps allowing us to avoid actions that are self-defeating. Stories are the most useful tool we have in the mental world. They have a unique power to sneak up on people and change the way they think and behave.

Even though it makes us uncomfortable, we should think about actively seeking out dissonance. Our minds are geared to quickly reduce it before we even become conscious of it, but it is dissonance that teaches us and changes the way we think. That critical feedback we dread stops us and makes us reflect. A position that conflicts with ours broadens our thinking and leads us to bigger ideas. From pondering the phi phenomenon to seeing our theory of human behavior fail, the dissonant is what broadens us and makes us grow. We shouldn't shun it or rationalize it away. We should seek it out and savor it.

Perhaps the most important thing to think about is that the world is of our own making. In the world of Newton and Aristotle, we're subject to the slings and arrows of outrageous fortune, and our defense is to counter them with force. It's easy for us to see ourselves as victims of that forbidding and hostile world out there. But according to neuroscience, we are the creators of the world, and we can change it just by changing our thinking. We may no longer have the comfort of seeing ourselves as victims, but we can make the world anything we want it to be.

Paradoxically, one last thing we should think about is to spend less time thinking. Consciousness gave Odysseus the ability to stop and think rather than simply responding emotionally the way Achilles did. It is this ability that allows us to delay immediate gratification for the promise of greater gratification in the future. Rather than spending their days lounging around and eating what was at hand, our ancestors decided to till a field, plant seeds, and tend crops, for the bigger payoff of a harvest in the future. As both Odysseus' success and a trip to the supermarket show, acquiring conscious-ness wasn't such a bad deal.

But once this pattern of thinking is established, it becomes a habit of mind. It's applied to everything, and all of our behavior becomes goal-oriented. We focus on the reward we'll achieve, the promotion we'll get, and the career we'll enjoy. But this runs counter to the way the mind works. The nucleus accumbens releases its dop-amine when we're engaged in the work that leads to the accomplish-ment of our goals, not when we accomplish the goals. It's the work itself that is rewarding. If we're always anticipating the payoff in the future, we never get to enjoy the present moment, nor apparently do we bring our full capability to what we do.

Psychologist Mihály Csikszentmihályi found that when people were able to exclusively focus on the work at hand, they felt happy, self-fulfilled, and performed at peak levels. He called this *flow:* "the state in which people are so involved in an activity that nothing else seemed to matter . . . people will do it even at great cost, for the sheer sake of doing it." The pleasure, Csikszentmihályi believes, results "because a person must concentrate attention on the task at hand and momentarily forget everything else." Consciousness is focused and dopamine is flowing freely.

It's ironic, but the strategic brain that makes us so good at man-aging human acitivity prevents us from performing at peak levels and experiencing the pleasure that comes from total immersion in our work. As in so many aspects of the world according to neurosci-ence, the solution is to subtly shift our attention. When we need to be strategic about human affairs, we pull our minds back to the big picture. But when we're involved in our work, we zero in on the task at hand with a laserlike focus.

A century and a half ago, the novelist George Eliot wrestled with this same dilemma in the story she told of a young man who asks if he will ever become good at his work. His boss answers yes, but explains that "you must love your work, and not be always looking over the edge of it waiting for your play to begin." For all of its great discoveries and insights, neuroscience has no better advice to offer us than this simple little story.

NOTES

CHAPTER 1: BRAIN SCIENCE

7: **"historian of science:"** Thomas Kuhn, *The Structure of Scientific Revolutions* (Chicago: University of Chicago Press, 1996).

10–12: **"according to the neurologist:"** Antonio R. Damasio, *Descartes' Error* (New York: Picador, 1994) 212–17.

15: **"according to a person's memories:"** John J. Ratey, *A User's Guide to the Brain* (New York: Vintage, 2002) 91.

15: **"Unlike the cells:"** Number of neurons: Ratey, 9.

16: **"study of sea snail neurons:"** Eric Kandel, *In Search of Memory* (New York: Norton 2006).

17: **"supersystem of systems:"** Damasio, *Descartes' Error*, 30.

17: **"changes driven by high-level networks:"** Zindel Segal, "Brain Mapping May Guide Treatment for Depression," *Boston Globe*, Jan. 6, 2004, A 1, 13.

18: **"a patient at Memorial Sloan-Kettering:"** Michael Gazzaniga, *Human* (New York: Harper Collins, 2008) 299–300.

CHAPTER 2: FROM BRAIN TO MIND

28: **"My love:"** Robert Burns, "A Red, Red Rose," in *Eighteenth Century Poetry* (New York: Ronald Press, ed. 1956), Louis I. Bredvold, Alan D. McKillop, and Lois Whitney, 965.

29: **"the way we think:"** George Lakoff and Mark Turner, *Metaphors We Live By* (Chicago: University of Chicago Press, 2003) 3.

29: **"the source of these:"** Theodore L. Brown, *Making Truth* (Champaign: University of Illinois Press, 2003) 40.

31: **"what you see:"** Richard E. Rubenstein, *Aristotle's Children* (New York: Harcourt, 2003) 28.

32: **"our nonrandom 'designed' solutions:"** Robert Aunger, *The Electric Meme* (New York: Free Press, 2002) 220.

34: **"Story is a basic principle of mind:"** Mark Turner, *The Literary Mind* (New York: Oxford University Press, 1998) v.

35: **"Our tales are spun:"** Daniel Dennett, *Consciousness Explained* (Boston: Little, Brown, 1991) 418.

35: **"taking it as our own:"** For a fuller treatment of our identification with stories, see Michael D. Slater, "Entertainment Education and the Persuasive Impact of Narratives," in *Narrative Impact* (Mahwah, NJ: Lawrence Erlbaum, 2002) ed. Melanie C. Green, Jeffrey J. Strange, and Timothy C. Brock, 172.

36: **"the ability to read other minds:"** Jerome Bruner, *Making Stories* (Cambridge, MA: Harvard University Press, 2002) 43.

36: **"a variation of the quest masterplot:"** H. Porter Abbott, *The Cambridge Introduction to Narrative* (Cambridge, UK: Cambridge University Press, 2002) 43.

37: **"People of a particular character:"** Turner, 133.

37: **"the rogue CEO:"** Jack Hitt, "American Kabuki: The Ritual of Scandal," *New York Times*, Jul. 18, 2004.

CHAPTER 3: WORKING RELATIONSHIPS

47: **"tit for tat:"** See Robert Axelrod, *The Evolution of Cooperation* (New York: Basic Books, 1984).

48: **"One heard a news story:"** Gary Marcus, *Kluge* (Boston: Houghton Mifflin, 2008) 88.

50: **"when we speak of the 'response':"** Ervin Laszlo, *The Systems View of the World* (Cresskill, NJ: Hampton Press, 1996) 113.

54: **"mirror neurons:"** For more detail, see Gazzaniga, 100–101.

54: **"mirror neurons for emotions:"** Gazzaniga, 178–79.

54: **"theory of mind:"** Gazzaniga, 49, 261.

55: **"step into others' shoes:"** Attributed to the sales trainer, Larry Wilson.

55: **"reappraise an emotion:"** Gazzaniga, 183–84.

60: **"In the early 1980s:"** John Gabarro and John Kotter, "Managing Your Boss," *Harvard Business Review*, Jan. 8, 2008.

61: **"a scientific approach:"** See Robert Cialdini, *Influence: Science and Practice*, 4th ed. (Old Tappan, NJ: Allyn & Bacon, 2000).

CHAPTER 4: MANAGING UPSIDE DOWN

67: **"I watched, amazed:"** Jane Goodall, *Through a Window* (Boston: Houghton Mifflin, 1990) 13.

68: **"behavioral displays:"** Goodall, 43.

68: **"highly developed social skills:"** Goodall, 23.

69: **"the goal of becoming the alpha male:"** Gazzaniga, 73.

70–73: **"Frederick Winslow Taylor:"** For a complete biography, see Robert Kanigel, *The One Best Way* (Boston: Little, Brown, 1997).

72: **"cog in the machine:"** See Kanigel.

72: **"not a whit for the thinking:"** See Kanigel.

73: **"landmark study at General Electric:"** For the full study, see Herbert H. Meyer, Emmanuel Kay, and John R. P. French Jr., "Split Roles in Performance Appraisal," *Harvard Business Review*, Jan. 1, 1964.

74: **"perform boring tasks:"** Eliot Aronson, "Dissonance, Hypocrisy, and the Self-Concept," in *Cognitive Dissonance*, ed. Eddie Harmon-Jones & Judson Mills (Washington, DC: American Psychological Association, 1999) 108–9.

75: **"human beings think:"** Aronson, 107–8.

76: **"a study on reward:"** Eliot Aronson, Timothy D. Wilson, and Robin M. Akert, *Social Psychology* (Old Tappan, NJ: Prentice Hall, 2005) 147–48.

77: **"rewarding the performance:"** Aronson, et al., 147.

77: **"two groups of children:"** Aronson, et al., 181.

78: **"Unlike rats and pigeons:"** Aronson, et al., 20.

79: **"When a person's action:"** George Caspar Homans, *Social Behavior* (New York: Harcourt Brace Jovanovich, 1974) 37.

80: **"a reward he expected:"** Homans, 39.

82: **"perceived as manipulative:"** Alfie Kohn, *Punished by Rewards* (Boston: Houghton Mifflin, 1993) 119–41.

CHAPTER 5: ORGANIZING LEVERAGE

91: **"Slime mold can teach us:"** Adapted from John Bleibtreu, *The Parable of the Beast* (New York: Collier, 1968) 215–22.

93: **"the selfish gene:"** Richard Dawkins, *The Selfish Gene*, 3d ed. (New York: Oxford University Press, 2006).

93: **"Twenty-two boys were divided:"** Muzafer Sherif, *The Robbers Cave Experiment* (Middletown, CT: Wesleyan University Press, 1988).

93: **"sticks and stones:"** Judith Rich Harris, *The Nurture Assumption* (New York: Free Press, 1998) 125–27.

95: **"making pins:"** Adam Smith, *An Inquiry Into the Nature and Causes of the Wealth of Nations* (1776; 1904), www.econlib.org/LIBRARY/Smith/smWN.html, accessed Nov. 24, 2008.

96ff: **"what happened with the railroads:"** For a full discussion of the railroads, see Alfred Chandler, *The Visible Hand* (Cambridge, MA: Belknap Press, 1993).

98: **"line A or line B:"** Lauren Slater, *Opening Skinner's Box* (New York: Norton, 2004) 41.

99: **"kin selection:"** See Dawkins, 90–93, and Robert Wright, *The Moral Animal* (New York: Vintage, 1994) 156–58.

100: **"married student housing:"** For a fascinating discussion of group dynamics, see George Homans, *The Human Group* (London: Routledge & Kegan Paul, 1950).

109: **"shared stories:"** Ronald N. Jacobs, "The Narrative Integration of Personal and Collective Identity in Social Movements," in *Narrative Impact*, 206.

109: **"emphasize agency and ultimate success:"** Jacobs, 208.

109: **"a utopian future:"** Jacobs, 219.

CHAPTER 6: THINKING STRATEGICALLY

113ff: **"she must be returned:"** For the full story, see Homer, *The Iliad* (New York: Penguin, 1990), trans. Robert Fagels.

114: **"They're not thinking:"** Julian Jaynes, *The Origin of Consciousness in the Breakdown of the Bicameral Brain* (Boston: Houghton Mifflin, 1976) 60.

114ff: **"Odysseus . . . wins the war:"** For the full story of his travels, see Homer, *The Odyssey* (New York: Penguin, 1996), trans. Robert Fagels.

119: **"Sperry's research:"** For a more in-depth treatment, see Michael Gazzaniga, *The Mind's Past* (Berkeley: University of California Press, 2000).

120: **"pathologically driven:"** Marcus, 143.

121: **"torn in thought:"** Homer, *Odyssey*, Book XX, l. 7–8.

121: **"Bear up old heart:"** Homer, *Odyssey*, Book XX, l. 13.

122–24: **"Henry V's classic battle:"** For a fuller description, see Christopher Allmand, *Henry V* (Berkeley: University of California Press, 1992).

125–33: **"People Express:"** See Leonard A. Schlesinger and Debra Whitestone, "People Express (A)," (Boston: Harvard Business Publishing, 1983).

130–32: **"Stanford Marshmallow Test:"** Carey Goldberg, "Marshmallow Temptations," *Boston Globe Online*, Oct. 22, 2008, www.boston.com/news/nation/articles/2008/10/22/marshmallow_temptations_brain_scans_could_yield_vital_lessons_in_self_control/.

132: **"like a 'cloud':"** Goldberg.

132: **"Jeremy Gray:"** Goldberg.

CHAPTER 7: CHANGING MINDS

139–41: **"drive a dolphin crazy:"** Morris Berman, *The Reenchantment of the World* (Ithaca, NY: Cornell University Press, 1984) 229–30.

142: **"reversals of logic:"** Arthur Koestler, *The Act of Creation* (1967) 65.

148: **"generate opposite results:"** Jamshid Gharajedaghi, *Systems Thinking* (Burlington, MA: Elsevier, 1999) 48.

150: **"processing novel information:"** Elkhonon Goldberg, *The Executive Brain* (New York: Oxford University Press, 2001) 43.

151: **"cognitive restructuring:"** Michael R. Leippe and Donna Eisenstadt, "A Self-Accountability Model of Dissonance Reduction," in *Cognitive Dissonance*, 204.

152: **"embedded in a large network:"** Leippe and Eisenstadt, 205.

152: **"a growing number of law enforcement professionals:"** Johann Hari, "What Will the Candidates Do to End the Unwinnable War on Drugs? *Huffington Post*, Aug. 13, 2008, www.huffingtonpost.com/johann-hari/what-will-the-candidates_b_118045.html, accessed Nov. 24, 2008.

153: **"two different types of change:"** Paul Watzlawick, John Weakland, and Richard Fisch, *Change* (1974), 10–11.

154: **"a couple on a sailboat:"** Watzlawick, et al., 37.

155: **"overly dependent children:"** Watzlawick, et al., 116–19.

155: **"emotional setting or viewpoint:"** Watzlawick, et al., 95.

158: **"expectation gone awry:"** Bruner, 28.

158: **"peripeteia:"** Aristotle, *Introduction to Aristotle*, ed. Richard McKeon (New York: Modern Library, 1992) 679.
159: **"some sort of resolution:"** Bruner, 16–17.

CHAPTER 8: LEADING IDEAS

165: **"we think of these as 'multiple drafts':** Dennett, 113.
165: **"narrative stream:"** Dennett, 113.
167: **"the movie *Patton*:"** *Patton* (Twentieth Century Fox, 1970).
168: **"authoritarian leadership:"** Bernard M. Bass, *Bass & Stogdill's Handbook of Leadership* (New York: Free Press, 1990) 442.
170: **"pay-for-performance:"** Bass, 362.
170: **"repetitive, boring, and tedious:"** Bass, 364.
170: **"the manager's reasons:"** Bass, 365.
171: **"definitions of leadership:"** Jay A. Conger, *Learning to Lead* (San Francisco: Jossey-Bass, 1992) 18.
171: **"360-degree feedback:"** Bass, 514.
172: **"'transactional' and 'transformational':"** James McGregor Burns, *Leadership* (New York: Harper Collins, 1978).
172: **"transformational leaders consistently outperform:"** Bass, 525.
172: **"supplement transactional leadership:"** Bass, 525.
173–75: **"Henry's response":** All quotes from *Shakespeare: The Complete Works*, ed. G.B. Harrison (1968).
176: **"what ... transformational leaders do:"** Bass, 184–221.
177: **"studies demonstrating ... participation:"** Bass, 436–71.
177: **"less participative:"** Bass, 441.
179: **"create ... rather than record:"** Joseph LeDoux, *Synaptic Self* (New York: Viking Penguin, 2002) 319.
179: **"A college class:"** Aronson, et al., 62.
179: **"bloomers:"** Aronson, et al., 70.
180: **"the performance of salespeople:"** J. Sterling Livingston, "The Pygmalion Effect," *Harvard Business Review*, Jan. 1, 2006.
180: **"a seminal article:"** Abraham Zaleznik, "Managers and Leaders: Are They Different?" *Harvard Business Review*, Jan. 1, 2004.
184: **"expectation ... charismatic:"** Bass, 197.

CHAPTER 9: ALL THINGS ARE READY

195: **"civilization's greatest economic powers:"** See David Landes, *The Wealth and Poverty of Nations* (New York: Norton, 1998) 213–23.
201: **"the sheer sake of doing it:"** Mihály Csikszentmihályi, *Flow* (New York: Harper Collins, 1990) 4.
201: **"forget everything else:"** Csikszentmihályi, 6.
202: **"you must love your work:"** George Eliot, *Middlemarch* (1872; 1965) 606.

ACKNOWLEDGMENTS

The ideas in this book just build on our three-thousand-year-old tradition of speculating on how the mind works and how best to use it. But in the twenty-first century, we have an advantage: the *f*MRI that enables us to actually see the brain at work. Scientists Stephen Pinker, Antonio Damasio, Michael Gazzaniga, and others have taken the discoveries of neuroscience and demonstrated what they mean for the way we live. My work would not have been possible without their insights.

Nor would it have been possible without the clients who have invited me into their companies and allowed me to be part of their efforts to transform their businesses. I know that I've learned at least as much from them as they've learned from me. In particular, I'm indebted to my client and friend Ben Levitan. He's become my barometer on trends in the business world and a sure-fire connection to anybody anywhere. His help and encouragement have been invaluable.

I've also been fortunate to have as my agents Kristina and

Michael of the Ebeling Agency. They embody the heart of the new approach to business that I present in this book. They challenged accepted practice and rewrote the rules of author representation to place my book with a great publisher in record time. They have continued to provide much needed counsel and advice.

But my greatest debt is to my editor, Courtney Young. She took my ideas and taught me how to make what might have been a difficult subject easily accessible. The packaging of the book, its structure, and the clarity of the writing are all due to her efforts. While she set challenging expectations, she was always first and foremost a true partner in the work. Without her, there wouldn't be a *Management Rewired*. And without the diligent efforts of my publicist at Portfolio, Courtney Nobile, probably nobody would even know about the book. My thanks to a great team.

INDEX